GOD

IS NOT

GREAT

GOD

IS NOT

GREAT

THE CASE AGAINST RELIGION

Christopher Hitchens

Atlantic Books
LONDON

First published in the United States of America in 2007 by Twelve, an imprint of Warner
Books, Inc., Hachette Book Group USA, 237 Park Avenue,
New York, NY 10169, USA.

First published in Great Britain in hardback in 2007 by Atlantic Books,
an imprint of Grove Atlantic Ltd.

3 5 7 9 8 6 4

Frontispiece: The Sleep of Reason Produces Monsters, from 'Los Caprichos'
(engraving) (b/w photo) (see also 81662) by Goya y Lucientes,
Francisco Jose de (1746-1828) ©Bibliotheque Nationale, Paris, France/ The
Bridgeman Art Library (image number XIR158286) Nationality / copyright status:
Spanish / out of copyright

A CIP catalogue record for this book is available from the British Library.

Hardback ISBN 978 1 84354 586 6
Trade Paperback ISBN 978 1 84354 573 6

Printed in Great Britain by MPG Books Ltd, Bodmin, Cornwall

Atlantic Books
An imprint of Grove Atlantic Ltd
Ormond House
26–27 Boswell Street
London WC1N 3JZ

For Ian McEwan
In serene recollection of
La Refulgencia

Contents

god

is not

Great

Oh, wearisome condition of humanity,
Born under one law, to another bound;
Vainly begot, and yet forbidden vanity,
Created sick, commanded to be sound.
—FULKE GREVILLE, *Mustapha*

And do you think that unto such as you
A maggot-minded, starved, fanatic crew
God gave a secret, and denied it me?
Well, well—what matters it? Believe that, too!
—*THE RUBAIYAT OF OMAR KHAYYAM*
(RICHARD LE GALLIENNE TRANSLATION)

Peacefully they will die, peacefully they will expire in your name, and beyond the grave they will find only death. But we will keep the secret, and for their own happiness we will entice them with a heavenly and eternal reward.
—THE GRAND INQUISITOR TO HIS "SAVIOR" in
THE BROTHERS KARAMAZOV

Chapter One

Putting It Mildly

If the intended reader of this book should want to go beyond disagreement with its author and try to identify the sins and deformities that animated him to write it (and I have certainly noticed that those who publicly affirm charity and compassion and forgiveness are often inclined to take this course), then he or she will not just be quarreling with the unknowable and ineffable creator who—presumably—opted to make me this way. They will be defiling the memory of a good, sincere, simple woman, of stable and decent faith, named Mrs. Jean Watts.

It was Mrs. Watts's task, when I was a boy of about nine and attending a school on the edge of Dartmoor, in southwestern England, to instruct me in lessons about nature, and also about scripture. She would take me and my fellows on walks, in an especially lovely part of my beautiful country of birth, and teach us to tell the different birds, trees, and plants from one another. The amazing variety to be found in a hedgerow; the wonder of a clutch of eggs found in an intricate nest; the way that if the nettles stung your legs (we had to wear shorts) there would be a soothing dock leaf planted near to hand: all this has stayed in my mind, just like the "gamekeeper's museum," where the local peasantry would display the corpses of rats, weasels, and other vermin and predators, presumably supplied by some less kindly deity. If you read John Clare's imperishable rural poems you will catch the music of what I mean to convey.

At later lessons we would be given a printed slip of paper entitled "Search the Scriptures," which was sent to the school by whatever national authority supervised the teaching of religion. (This, along with daily prayer services, was compulsory and enforced by the state.) The slip would contain a single verse from the Old or New Testament, and the assignment was to look up the verse and then to tell the class or the teacher, orally or in writing, what the story and the moral was. I used to love this exercise, and even to excel at it so that (like Bertie Wooster) I frequently passed "top" in scripture class. It was my first introduction to practical and textual criticism. I would read all the chapters that led up to the verse, and all the ones that followed it, to be sure that I had got the "point" of the original clue. I can still do this, greatly to the annoyance of some of my enemies, and still have respect for those whose style is sometimes dismissed as "merely" Talmudic, or Koranic, or "fundamentalist." This is good and necessary mental and literary training.

However, there came a day when poor, dear Mrs. Watts overreached herself. Seeking ambitiously to fuse her two roles as nature instructor and Bible teacher, she said, "So you see, children, how powerful and generous God is. He has made all the trees and grass to be green, which is exactly the color that is most restful to our eyes. Imagine if instead, the vegetation was all purple, or orange, how awful that would be."

And now behold what this pious old trout hath wrought. I liked Mrs. Watts: she was an affectionate and childless widow who had a friendly old sheepdog who really was named Rover, and she would invite us for sweets and treats after hours to her slightly ramshackle old house near the railway line. If Satan chose her to tempt me into error he was much more inventive than the subtle serpent in the Garden of Eden. She never raised her voice or offered violence—which couldn't be said for all my teachers—and in general was one of those people, of the sort whose memorial is in *Middlemarch*, of whom it may be said that if "things are not so ill with you and me as they might have been," this is "half-owing to the number who lived faithfully a hidden life, and rest in unvisited tombs."

However, I was frankly appalled by what she said. My little ankle-strap sandals curled with embarrassment for her. At the age of nine I had not even a conception of the argument from design, or of Darwinian evolution as its rival, or of the relationship between photosynthesis and chlorophyll. The secrets of the genome were as hidden from me as they were, at that time, to everyone else. I had not then visited scenes of nature where almost everything was hideously indifferent or hostile to human life, if not life itself. I simply *knew*, almost as if I had privileged access to a higher authority, that my teacher had managed to get everything wrong in just two sentences. The eyes were adjusted to nature, and not the other way about.

I must not pretend to remember everything perfectly, or in order, after this epiphany, but in a fairly short time I had also begun to notice other oddities. Why, if god was the creator of all things, were we supposed to "praise" him so incessantly for doing what came to him naturally? This seemed servile, apart from anything else. If Jesus could heal a blind person he happened to meet, then why not heal blindness? What was so wonderful about his casting out devils, so that the devils would enter a herd of pigs instead? That seemed sinister: more like black magic. With all this continual prayer, why no result? Why did I have to keep saying, in public, that I was a miserable sinner? Why was the subject of sex considered so toxic? These faltering and childish objections are, I have since discovered, extremely commonplace, partly because no religion can meet them with any satisfactory answer. But another, larger one also presented itself. (I say "presented itself" rather than "occurred to me" because these objections are, as well as insuperable, inescapable.) The headmaster, who led the daily services and prayers and held the Book, and was a bit of a sadist and a closeted homosexual (and whom I have long since forgiven because he ignited my interest in history and lent me my first copy of P. G. Wodehouse), was giving a no-nonsense talk to some of us one evening. "You may not see the point of all this faith now," he said. "But you will one day, when you start to lose loved ones."

Again, I experienced a stab of sheer indignation as well as disbelief. Why, that would be as much as saying that religion might not be true, but never mind that, since it can be relied upon for comfort. How contemptible. I was then nearing thirteen, and becoming quite the insufferable little intellectual. I had never heard of Sigmund Freud—though he would have been very useful to me in understanding the headmaster—but I had just been given a glimpse of his essay *The Future of an Illusion*.

I am inflicting all this upon you because I am not one of those whose chance at a wholesome belief was destroyed by child abuse or brutish indoctrination. I know that millions of human beings have had to endure these things, and I do not think that religions can or should be absolved from imposing such miseries. (In the very recent past, we have seen the Church of Rome befouled by its complicity with the unpardonable sin of child rape, or, as it might be phrased in Latin form, "no child's behind left.") But other nonreligious organizations have committed similar crimes, or even worse ones.

There still remain four irreducible objections to religious faith: that it wholly misrepresents the origins of man and the cosmos, that because of this original error it manages to combine the maximum of servility with the maximum of solipsism, that it is both the result and the cause of dangerous sexual repression, and that it is ultimately grounded on wish-thinking.

I do not think it is arrogant of me to claim that I had already discovered these four objections (as well as noticed the more vulgar and obvious fact that religion is used by those in temporal charge to invest themselves with authority) before my boyish voice had broken. I am morally certain that millions of other people came to very similar conclusions in very much the same way, and I have since met such people in hundreds of places, and in dozens of different countries. Many of them never believed, and many of them abandoned faith after a difficult struggle. Some of them had blinding moments of un-conviction that were every bit as instantaneous, though perhaps less epileptic and apocalyptic (and later more rationally and more morally justified) than Saul of Tarsus on the Damascene road. And here is the point, about myself and my co-thinkers. Our belief is not a be-lief. Our principles are not a faith. We do not rely solely upon sci-ence and reason, because these are necessary rather than sufficient factors, but we distrust anything that contradicts science or outrages reason. We may differ on many things, but what we respect is free inquiry, openmindedness, and the pursuit of ideas for their own sake. We do not hold our convictions dogmatically: the disagreement be-tween Professor Stephen Jay Gould and Professor Richard Dawkins, concerning "punctuated evolution" and the unfilled gaps in post-Darwinian theory, is quite wide as well as quite deep, but we shall resolve it by evidence and reasoning and not by mutual excommuni-cation. (My own annoyance at Professor Dawkins and Daniel Den-nett, for their cringe-making proposal that atheists should conceitedly nominate themselves to be called "brights," is a part of a continuous argument.) We are not immune to the lure of wonder and mystery and awe: we have music and art and literature, and find that the seri-ous ethical dilemmas are better handled by Shakespeare and Tolstoy and Schiller and Dostoyevsky and George Eliot than in the mythical morality tales of the holy books. Literature, not scripture, sustains the mind and—since there is no other metaphor—also the soul. We do not believe in heaven or hell, yet no statistic will ever find that without these blandishments and threats we commit more crimes of greed or violence than the faithful. (In fact, if a proper statistical inquiry could ever be made, I am sure the evidence would be the other way.) We are reconciled to living only once, except through our children, for whom we are perfectly happy to notice that we must make way, and room. We speculate that it is at least possible that, once people accepted the fact of their short and struggling lives, they might behave better toward each other and not worse. We believe with certainty that an ethical life can be lived without religion. And we know for a fact that the corollary holds true—that religion has caused innumerable people not just to conduct themselves no better than others, but to award themselves permission to behave in ways that would make a brothel-keeper or an ethnic cleanser raise an eyebrow.

Most important of all, perhaps, we infidels do not need any machinery of reinforcement. We are those who Blaise Pascal took into account when he wrote to the one who says, "I am so made that I cannot believe." In the village of Montaillou, during one of the great medieval persecutions, a woman was asked by the Inquisitors to tell them from whom she had acquired her heretical doubts about hell and resurrection. She must have known that she stood in terrible danger of a lingering death administered by the pious, but she responded that she took them from nobody and had evolved them all by herself. (Often, you hear the believers praise the simplicity of their flock, but not in the case of this unforced and conscientious sanity and lucidity, which has been stamped out and burned out in the cases of more humans than we shall ever be able to name.)

There is no need for us to gather every day, or every seven days, or on any high and auspicious day, to proclaim our rectitude or to grovel and wallow in our unworthiness. We atheists do not require any priests, or any hierarchy above them, to police our doctrine. Sacrifices and ceremonies are abhorrent to us, as are relics and the worship of any images or objects (even including objects in the form of one of man's most useful innovations: the bound book). To us no spot on earth is or could be "holier" than another: to the ostentatious absurdity of the pilgrimage, or the plain horror of killing civilians in the name of some sacred wall or cave or shrine or rock, we can counterpose a leisurely or urgent walk from one side of the library or the gallery to another, or to lunch with an agreeable friend, in pursuit of truth or beauty. Some of these excursions to the bookshelf or the lunch or the gallery will obviously, if they are serious, bring us into contact with belief and believers, from the great devotional painters and composers to the works of Augustine, Aquinas, Maimonides, and Newman. These mighty scholars may have written many evil things or many foolish things, and been laughably ignorant of the germ theory of disease or the place of the terrestrial globe in the solar system, let alone the universe, and this is the plain reason why there are no more of them today, and why there will be no more of them tomorrow. Religion spoke its last intelligible or noble or inspiring words a long time ago: either that or it mutated into an admirable but nebulous humanism, as did, say, Dietrich Bonhoeffer, a brave Lutheran pastor hanged by the Nazis for his refusal to collude with them. We shall have no more prophets or sages from the ancient quarter, which is why the devotions of today are only the echoing repetitions of yesterday, sometimes ratcheted up to screaming point so as to ward off the terrible emptiness.

While some religious apology is magnificent in its limited way—one might cite Pascal—and some of it is dreary and absurd—here one cannot avoid naming C. S. Lewis—both styles have something in common, namely the appalling load of strain that they have to bear. How much effort it takes to affirm the incredible! The Aztecs had to tear open a human chest cavity *every day* just to make sure that the sun would rise. Monotheists are supposed to pester their deity more times than that, perhaps, lest he be deaf. How much vanity must be concealed—not too effectively at that—in order to pretend that one is the personal object of a divine plan? How much self-respect must be sacrificed in order that one may squirm continually in an awareness of one's own sin? How many needless assumptions must be made, and how much contortion is required, to receive every new insight of science and manipulate it so as to "fit" with the revealed words of ancient man-made deities? How many saints and miracles and councils and conclaves are required in order first to be able to establish a dogma and then—after infinite pain and loss and absurdity and cruelty—to be forced to rescind one of those dogmas? God did not create man in his own image. Evidently, it was the other way about, which is the painless explanation for the profusion of gods and religions, and the fratricide both between and among faiths, that we see all about us and that has so retarded the development of civilization.

Past and present religious atrocities have occurred not because we are evil, but because it is a fact of nature that the human species is, biologically, only partly rational. Evolution has meant that our prefrontal lobes are too small, our adrenal glands are too big, and our reproductive organs apparently designed by committee; a recipe which, alone or in combination, is very certain to lead to some unhappiness and disorder. But still, what a difference when one lays aside the strenuous believers and takes up the no less arduous work of a Darwin, say, or a Hawking or a Crick. These men are more enlightening when they are wrong, or when they display their inevitable biases, than any falsely modest person of faith who is vainly trying to square the circle and to explain how he, a mere creature of the Creator, can possibly know what that Creator intends. Not all can be agreed on matters of aesthetics, but we secular humanists and atheists and agnostics do not wish to deprive humanity of its wonders or consolations. Not in the least. If you will devote a little time to studying the staggering photographs taken by the Hubble telescope, you will be scrutinizing things that are far more awesome and mysterious and beautiful—and more chaotic and overwhelming and forbidding—than any creation or "end of days" story. If you read Hawking on the "event horizon," that theoretical lip of the "black hole" over which one could in theory plunge and see the past and the future (except that one would, regrettably and by definition, not have enough "time"), I shall be surprised if you can still go on gaping at Moses and his unimpressive "burning bush." If you examine the beauty and symmetry of the double helix, and then go on to have your own genome sequence fully analyzed, you will be at once impressed that such a near-perfect phenomenon is at the core of your being, and reassured (I hope) that you have so much in common with other tribes of the human species—"race" having gone, along with "creation" into the ashcan—and further fascinated to learn how much you are a part of the animal kingdom as well. Now at last you can be properly humble in the face of your maker, which turns out not to be a "who," but a process of mutation with rather more random elements than our vanity might wish. This is more than enough mystery and marvel for any mammal to be getting along with: the most educated person in the world now has to admit—I shall *not* say confess—that he or she knows less and less but at least knows less and less about more and more.

As for consolation, since religious people so often insist that faith answers this supposed need, I shall simply say that those who offer false consolation are false friends. In any case, the critics of religion do not simply deny that it has a painkilling effect. Instead, they warn against the placebo and the bottle of colored water. Probably the most popular misquotation of modern times—certainly the most popular in this argument—is the assertion that Marx dismissed religion as "the opium of the people." On the contrary, this son of a rabbinical line took belief very seriously and wrote, in his *Contribution to the Critique of Hegel's Philosophy of Right*, as follows:

> Religious distress is at the same time the expression of real distress and the *protest* against real distress. Religion is the sigh of the oppressed creature, the heart of a heartless world, just as it is the spirit of a spiritless situation. It is the opium of the people.
>
> The abolition of religion as the illusory happiness of the people is required for their real happiness. The demand to give up the illusions about its condition is the demand to give up a condition that needs illusions. The criticism of religion is therefore in embryo the criticism of the vale of woe, the halo of which is religion. Criticism has plucked the imaginary flowers from the chain, not so that man will wear the chain without any fantasy

or consolation but so that he will shake off the chain and cull the living flower.

So the famous misquotation is not so much a "misquotation" but rather a very crude attempt to misrepresent the philosophical case against religion. Those who have believed what the priests and rabbis and imams tell them about what the unbelievers think and about how they think, will find further such surprises as we go along. They will perhaps come to distrust what they are told—or not to take it "on faith," which is the problem to begin with.

Marx and Freud, it has to be conceded, were not doctors or exact scientists. It is better to think of them as great and fallible imaginative essayists. When the intellectual universe alters, in other words, I don't feel arrogant enough to exempt myself from self-criticism. And I am content to think that some contradictions will remain contradictory, some problems will never be resolved by the mammalian equipment of the human cerebral cortex, and some things are indefinitely unknowable. If the universe was found to be finite or infinite, either discovery would be equally stupefying and impenetrable to me. And though I have met many people much wiser and more clever than myself, I know of nobody who could be wise or intelligent enough to say differently.

Thus the mildest criticism of religion is also the most radical and the most devastating one. Religion is man-made. Even the men who made it cannot agree on what their prophets or redeemers or gurus actually said or did. Still less can they hope to tell us the "meaning" of later discoveries and developments which were, when they began, either obstructed by their religions or denounced by them. And yet—the believers still claim to know! Not just to know, but to know *everything*. Not just to know that god exists, and that he created and supervised the whole enterprise, but also to know what "he" demands of us—from our diet to our observances to our sexual morality. In other words, in a vast and complicated discussion where we know

more and more about less and less, yet can still hope for some enlightenment as we proceed, one faction—itself composed of mutually
warring factions—has the sheer arrogance to tell us that we already
have all the essential information we need. Such stupidity, combined
with such pride, should be enough on its own to exclude "belief" from
the debate. The person who is certain, and who claims divine warrant
for his certainty, belongs now to the infancy of our species. It may be
a long farewell, but it has begun and, like all farewells, should not be
protracted.

I trust that if you met me, you would not necessarily know that this
was my view. I have probably sat up later, and longer, with religious
friends than with any other kind. These friends often irritate me by
saying that I am a "seeker," which I am not, or not in the way they
think. If I went back to Devon, where Mrs. Watts has her unvisited
tomb, I would surely find myself sitting quietly at the back of some
old Celtic or Saxon church. (Philip Larkin's lovely poem "Church-
going" is the perfect capture of my own attitude.) I once wrote a book
about George Orwell, who might have been my hero if I had heroes,
and was upset by his callousness about the burning of churches in
Catalonia in 1936. Sophocles showed, well before the rise of monotheism, that Antigone spoke for humanity in her revulsion against
desecration. I leave it to the faithful to burn each other's churches and
mosques and synagogues, which they can always be relied upon to
do. When I go to the mosque, I take off my shoes. When I go to
the synagogue, I cover my head. I once even observed the etiquette
of an ashram in India, though this was a trial to me. My parents did
not try to impose any religion: I was probably fortunate in having
a father who had not especially loved his strict Baptist/Calvinist upbringing, and a mother who preferred assimilation—partly for my
sake—to the Judaism of her forebears. I now know enough about all
religions to know that I would always be an infidel at all times and
in all places, but my particular atheism is a Protestant atheism. It is
with the splendid liturgy of the King James Bible and the Cranmer

prayer book—liturgy that the fatuous Church of England has cheaply discarded—that I first disagreed. When my father died and was buried in a chapel overlooking Portsmouth—the same chapel in which General Eisenhower had prayed for success the night before D-Day in 1944—I gave the address from the pulpit and selected as my text a verse from the epistle of Saul of Tarsus, later to be claimed as "Saint Paul," to the Philippians (chapter 4, verse 8):

> Finally, brethren, whatsoever things are true, whatsoever things are honest, whatsoever things are just, whatsoever things are pure, whatsoever things are lovely, whatsoever things are of good report: if there be any virtue, and if there be any praise, think on these things.

I chose this because of its haunting and elusive character, which will be with me at the last hour, and for its essentially secular injunction, and because it shone out from the wasteland of rant and complaint and nonsense and bullying which surrounds it.

The argument with faith is the foundation and origin of all arguments, because it is the beginning—but not the end—of all arguments about philosophy, science, history, and human nature. It is also the beginning—but by no means the end—of all disputes about the good life and the just city. Religious faith is, precisely *because* we are still-evolving creatures, ineradicable. It will never die out, or at least not until we get over our fear of death, and of the dark, and of the unknown, and of each other. For this reason, I would not prohibit it even if I thought I could. Very generous of me, you may say. But will the religious grant me the same indulgence? I ask because there is a real and serious difference between me and my religious friends, and the real and serious friends are sufficiently honest to admit it. I would be quite content to go to their children's bar mitzvahs, to marvel at their Gothic cathedrals, to "respect" their belief that the Koran was dictated, though exclusively in Arabic, to an illiterate merchant, or to interest myself in Wicca and Hindu and Jain consolations. And as it happens, I will continue to do this without insisting on the polite reciprocal condition—which is *that they in turn leave me alone*. But this, religion is ultimately incapable of doing. As I write these words, and as you read them, people of faith are in their different ways planning your and my destruction, and the destruction of all the hard-won human attainments that I have touched upon. *Religion poisons everything.*

Chapter Two

Religion Kills

His aversion to religion, in the sense usually attached to the term, was of the same kind with that of Lucretius: he regarded it with the feelings due not to a mere mental delusion, but to a great moral evil. He looked upon it as the greatest enemy of morality: first, by setting up factitious excellencies—belief in creeds, devotional feelings, and ceremonies, not connected with the good of human kind—and causing these to be accepted as substitutes for genuine virtue: but above all, by radically vitiating the standard of morals; making it consist in doing the will of a being, on whom it lavishes indeed all the phrases of adulation, but whom in sober truth it depicts as eminently hateful.

—JOHN STUART MILL ON HIS FATHER, IN THE *AUTOBIOGRAPHY*

Tantum religio potuit suadere malorum.
(To such heights of evil are men driven by religion.)
—LUCRETIUS, *DE RERUM NATURA*

Imagine that you can perform a feat of which I am incapable. Imagine, in other words, that you can picture an infinitely benign and all-powerful creator, who conceived of you, then made and shaped you, brought you into the world he had made for you, and now supervises and cares for you even while you sleep. Imagine, further, that if you obey the rules and commandments that he has lovingly prescribed, you will qualify for an eternity of bliss and repose. I do not say that I envy you this belief (because to me it seems like the wish for a horrible form of benevolent and unalterable dictatorship), but I do have a sincere question. Why does such a belief not make its adherents happy? It must seem to them that they have come into possession of a marvelous secret, of the sort that they could cling to in moments of even the most extreme adversity.

Superficially, it does sometimes seem as if this is the case. I have been to evangelical services, in black and in white communities, where the whole event was one long whoop of exaltation at being saved, loved, and so forth. Many services, in all denominations and among almost all pagans, are exactly designed to evoke celebration and communal fiesta, which is precisely why I suspect them. There are more restrained and sober and elegant moments, also. When I was a member of the Greek Orthodox Church, I could feel, even if I could not believe, the joyous words that are exchanged between believers on Easter morning: *"Christos anesti!"* (Christ is risen!) *"Alethos anesti!"* (He is risen indeed!) I was a member of the Greek Orthodox Church, I might add, for a reason that explains why very many people profess an outward allegiance. I joined it to please my Greek parents-in-law. The archbishop who received me into his communion on the same day that he officiated at my wedding, thereby trousering two fees instead of the usual one, later became an enthusiastic cheerleader and fund-raiser for his fellow Orthodox Serbian mass murderers Radovan Karadzic and Ratko Mladic, who filled countless mass graves all over Bosnia. The next time I got married, which was by a Reform Jewish rabbi with an Einsteinian and Shakespearean bent, I had something a little more in common with the officiating person. But even he was aware that his lifelong homosexuality was, in principle, condemned as a capital offense, punishable by the founders of his religion by stoning. As to the Anglican Church into which I was originally baptized, it may look like a pathetic bleating sheep today, but as the descendant of a church that has always enjoyed a state subsidy and an intimate relationship with hereditary monarchy, it has a historic responsibility for the Crusades, for persecution of Catholics, Jews, and Dissenters, and for combat against science and reason.

The level of intensity fluctuates according to time and place, but it can be stated as a truth that religion does not, and in the long run cannot, be content with its own marvelous claims and sublime assurances. It *must* seek to interfere with the lives of nonbelievers, or heretics, or adherents of other faiths. It may speak about the bliss of the next world, but it wants power in this one. This is only to be expected. It is, after all, wholly man-made. And it does not have the confidence in its own various preachings even to allow coexistence between different faiths.

Take a single example, from one of the most revered figures that modern religion has produced. In 1996, the Irish Republic held a referendum on one question: whether its state constitution should still prohibit divorce. Most of the political parties, in an increasingly secular country, urged voters to approve of a change in the law. They did so for two excellent reasons. It was no longer thought right that the Roman Catholic Church should legislate its morality for all citizens, and it was obviously impossible even to hope for eventual Irish reunification if the large Protestant minority in the North was continually repelled by the possibility of clerical rule. Mother Teresa flew all the way from Calcutta to help campaign, along with the church and its hard-liners, for a "no" vote. In other words, an Irish woman married to a wife-beating and incestuous drunk should never expect anything better, and might endanger her soul if she begged for a fresh start, while as for the Protestants, they could either choose the blessings of Rome or stay out altogether. There was not even the suggestion that Catholics could follow their own church's commandments while not imposing them on all other citizens. And this in the British Isles, in the last decade of the twentieth century. The referendum eventually amended the constitution, though by the narrowest of majorities. (Mother Teresa in the same year gave an interview saying that she hoped her friend Princess Diana would be happier after she had escaped from what was an obviously miserable marriage, but it's less of a surprise to find the church applying sterner laws to the poor, or offering indulgences to the rich.)

A week before the events of September 11, 2001, I was on a panel with Dennis Prager, who is one of America's better-known religious broadcasters. He challenged me in public to answer what he called a "straight yes/no question," and I happily agreed. Very well, he said. I was to imagine myself in a strange city as the evening was coming on. Toward me I was to imagine that I saw a large group of men approaching. Now—would I feel safer, or less safe, if I was to learn that they were just coming from a prayer meeting? As the reader will see, this is not a question to which a yes/no answer can be given. But I was able to answer it as if it were not hypothetical. "Just to stay within the letter 'B,' I have actually had that experience in Belfast, Beirut, Bombay, Belgrade, Bethlehem, and Baghdad. In each case I can say absolutely, and can give my reasons, why I would feel immediately threatened if I thought that the group of men approaching me in the dusk were coming from a religious observance."

Here, then, is a very brief summary of the religiously inspired cruelty I witnessed in these six places. In Belfast, I have seen whole streets burned out by sectarian warfare between different sects of Christianity, and interviewed people whose relatives and friends have been kidnapped and killed or tortured by rival religious death squads, often for no other reason than membership of another confession. There is an old Belfast joke about the man stopped at a roadblock and asked his religion. When he replies that he is an atheist he is asked, "Protestant or Catholic atheist?" I think this shows how the obsession has rotted even the legendary local sense of humor. In any case, this did actually happen to a friend of mine and the experience was decidedly not an amusing one. The ostensible pretext for this mayhem is rival nationalisms, but the street language used by opposing rival tribes consists of terms insulting to the other confession ("Prods" and "Teagues"). For many years, the Protestant establishment wanted Catholics to be both segregated and suppressed. Indeed, in the days when the Ulster state was founded, its slogan was: "A Protestant Parliament for a Protestant People." Sectarianism is conveniently self-generating and can always be counted upon to evoke a reciprocal sectarianism. On the main point, the Catholic leadership was in agreement. It desired clerical-dominated schools and segregated neighborhoods, the better to exert its control. So, in the name of god, the old hatreds were drilled into new generations of schoolchildren, and are still being drilled. (Even the word "drill" makes me queasy: a power tool of that kind was often used to destroy the kneecaps of those who fell foul of the religious gangs.)

When I first saw Beirut, in the summer of 1975, it was still recognizable as "the Paris of the Orient." Yet this apparent Eden was infested with a wide selection of serpents. It suffered from a positive surplus of religions, all of them "accommodated" by a sectarian state constitution. The president by law had to be a Christian, usually a Maronite Catholic, the speaker of the parliament a Muslim, and so on. This never worked well, because it institutionalized differences of belief as well as of caste and ethnicity (the Shia Muslims were at the bottom of the social scale, the Kurds were disenfranchised altogether).

The main Christian party was actually a Catholic militia called the Phalange, or "Phalanx," and had been founded by a Maronite Lebanese named Pierre Gemayel who had been very impressed by his visit to Hitler's Berlin Olympics in 1936. It was later to achieve international notoriety by conducting the massacre of Palestinians at the Sabra and Chatila refugee camps in 1982, while acting under the orders of General Sharon. That a Jewish general should collaborate with a fascist party may seem grotesque enough, but they had a common Muslim enemy and that was enough. Israel's irruption into Lebanon that year also gave an impetus to the birth of Hezbollah, the modestly named "Party of God," which mobilized the Shia underclass and gradually placed it under the leadership of the theocratic dictatorship in Iran that had come to power three years previously. It was in lovely

Lebanon, too, having learned to share the kidnapping business with the ranks of organized crime, that the faithful moved on to introduce us to the beauties of suicide bombing. I can still see that severed head in the road outside the near-shattered French embassy. On the whole, I tended to cross the street when the prayer meetings broke up.

Bombay also used to be considered a pearl of the Orient, with its necklace of lights along the corniche and its magnificent British Raj architecture. It was one of India's most diverse and plural cities, and its many layers of texture have been cleverly explored by Salman Rushdie—especially in *The Moor's Last Sigh*—and in the films of Mira Nair. It is true that there had been intercommunal fighting there, during the time in 1947–48 when the grand historic movement for Indian self-government was being ruined by Muslim demands for a separate state and by the fact that the Congress Party was led by a pious Hindu. But probably as many people took refuge in Bombay during that moment of religious bloodlust as were driven or fled from it. A form of cultural coexistence resumed, as often happens when cities are exposed to the sea and to influences from outside. Parsis—former Zoroastrians who had been persecuted in Persia—were a prominent minority, and the city was also host to a historically significant community of Jews. But this was not enough to content Mr. Bal Thackeray and his Shiv Sena Hindu nationalist movement, who in the 1990s decided that Bombay should be run by and for his coreligionists, and who loosed a tide of goons and thugs onto the streets. Just to show he could do it, he ordered the city renamed as "Mumbai," which is partly why I include it in this list under its traditional title.

Belgrade had until the 1980s been the capital of Yugoslavia, or the land of the southern Slavs, which meant by definition that it was the capital of a multiethnic and multiconfessional state. But a secular Croatian intellectual once gave me a warning that, as in Belfast, took the form of a sour joke. "If I tell people that I am an atheist and a Croat," he said, "people ask me how I can prove I am not a Serb." To be Croatian, in other words, is to be Roman Catholic. To be a Serb is to be Christian Orthodox. In the 1940s, this meant a Nazi puppet state, set up in Croatia and enjoying the patronage of the Vatican, which naturally sought to exterminate all the Jews in the region but also undertook a campaign of forcible conversion directed at the other Christian community. Tens of thousands of Orthodox Christians were either slaughtered or deported in consequence, and a vast concentration camp was set up near the town of Jasenovacs. So disgusting was the regime of General Ante Pavelic and his Ustashe party that even many German officers protested at having to be associated with it.

By the time I visited the site of the Jasenovacs camp in 1992, the jackboot was somewhat on the other foot. The Croatian cities of Vukovar and Dubrovnik had been brutally shelled by the armed forces of Serbia, now under the control of Slobodan Milosevic. The mainly Muslim city of Sarajevo had been encircled and was being bombarded around the clock. Elsewhere in Bosnia-Herzegovina, especially along the river Drina, whole towns were pillaged and massacred in what the Serbs themselves termed "ethnic cleansing." In point of fact, "religious cleansing" would have been nearer the mark. Milosevic was an ex-Communist bureaucrat who had mutated into a xenophobic nationalist, and his anti-Muslim crusade, which was a cover for the annexation of Bosnia to a "Greater Serbia," was to a large extent carried out by unofficial militias operating under his "deniable" control. These gangs were made up of religious bigots, often blessed by Orthodox priests and bishops, and sometimes augmented by fellow Orthodox "volunteers" from Greece and Russia. They made a special attempt to destroy all evidence of Ottoman civilization, as in the specially atrocious case of the dynamiting of several historic minarets in Banja Luka, which was done during a cease-fire and not as the result of any battle.

The same was true, as is often forgotten, of their Catholic counterparts. The Ustashe formations were revived in Croatia and made a vicious attempt to take over Herzegovina, as they had during the Second World War. The beautiful city of Mostar was also shelled and besieged, and the world-famous Stari Most, or "Old Bridge,"

dating from Turkish times and listed by UNESCO as a cultural site
of world importance, was bombarded until it fell into the river below.
In effect, the extremist Catholic and Orthodox forces were collud-
ing in a bloody partition and cleansing of Bosnia-Herzegovina. They
were, and still are, largely spared the public shame of this, because the
world's media preferred the simplication of "Croat" and "Serb," and
only mentioned religion when discussing "the Muslims." But the triad
of terms "Croat," "Serb," and "Muslim" is unequal and misleading, in
that it equates two nationalities and one religion. (The same blunder
is made in a different way in coverage of Iraq, with the "Sunni-Shia-
Kurd" trilateral.) There were at least ten thousand Serbs in Sarajevo
throughout the siege, and one of the leading commanders of its defense, an officer and gentleman named General Jovan Divjak, whose
hand I was proud to shake under fire, was a Serb also. The city's
Jewish population, which dated from 1492, also identified itself for
the most part with the government and the cause of Bosnia. It would
have been far more accurate if the press and television had reported
that "today the Orthodox Christian forces resumed their bombard-
ment of Sarajevo," or "yesterday the Catholic militia succeeded in collapsing the Stari Most." But confessional terminology was reserved
only for "Muslims," even as their murderers went to all the trouble
of distinguishing themselves by wearing large Orthodox crosses over
their bandoliers, or by taping portraits of the Virgin Mary to their
rifle butts. Thus, once again, *religion poisons everything*, including our
own faculties of discernment.

As for Bethlehem, I suppose I would be willing to concede to Mr.
Prager that on a good day, I would feel safe enough standing around
outside the Church of the Nativity as evening came on. It is in Bethlehem, not far from Jerusalem, that many believe that, with the cooperation of an immaculately conceived virgin, god was delivered of
a son.

"Now the birth of Jesus Christ was in this wise. When his mother,
Mary, was espoused to Joseph, before they came together she was

found with child of the Holy Ghost." Yes, and the Greek demigod Perseus was born when the god Jupiter visited the virgin Danaë as a shower of gold and got her with child. The god Buddha was born through an opening in his mother's flank. Catlicus the serpent-skirted caught a little ball of feathers from the sky and hid it in her bosom, and the Aztec god Huitzilopochtli was thus conceived. The virgin Nana took a pomegranate from the tree watered by the blood of the slain Agdestris, and laid it in her bosom, and gave birth to the god Attis. The virgin daughter of a Mongol king awoke one night and found herself bathed in a great light, which caused her to give birth to Genghis Khan. Krishna was born of the virgin Devaka. Horus was born of the virgin Isis. Mercury was born of the virgin Maia. Romulus was born of the virgin Rhea Sylvia. For some reason, many religions force themselves to think of the birth canal as a one-way street, and even the Koran treats the Virgin Mary with reverence. However, this made no difference during the Crusades, when a papal army set out to recapture Bethlehem and Jerusalem from the Muslims, incidentally destroying many Jewish communities and sacking heretical Christian Byzantium along the way, and inflicted a massacre in the narrow streets of Jerusalem, where, according to the hysterical and gleeful chroniclers, the spilled blood reached up to the bridles of the horses.

Some of these tempests of hatred and bigotry and bloodlust have passed away, though new ones are always impending in this area, but meanwhile a person can feel relatively unmolested in and around "Manger Square," which is the center, as its name suggests, of a tourist trap of such unrelieved tawdriness as to put Lourdes itself to shame. When I first visited this pitiful town, it was under the nominal control of a largely Christian Palestinian municipality, linked to one particular political dynasty identified with the Freij family. When I have seen it since, it has generally been under a brutal curfew imposed by the Israeli military authorities—whose presence on the West Bank is itself not unconnected with belief in certain ancient scriptural prophecies, though this time with a different promise made by a different god to a different people. Now comes the turn of still another religion. The forces of Hamas, who claim the whole of Palestine as an Islamic *waqf* or holy dispensation sacred to Islam, have begun to elbow aside the Christians of Bethlehem. Their leader, Mahmoud al-Zahar, has announced that all inhabitants of the Islamic state of Palestine will be expected to conform to Muslim law. In Bethlehem, it is now proposed that non-Muslims be subjected to the *al-Jeziya* tax, the historic levy imposed on *dhimmis* or unbelievers under the old Ottoman Empire. Female employees of the municipality are forbidden to greet male visitors with a handshake. In Gaza, a young woman named Yusra al-Azami was shot dead in April 2005, for the crime of sitting unchaperoned in a car with her fiancé. The young man escaped with only a vicious beating. The leaders of the Hamas "vice and virtue" squad justified this casual murder and torture by saying that there had been "suspicion of immoral behavior." In once secular Palestine, mobs of sexually repressed young men are conscripted to snoop around parked cars, and given permission to do what they like.

I once heard the late Abba Eban, one of Israel's more polished and thoughtful diplomats and statesmen, give a talk in New York. The first thing to strike the eye about the Israeli-Palestinian dispute, he said, was the ease of its solubility. From this arresting start he went on to say, with the authority of a former foreign minister and UN representative, that the essential point was a simple one. Two peoples of roughly equivalent size had a claim to the same land. The solution was, obviously, to create two states side by side. Surely something so self-evident was within the wit of man to encompass? And so it would have been, decades ago, if the messianic rabbis and mullahs and priests could have been kept out of it. But the exclusive claims to god-given authority, made by hysterical clerics on both sides and further stoked by Armageddon-minded Christians who hope to bring on the Apocalypse (preceded by the death or conversion of all Jews), have made the situation insufferable, and put the whole of humanity in the position of hostage to a quarrel that now features the threat of nuclear war. *Religion poisons everything.* As well as a menace to civilization, it has become a threat to human survival.

To come last to Baghdad. This is one of the greatest centers of learning and culture in history. It was here that some of the lost works of Aristotle and other Greeks ("lost" because the Christian authorities had burned some, suppressed others, and closed the schools of philosophy, on the grounds that there could have been no useful reflections on morality before the preaching of Jesus) were preserved, retranslated, and transmitted via Andalusia back to the ignorant "Christian" West. Baghdad's libraries and poets and architects were renowned. Many of these attainments took place under Muslim caliphs, who sometimes permitted and as often repressed their expression, but Baghdad also bears the traces of ancient Chaldean and Nestorian Christianity, and was one of the many centers of the Jewish diaspora. Until the late 1940s, it was home to as many Jews as were living in Jerusalem.

I am not here going to elaborate a position on the overthrow of Saddam Hussein in April 2003. I shall simply say that those who regarded his regime as a "secular" one are deluding themselves. It is true that the Ba'ath Party was founded by a man named Michel Aflaq, a sinister Christian with a sympathy for fascism, and it is also true that membership of that party was open to all religions (though its Jewish membership was, I have every reason to think, limited). However, at least since his calamitous invasion of Iran in 1979, which led to furious accusations from the Iranian theocracy that he was an "infidel," Saddam Hussein had decked out his whole rule—which was based in any case on a tribal minority of the Sunni minority—as one of piety and jihad. (The Syrian Ba'ath Party, also based on a confessional fragment of society aligned with the Alawite minority, has likewise enjoyed a long and hypocritical relationship with the Iranian mullahs.) Saddam had inscribed the words *"Allahuh Akhbar"*—"God Is Great"—on the Iraqi flag. He had sponsored a huge international conference of holy warriors and mullahs, and maintained very warm relations with their other chief state sponsor in the region, namely the genocidal government of Sudan. He had built the largest mosque in the region, and named it the "Mother of All Battles" mosque, complete with a Koran written in blood that he claimed to be his own. When launching his own genocidal campaign against the (mainly Sunni) people of Kurdistan—a campaign that involved the thoroughgoing use of chemical atrocity weapons and the murder and deportation of hundreds of thousands of people—he had called it "Operation *Anfal*," borrowing by this term a Koranic justification—"The Spoils" of sura 8—for the despoilment and destruction of nonbelievers. When the Coalition forces crossed the Iraqi border, they found Saddam's army dissolving like a sugar lump in hot tea, but met with some quite tenacious resistance from a paramilitary group, stiffened with foreign jihadists, called the Fedayeen Saddam. One of the jobs of this group was to execute anybody who publicly welcomed the Western intervention, and some revolting public hangings and mutilations were soon captured on video for all to see.

At a minimum, it can be agreed by all that the Iraqi people had endured much in the preceding thirty-five years of war and dictatorship, that the Saddam regime could not have gone on forever as an outlaw system within international law, and therefore that—whatever objections there might be to the actual means of "regime change"— the whole society deserved a breathing space in which to consider reconstruction and reconciliation. Not one single minute of breathing space was allowed.

Everybody knows the sequel. The supporters of al-Qaeda, led by a Jordanian jailbird named Abu Musab al-Zarqawi, launched a frenzied campaign of murder and sabotage. They not only slew unveiled women and secular journalists and teachers. They not only set off bombs in Christian churches (Iraq's population is perhaps 2 percent Christian) and shot or maimed Christians who made and sold alcohol. They not only made a video of the mass shooting and throat-cutting of a contingent of Nepalese guest workers, who were assumed to be Hindu and thus beyond all consideration. These atrocities might be counted as more or less routine. They directed the most toxic part of their campaign of terror at fellow Muslims. The mosques and funeral processions of the long-oppressed Shiite majority were blown up. Pilgrims coming long distances to the newly accessible shrines at Karbala and Najaf did so at the risk of their lives. In a letter to his leader Osama bin Laden, Zarqawi gave the two main reasons for this extraordinarily evil policy. In the first place, as he wrote, the Shiites were heretics who did not take the correct Salafist path of purity. They were thus a fit prey for the truly holy. In the second place, if a religious war could be induced within Iraqi society, the plans of the "crusader" West could be set at naught. The obvious hope was to ignite a counterresponse from the Shia themselves, which would drive Sunni Arabs into the arms of their bin Ladenist "protectors." And, despite some noble appeals for restraint from the Shiite grand ayatollah Sistani, it did not prove very difficult to elicit such a response. Before long, Shia death squads, often garbed in police uniforms, were killing and torturing random members of the Sunni Arab faith. The surreptitious influence of the neighboring "Islamic Republic" of Iran was not difficult to detect, and in some Shia areas also it became dangerous to be an unveiled woman or a secular person. Iraq boasts quite a long history of intermarriage and intercommunal cooperation. But a few years of this hateful dialectic soon succeeded in creating an atmosphere of misery, distrust, hostility, and sect-based politics. Once again, *religion had poisoned everything.*

In all the cases I have mentioned, there were those who protested in the name of religion and who tried to stand athwart the rising tide of fanaticism and the cult of death. I can think of a handful of priests and bishops and rabbis and imams who have put humanity ahead of their own sect or creed. History gives us many other such examples, which I am going to discuss later on. But this is a compliment to humanism, not to religion. If it comes to that, these crises have also caused me, and many other atheists, to protest on behalf of Catholics suffering discrimination in Ireland, of Bosnian Muslims facing extermination in the Christian Balkans, of Shia Afghans and

Iraqis being put to the sword by Sunni jiahdists, and vice versa, and numberless other such cases. To adopt such a stand is the elementary duty of a self-respecting human. But the general reluctance of clerical authorities to issue unambiguous condemnation, whether it is the Vatican in the case of Croatia or the Saudi or Iranian leaderships in the case of their respective confessions, is uniformly disgusting. And so is the willingness of each "flock" to revert to atavistic behavior under the least provocation.

No, Mr. Prager, I have not found it a prudent rule to seek help as the prayer meeting breaks up. And this, as I told you, is only the letter "B." In all these cases, anyone concerned with human safety or dignity would have to hope fervently for a mass outbreak of democratic and republican secularism.

I DID NOT HAVE TO TRAVEL to all these exotic places in order to see the poison doing its work. Long before the critical day of September 11, 2001, I could sense that religion was beginning to reassert its challenge to civil society. When I am not operating as a tentative and amateur foreign correspondent, I lead a rather tranquil and orderly life: writing books and essays, teaching my students to love English literature, attending agreeable conferences of literary types, taking part in the transient arguments that arise in publishing and the academy. But even this rather sheltered existence has been subject to outrageous invasions and insults and challenges. On February 14, 1989, my friend Salman Rushdie was hit by a simultaneous death sentence and life sentence, for the crime of writing a work of fiction. To be more precise, the theocratic head of a foreign state—the Ayatollah Khomeini of Iran—publicly offered money, in his own name, to suborn the murder of a novelist who was a citizen of another country. Those who were encouraged to carry out this bribed assassination scheme, which extended to "all those involved in the publication" of *The Satanic Verses*, were offered not just the cold cash but also a free ticket to paradise. It is impossible to imagine a greater affront to every value of free expression. The ayatollah had not read, and probably could not read, and in any case forbade everyone else to read, the novel. But he succeeded in igniting ugly demonstrations, among Muslims in Britain as well as across the world, where crowds burned the book and screamed for the author to be fed to the flames as well.

This episode—part horrifying and part grotesque—of course had its origins in the material or "real" world. The ayatollah, having flung away hundreds of thousands of young Iranian lives in an attempt to prolong the war which Saddam Hussein had started, and thereby to turn it into a victory for his own reactionary theology, had recently been forced to acknowledge reality and to agree to the United Nations cease-fire resolution that he had sworn he would drink poison before signing. He was in need, in other words, of an "issue." A group of reactionary Muslims in South Africa, who sat in the puppet parliament of the apartheid regime, had announced that if Mr. Rushdie attended a book fair in their country he would be killed. A fundamentalist group in Pakistan had shed blood on the streets. Khomeini had to prove that he could not be outdone by anybody.

As it happens, there are some statements allegedly made by the Prophet Muhammad, which are difficult to reconcile with Muslim teaching. Koranic scholars had attempted to square this circle by suggesting that, in these instances, the Prophet was accidentally taking dictation from Satan instead of from God. This ruse—which would not have disgraced the most sinuous school of medieval Christian apologetics—provided an excellent opportunity for a novelist to explore the relationship between holy writ and literature. But the literal mind does not understand the ironic mind, and sees it always as a source of danger. Moreover, Rushdie had been brought up as a Muslim and had an understanding of the Koran, which meant in effect that he was an apostate. And "apostasy," according to the Koran, is punishable by death. There is no right to change religion, and all religious states have always insisted on harsh penalties for those who try it.

A number of serious attempts were made to kill Rushdie by religious death squads supported from Iranian embassies. His Italian and Japanese translators were criminally assaulted, apparently in one case in the absurd belief that the translator might know his whereabouts, and one of them was savagely mutilated as he lay dying. His Norwegian publisher was shot in the back several times with a high-velocity rifle and left for dead in the snow, but astonishingly survived. One might have thought that such arrogant state-sponsored homicide, directed at a lonely and peaceful individual who pursued a life devoted to language, would have called forth a general condemnation. But such was not the case. In considered statements, the Vatican, the archbishop of Canterbury, and the chief sephardic rabbi of Israel all took a stand in sympathy with—the ayatollah. So did the cardinal archbishop of New York and many other lesser religious figures. While they usually managed a few words in which to deplore the resort to violence, all these men stated that the main problem raised by the publication of *The Satanic Verses* was not murder by mercenaries, but blasphemy. Some public figures not in holy orders, such as the Marxist writer John Berger, the Tory historian Hugh Trevor-Roper, and the doyen of espionage authors John Le Carré, also pronounced that Rushdie was the author of his own troubles, and had brought them on himself by "offending" a great monotheistic religion. There seemed nothing fantastic, to these people, in the British police having to defend an Indian-born ex-Muslim citizen from a concerted campaign to take his life in the name of god.

Sheltered as my own life normally is, I had a taste of this surreal situation when Mr. Rushdie came to Washington over the Thanksgiving weekend of 1993, in order to keep an appointment with President Clinton, and stayed for a night or two in my apartment. An enormous and forbidding security operation was necessary to bring this about, and when the visit was over I was asked to pay a visit to the Department of State. There I was informed by a senior official that believable "chatter" had been intercepted expressing the intention of revenge on me and on my family. I was advised to change my address and my telephone number, which seemed an unlikely way of avoiding reprisal. However, it did put me on notice of what I already knew. It is not possible for me to say, Well, you pursue your Shiite dream of a hidden imam and I pursue my study of Thomas Paine and George Orwell, and the world is big enough for both of us. The true believer cannot rest until the whole world bows the knee. Is it not obvious to all, say the pious, that religious authority is paramount, and that those who decline to recognize it have forfeited their right to exist?

It was, as it happens, the *murderers* of the Shia who forced this point upon the world's attention a few years later. So ghastly had been the regime of the Taliban in Afghanistan, which slaughtered the Shiite Hazara population, that Iran itself had considered invading the country in 1999. And so great was the Taliban's addiction to profanity that it had methodically shelled and destroyed one of the world's greatest cultural artifacts—the twin Buddha statues at Bamiyan, which in their magnificence showed the fusion of Hellenic and other styles in the Afghan past. But, pre-Islamic as they undoubtedly were, the statues were a standing insult to the Taliban and their al-Qaeda guests, and the reduction of Bamiyan to shards and rubble foreshadowed the incineration of two other twin structures, as well as almost three thousand human beings, in downtown Manhattan in the fall of 2001.

Everybody has their own 9/11 story: I shall skip over mine except to say that someone I slightly knew was flown into the wall of the Pentagon having managed to call her husband and give a description of her murderers and their tactics (and having learned from him that it was not a hijack and that she was going to die). From the roof of my building in Washington, I could see the smoke rising from the other side of the river, and I have never since passed the Capitol or the White House without thinking of what might have happened were it not for the courage and resourcefulness of the passengers on the fourth plane, who managed to bring it down in a Pennsylvanian field only twenty minutes' flying time from its destination.

Well, I was able to write in a further reply to Dennis Prager, now you have your answer. The nineteen suicide murderers of New York and Washington and Pennsylvania were beyond any doubt the most sincere believers on those planes. Perhaps we can hear a little less about how "people of faith" possess moral advantages that others can only envy. And what is to be learned from the jubilation and the ecstatic propaganda with which this great feat of fidelity has been greeted in the Islamic world? At the time, the United States had an attorney general named John Ashcroft, who had stated that America had "no king but Jesus" (a claim that was exactly two words too long). It had a president who wanted to hand over the care of the poor to "faith-based" institutions. Might this not be a moment where the light of reason, and the defense of a society that separated church and state and valued free expression and free inquiry, be granted a point or two?

The disappointment was, and to me remains, acute. Within hours, the "reverends" Pat Robertson and Jerry Falwell had announced that the immolation of their fellow creatures was a divine judgment on a secular society that tolerated homosexuality and abortion. At the solemn memorial service for the victims, held in the beautiful National Cathedral in Washington, an address was permitted from Billy Graham, a man whose record of opportunism and anti-Semitism is in itself a minor national disgrace. His absurd sermon made the claim that all the dead were now in paradise and would not return to us even if they could. I say absurd because it is impossible even in the most lenient terms to believe that a good number of sinful citizens had not been murdered by al-Qaeda that day. And there is no reason to believe that Billy Graham knew the current whereabouts of their souls, let alone their posthumous desires. But there was also something sinister in hearing detailed claims to knowledge of paradise, of the sort that bin Laden himself was making on behalf of the assassins.

Matters continued to deteriorate in the interval between the removal of the Taliban and the overthrow of Saddam Hussein. A senior military official named General William Boykin announced that he had been vouchsafed a vision while serving earlier during the fiasco in Somalia. Apparently the face of Satan himself had been detected by some aerial photography of Mogadishu, but this had only increased the confidence of the general that his god was stronger than the evil deity of the opposition. At the U.S. Air Force Academy in Colorado Springs, it was revealed that Jewish and agnostic cadets were being viciously bullied by a group of unpunished "born again" cadres, who insisted that only those accepting Jesus as a personal savior were qualified to serve. The deputy commander of the academy sent out e-mails proselytizing for a national day of (Christian) prayer. A chaplain named MeLinda Morton, who complained about this hysteria and intimidation, was abruptly transferred to a faraway base in Japan. Meanwhile, empty-headed multiculturalism also contributed its portion, by among other means ensuring the distribution of cheap and mass-produced Saudi editions of the Koran, for use in America's prison system. These Wahhabi texts went even further than the original in recommending holy war against all Christians and Jews and secularists. To observe all this was to witness a kind of cultural suicide: an "assisted suicide" at which believers and unbelievers were both prepared to officiate.

It ought to have been pointed out at once that this sort of thing, as well as being unethical and unprofessional, was also flat-out unconstitutional and anti-American. James Madison, the author of the First Amendment to the Constitution, prohibiting any law respecting an establishment of religion, was also an author of Article VI, which states unambiguously that "no religious test shall ever be required as a qualification to any office or public trust." His later *Detached Memoranda* make it very plain that he opposed the government appointment of chaplains in the first place, either in the armed forces or at the opening ceremonies of Congress. "The establishment of the chaplainship to Congress is a palpable violation of equal rights, as well as of Constitutional principles." As to clerical presence in the armed forces, Madison wrote, "The object of this establishment is seducing; the motive to it is laudable. But is it not safer to adhere to a right principle, and trust to its consequences, than confide in the reasoning however specious in favor of a wrong one? Look thro' the armies and navies of the world, and say whether in the appointment of their ministers of religion, the spiritual interest of the flocks or the temporal interest of the Shepherd be most in view?" Anyone citing Madison today would very likely be thought either subversive or insane, and yet without him and Thomas Jefferson, coauthors of the Virginia Statute on Religious Freedom, the United States would have gone on as it was—with Jews prohibited from holding office in some states, Catholics in others, and Protestants in Maryland: the latter a state where "profane words concerning the Holy Trinity" were punishable by torture, branding, and, at the third offense, "death without benefit of clergy." Georgia might have persisted in maintaining that its official state faith was "Protestantism"—whichever one of Luther's many hybrids that might have turned out to be.

As the debate over intervention in Iraq became more heated, positive torrents of nonsense poured from the pulpits. Most churches opposed the effort to remove Saddam Hussein, and the pope disgraced himself utterly by issuing a personal invitation to the wanted war criminal Tariq Aziz, a man responsible for the state murder of children. Not only was Aziz welcomed at the Vatican as the senior Catholic member of a ruling fascist party (not the first time that such an indulgence had been granted), he was then taken to Assisi for a personal session of prayer at the shrine of Saint Francis, who apparently used to lecture to birds. This, he must have thought, was altogether too easy. On the other side of the confessional span, some but not all American evangelicals thundered joyously about the prospect of winning the Muslim world for Jesus. (I say "some but not all" because one fundamentalist splinter group has since taken to picketing the funerals of American soldiers killed in Iraq, claiming that their murders are god's punishment for American homosexuality. One especially tasteful sign, waved in the faces of the mourners, is "Thank God for IEDs," the roadside bombs placed by equally anti-gay Muslim fascists. It is not my problem to decide which theology is the correct one here: I would say the chances of either being right are approximately the same.) Charles Stanley, whose weekly sermons from the First Baptist Church in Atlanta are watched by millions, could have been any demagogic imam as he said, "We should offer to serve the war effort in any way possible. God battles with people who oppose him, who fight against him and his followers." His organization's Baptist Press news service printed an article from a missionary exulting that "American foreign policy, and military might, have opened an opportunity for the gospel in the land of Abraham, Isaac and Jacob." Never to be outdone, Tim LaHaye decided to go even further. Best-known as the coauthor of the best-selling *Left Behind* pulp novel series, which readies the average American for the "rapture" and then for Armageddon, he spoke of Iraq as "a focal point of end-time events." Other biblical enthusiasts tried to link Saddam Hussein with the wicked King Nebuchadnezzar of ancient Babylon, a comparison that the dictator himself would probably have approved, given his rebuilding of the old walls at Babylon with bricks that had his name inscribed on every one of them. Thus, instead of a rational discussion about the best way to contain and defeat religious fanaticism, one had the mutual reinforcement of two forms of that mania: the jihadist assault reconjured the bloodstained specter of the Crusaders.

In this respect, religion is not unlike racism. One version of it inspires and provokes the other. I was once asked another trick question, slightly more searching than Dennis Prager's, that was designed to uncover my level of latent prejudice. You are on a subway platform in New York, late at night, in a deserted station. Suddenly a group of a dozen black men appears. Do you stay where you are or move to the exit? I was able again to reply that I had had this exact experience. Waiting alone for a train, well after midnight, I had been suddenly joined by a crew of repairmen exiting the tunnel with their tools and work gloves. All of them were black. I felt instantly safer, and moved toward them. I have no idea what their religious affiliation was. But in every other case that I have cited, religion has been an enormous multiplier of tribal suspicion and hatred, with members of each group talking of the other in precisely the tones of the bigot. The Christians and Jews eat defiled pig meat and swill poisonous alcohol. Buddhist and Muslim Sri Lankans blamed the wine-oriented Christmas celebrations of 2004 for the immediately following tsunami. Catholics are dirty and have too many children. Muslims breed like rabbits and wipe their bottoms with the wrong hand. Jews have lice in their beards and seek the blood of Christian children to add flavor and zest to their Passover matzos. And so it goes on.

Chapter Three

A Short Digression on the Pig; or, Why Heaven Hates Ham

All religions have a tendency to feature some dietary injunction or prohibition, whether it is the now lapsed Catholic injunction to eat fish on Fridays, or the adoration by Hindus of the cow as a consecrated and invulnerable animal (the government of India even offered to import and protect all the cattle facing slaughter as a result of the bovine encephalitic, or "mad cow," plague that swept Europe in the 1990s), or the refusal by some other Eastern cults to consume any animal flesh, or to injure any other creature be it rat or flea. But the oldest and most tenacious of all fetishes is the hatred and even fear of the pig. It emerged in primitive Judaea, and was for centuries one of the ways—the other being circumcision—by which Jews could be distinguished.

Even though sura 5.60 of the Koran condemns particularly Jews but also other unbelievers as having been turned into pigs and monkeys—a very intense theme in recent Salafist Muslim preaching—and the Koran describes the flesh of swine as unclean or even "abominable," Muslims appear to see nothing ironic in the adoption of this uniquely Jewish taboo. Real horror of the porcine is manifest all over the Islamic world. One good instance would be the continued prohibition of George Orwell's *Animal Farm*, one of the most charming and useful fables of modern times, of the reading of which Muslim schoolchildren are deprived. I have perused some of the solemn prohibition orders written by Arab education ministries, which are so stupid that they fail to notice the evil and dictatorial role played by the pigs in the story itself.

Orwell actually did dislike pigs, as a consequence of his failure as a small farmer, and this revulsion is shared by many adults who have had to work with these difficult animals in agricultural conditions. Crammed together in sties, pigs tend to act swinishly, as it were, and to have noisy and nasty fights. It is not unknown for them to eat their own young and even their own excrement, while their tendency to random and loose gallantry is often painful to the more fastidious eye. But it has often been noticed that pigs left to their own devices, and granted sufficient space, will keep themselves very clean, arrange little bowers, bring up families, and engage in social interaction with other pigs. The creatures also display many signs of intelligence, and it has been calculated that the crucial ratio—between brain weight and body weight—is almost as high with them as it is in dolphins. There is great adaptability between the pig and its environment, as witness wild boars and "feral pigs" as opposed to the placid porkers and frisky piglets of our more immediate experience. But the cloven hoof, or trotter, became a sign of diabolism to the fearful, and I daresay that it is easy to surmise which came first—the devil or the pig. It would be merely boring and idiotic to wonder how the designer of all things conceived such a versatile creature and then commanded his higher-mammal creation to avoid it altogether or risk his eternal displeasure. But many otherwise intelligent mammals affect the belief that heaven hates ham.

I hope that you have guessed by now what we know in any case—that this fine beast is one of our fairly close cousins. It shares a great deal of our DNA, and there have lately been welcome transplants of skin, heart valves, and kidneys from pigs to humans. If—which I heartily trust does not happen—a new Dr. Moreau could corrupt recent advances in cloning and create a hybrid, a "pig-man" is widely feared as the most probable outcome. Meanwhile, almost everything about the pig is useful, from its nutritious and delicious meat to its tanned hide for leather and its bristles for brushes. In Upton Sinclair's graphic novel of the Chicago slaughterhouse, *The Jungle*, it is agonizing to read about the way that pigs are borne aloft on hooks, screaming as their throats are cut. Even the strongest nerves of the most hardened workers are shaken by the experience. There is something about that shriek . . .

To press this a little further, one may note that children if left unmolested by rabbis and imams are very drawn to pigs, especially to baby ones, and that firefighters in general do not like to eat roast pork or crackling. The barbaric vernacular word for roasted human in New Guinea and elsewhere was "long pig": I have never had the relevant degustatative experience myself, but it seems that we do, if eaten, taste very much like pigs.

This helps to make nonsense of the usual "secular" explanations of the original Jewish prohibition. It is argued that the ban was initially rational, since pig meat in hot climates can become rank and develop the worms of trichinosis. This objection—which perhaps does apply in the case of non-kosher shellfish—is absurd when applied to the actual conditions. First, trichinosis is found in all climates, and in fact occurs more in cold than in hot ones. Second, ancient Jewish settlements in the land of Canaan can easily be distinguished by archaeologists by the absence of pig bones in their rubbish tips, as opposed to the presence of such bones in the middens of other communities. The non-Jews did not sicken and die from eating pork, in other words. (Quite apart from anything else, if they *had* died for this reason there would have been no need for the god of Moses to urge their slaughter by non-pig-eaters.)

There must therefore be another answer to the conundrum. I claim my own solution as original, though without the help of Sir James Frazer and the great Ibn Warraq I might not have hit upon it. According to many ancient authorities, the attitude of early Semites to swine was one of reverence as much as disgust. The eating of pig flesh was considered as something special, even privileged and ritualistic. (This mad confusion between the sacred and the profane is found in all faiths at all times.) The simultaneous attraction and repulsion derived from an anthropomorphic root: the look of the pig, and the taste of the pig, and the dying yells of the pig, and the evident intelligence of the pig, were too uncomfortably reminiscent of the human. Porcophobia—and porcophilia—thus probably originate in a nighttime of human sacrifice and even cannibalism at which the "holy" texts often do more than hint. Nothing optional—from homosexuality to adultery—is ever made punishable unless those who do the prohibiting (and exact the fierce punishments) have a repressed desire to participate. As Shakespeare put it in *King Lear*, the policeman who lashes the whore has a hot need to use her for the very offense for which he plies the lash.

Porcophilia can also be used for oppressive and repressive purposes. In medieval Spain, where Jews and Muslims were compelled on pain of death and torture to convert to Christianity, the religious authorities quite rightly suspected that many of the conversions were not sincere. Indeed, the Inquisition arose partly from the holy dread that secret infidels were attending Mass—where of course, and even more disgustingly, they were pretending to eat human flesh and drink human blood, in the person of Christ himself. Among the customs that arose in consequence was the offering, at most events formal and informal, of a plate of charcuterie. Those who have been fortunate enough to visit Spain, or any good Spanish restaurant, will be familiar with the gesture of hospitality: literally dozens of pieces of differently cured, differently sliced pig. But the grim origin of this lies in a constant effort to sniff out heresy, and to be unsmilingly watchful for giveaway expressions of distaste. In the hands of eager Christian fanatics, even the toothsome *jamón Ibérico* could be pressed into service as a form of torture.

Today, ancient stupidity is upon us again. Muslim zealots in Europe are demanding that the Three Little Pigs, and Miss Piggy, *Winnie-the-Pooh*'s Piglet, and other traditional pets and characters be removed from the innocent gaze of their children. The mirthless cretins of jihad have probably not read enough to know of the Empress of Blandings, and of the Earl of Emsworth's infinitely renewable delight in the splendid pages of the incomparable author Mr. Whiffle, *The Care of the Pig*, but there will be trouble when they get that far. An old statue of a wild boar, in an arboretum in Middle England, has already been threatened with mindless Islamic vandalism.

In microcosm, this apparently trivial fetish shows how religion and faith and superstition distort our whole picture of the world. The pig is so close to us, and has been so handy to us in so many respects, that a strong case is now made by humanists that it should not be factory-farmed, confined, separated from its young, and forced to live in its own ordure. All other considerations to one side, the resulting pink and spongy meat *is* somewhat rebarbative. But this is a decision that we can make in the plain light of reason and compassion, as extended to fellow creatures and relatives, and not as a result of incantations from Iron Age campfires where much worse offenses were celebrated in the name of god. "Pig's head on a stick," says the nervous but stouthearted Ralph in the face of the buzzing, suppurating idol (first killed and then worshipped) that has been set up by cruel, frightened schoolboys in *Lord of the Flies*. "Pig's head on a stick." And he was more right than he could have known, and much wiser than his elders as well as his delinquent juniors.

Chapter Four

A Note on Health, to Which Religion Can Be Hazardous

In dark ages people are best guided by religion, as in a pitch-black night a blind man is the best guide; he knows the roads and paths better than a man who can see. When daylight comes, however, it is foolish to use blind old men as guides.
—HEINRICH HEINE, *GEDANKEN UND EINFALLE*

In the fall of 2001 I was in Calcutta with the magnificent photographer Sebastião Salgado, a Brazilian genius whose studies with the camera have made vivid the lives of migrants, war victims, and those workers who toil to extract primary products from mines and quarries and forests. On this occasion, he was acting as an envoy of UNICEF and promoting his cause as a crusader—in the positive sense of that term—against the scourge of polio. Thanks to the work of inspired and enlightened scientists like Jonas Salk, it is now possible to immunize children against this ghastly malady for a negligible cost: the few cents or pennies that it takes to administer two drops of oral vaccine to the mouth of an infant. Advances in medicine had managed to put the fear of smallpox behind us, and it was confidently expected that another year would do the same for polio. Humanity itself had

43

seemingly united on this proposition. In several countries, including El Salvador, warring combatants had proclaimed cease-fires in order to allow the inoculation teams to move freely. Extremely poor and backward countries had mustered the resources to get the good news to every village: no more children need be killed, or made useless and miserable, by this hideous disease. Back home in Washington, where that year many people were still fearfully staying indoors after the trauma of 9/11, my youngest daughter was going dauntlessly door to door on Halloween, piping "Trick or Treat for UNICEF" and healing or saving, with every fistful of small change, children she would never meet. One had that rare sense of participating in an entirely positive enterprise.

The people of Bengal, and particularly the women, were enthusiastic and inventive. I remember one committee meeting, where staunch Calcutta hostesses planned without embarrassment to team up with the city's prostitutes to spread the word into the farthest corners of society. Bring your children, no questions asked, and let them swallow the two drops of fluid. Someone knew of an elephant a few miles out of town that might be hired to lead a publicity parade. Everything was going well: in one of the poorest cities and states of the world there was to be a new start. And then we began to hear of a rumor. In some outlying places, Muslim die-hards were spreading the story that the droplets were a plot. If you took this sinister Western medicine, you would be stricken by impotence and diarrhea (a forbidding and depressing combination).

This was a problem, because the drops have to be administered twice—the second time as a booster and confirmation of immunity—and because it takes only a few uninoculated people to allow the disease to survive and revive, and to spread back through contact and the water supply. As with smallpox, eradication must be utter and complete. I wondered as I left Calcutta if West Bengal would manage to meet the deadline and declare itself polio-free by the end of the next year. That would leave only pockets of Afghanistan and one or two other inaccessible regions, already devastated by religious fervor, before we could say that another ancient tyranny of illness had been decisively overthrown.

In 2005 I learned of one outcome. In northern Nigeria—a country that had previously checked in as provisionally polio-free—a group of Islamic religious figures issued a ruling, or fatwa, that declared the polio vaccine to be a conspiracy by the United States (and, amazingly, the United Nations) against the Muslim faith. The drops were designed, said these mullahs, to sterilize the true believers. Their intention and effect was genocidal. Nobody was to swallow them, or administer them to infants. Within months, polio was back, and not just in northern Nigeria. Nigerian travelers and pilgrims had already taken it as far as Mecca, and spread it back to several other polio-free countries, including three African ones and also faraway Yemen. The entire boulder would have to be rolled back right up to the top of the mountain.

You may say that this is an "isolated" case, which would be a grimly apt way of putting it. But you would be mistaken. Would you care to see my video of the advice given by Cardinal Alfonso Lopez de Trujillo, the vatican's president of the Pontifical Council for the Family, carefully warning his audience that all condoms are secretly made with many microscopic holes, through which the AIDS virus can pass? Close your eyes and try to picture what you might say if you had the authority to inflict the greatest possible suffering in the least number of words. Consider the damage that such a dogma has caused: presumably those holes permit the passage of other things too, which rather destroys the point of a condom in the first place. To make such a statement in Rome is wicked enough. But translate the message into the language of poor and stricken countries and see what happens. During carnival season in Brazil, the auxiliary bishop of Rio de Janeiro, Rafael Llano Cifuentes, told his congregation in a sermon that "the church is against condom use. Sexual relations between a man and a woman have to be natural. I have never seen a little dog using a condom during sexual intercourse with another dog." Senior clerical figures in several other countries—Cardinal Obando y Bravo of Nicaragua, the archbishop of Nairobi in Kenya, Cardinal Emmanuel Wamala of Uganda—have all told their flocks that condoms transmit AIDS. Cardinal Wamala, indeed, has opined that women who die of AIDS rather than employ latex protection should be considered as martyrs (though presumably this martyrdom must take place within the confines of marriage).

The Islamic authorities have been no better and sometimes worse. In 1995, the Council of Ulemas in Indonesia urged that condoms only be made available to married couples, and on prescription. In Iran, a worker found to be HIV-positive can lose his job, and doctors and hospitals have the right to refuse treatment to AIDS patients. An official of Pakistan's AIDS Control Program told *Foreign Policy* magazine in 2005 that the problem was smaller in his country because of "better social and Islamic values." This, in a state where the law allows a woman to be *sentenced* to be gang-raped in order to expiate the "shame" of a crime committed by her brother. This is the old religious combination of repression and denial: a plague like AIDS is assumed to be unmentionable because the teachings of the Koran are enough in themselves to inhibit premarital intercourse, drug use, adultery, and prostitution. Even a very brief visit to, say, Iran, will demonstrate the opposite. It is the mullahs themselves who profit from hypocrisy by licensing "temporary marriages," in which wedding certificates are available for a few hours, sometimes in specially designated houses, with a divorce declaration ready to hand at the conclusion of business. You could almost call it prostitution . . . The last time I was offered such a bargain it was just outside the ugly shrine to the Ayatollah Khomeini in south Tehran. But veiled and burqa-clad women, infected by their husbands with the virus, are expected to die in silence. It is a certainty that millions of other harmless and decent people will die, very miserably and quite needlessly, all over the world as a result of this obscurantism.

The attitude of religion to medicine, like the attitude of religion to science, is always necessarily problematic and very often necessarily hostile. A modern believer can say and even believe that his faith is quite compatible with science and medicine, but the awkward fact will always be that both things have a tendency to break religion's monopoly, and have often been fiercely resisted for that reason. What happens to the faith healer and the shaman when any poor citizen can see the full effect of drugs and surgeries, administered without ceremonies or mystifications? Roughly the same thing as happens to the rainmaker when the climatologist turns up, or to the diviner from the heavens when school-teachers get hold of elementary telescopes. Plagues of antiquity were held to be punishment from the gods, which did much to strengthen the hold of the priesthood and much to encourage the burning of infidels and heretics who were thought—in an alternative explanation—to be spreading disease by witchcraft or else poisoning the wells.

We may make allowances for the orgies of stupidity and cruelty that were indulged in before humanity had a clear concept of the germ theory of disease. Most of the "miracles" of the New Testament have to do with healing, which was of such great importance in a time when even minor illness was often the end. (Saint Augustine himself said that he would not have believed in Christianity if it were not for the miracles.) Scientific critics of religion such as Daniel Dennett have been generous enough to point out that apparently useless healing rituals may even have helped people get better, in that we know how important morale can be in aiding the body to fight injury and infection. But that would be an excuse only available in retrospect. By the time Dr. Jenner had discovered that a cowpox vaccine could ward off smallpox, this excuse had become void. Yet Timothy Dwight, a president of Yale University and to this day one of America's most respected "divines," was opposed to the smallpox vaccination because he regarded it as an interference with god's design. And this mentality is still heavily present, long after its pretext and justification in human ignorance has vanished.

It is interesting, and suggestive, that the archbishop of Rio makes his analogy with dogs. They do not trouble to roll on a condom: who are we to quarrel with their fidelity to "nature"? In the recent division in the Anglican Church over homosexuality and ordination, several bishops made the fatuous point that homosexuality is "unnatural" because it does not occur in other species. Leave aside the fundamental absurdity of this observation: are humans part of "nature" or not? Or, if they chance to be homosexual, are they created in god's image or not? Leave aside the well-attested fact that numberless kinds of birds and mammals and primates do engage in homosexual play. Who are the clerics to interpret nature? They have shown themselves quite unable to do so. A condom is, quite simply, a necessary but not a sufficient condition for avoiding the transmission of AIDS. All qualified authorities, including those who state that abstinence is even better, are agreed on this. Homosexuality is present in all societies, and its incidence would appear to be part of human "design." We must perforce confront these facts as we find them. We now know that the bubonic plague was spread not by sin or moral backsliding but by rats and fleas. Archbishop Lancelot Andrewes, during the celebrated "Black Death" in London in 1665, noticed uneasily that the horror fell upon those who prayed and kept the faith as well as upon those who did not. He came perilously close to stumbling upon a real point. As I was writing this chapter, an argument broke out in my hometown of Washington, D.C. The human papillomavirus (HPV) has long been known as a sexually transmitted infection that, at its worst, can cause cervical cancer in women. A vaccine is now available—these days, vaccines are increasingly swiftly developed—not to cure this malady but to immunize women against it. But there are forces in the administration who oppose the adoption of this measure on the grounds that it fails to discourage premarital sex. To accept the spread of cervical cancer in the name of god is no different, morally or intellectually, from sacrificing these women on a stone altar and thanking the deity for giving us the sexual impulse and then condemning it.

We do not know how many people in Africa have died or will die because of the AIDS virus, which was isolated and became treatable, in a great feat of humane scientific research, very soon after it made its lethal appearance. On the other hand, we do know that having sex with a virgin—one of the more popular local "cures"—does not in fact prevent or banish the infection. And we also know that the use of condoms can at least contribute, as a form of prophylaxis, to the limitation and containment of the virus. We are not dealing, as early missionaries might have liked to believe, with witch doctors and savages who resist the boons that the missionaries bring. We are instead dealing with the Bush administration, which, in a supposedly secular republic in the twenty-first century, refuses to share its foreign aid budget with charities and clinics that offer advice on family planning. At least two major and established religions, with millions of adherents in Africa, believe that the cure is much worse than the disease. They also harbor the belief that the AIDS plague is in some sense a verdict from heaven upon sexual deviance—in particular upon homosexuality. A single stroke of Ockham's potent razor eviscerates this half-baked savagery: female homosexuals not only do not contract AIDS (except if they are unlucky with a transfusion or a needle), they are also much freer of *all* venereal infection than even heterosexuals. Yet clerical authorities persistently refuse to be honest about even the existence of the lesbian. In doing so, they further demonstrate that religion continues to pose an urgent threat to public health.

I pose a hypothetical question. As a man of some fifty-seven years of age, I am discovered sucking the penis of a baby boy. I ask you to picture your own outrage and revulsion. Ah, but I have my explanation all ready. I am a mohel: an appointed circumciser and foreskin remover. My authority comes from an ancient text, which commands me to take a baby boy's penis in my hand, cut around the prepuce, and complete the action by taking his penis in my mouth, sucking off the foreskin, and spitting out the amputated flap along with a mouthful of blood and saliva. This practice has been abandoned by most Jews, either because of its unhygienic nature or its disturbing

associations, but it still persists among the sort of Hasidic fundamentalists who hope for the Second Temple to be rebuilt in Jerusalem. To
them, the primitive rite of the *peri'ah metsitsah* is part of the original
and unbreakable covenant with god. In New York City in the year
2005, the ritual, as performed by a fifty-seven-year-old mohel, was
found to have given genital herpes to several small boys, and to have
caused the deaths of at least two of them. In normal circumstances,
the disclosure would have led the public health department to forbid
the practice and the mayor to denounce it. But in the capital of the
modern world, in the first decade of the twenty-first century, such
was not the case. Instead, Mayor Bloomberg overrode the reports by
distinguished Jewish physicians who had warned of the danger of the
custom, and told his health care bureaucracy to postpone any verdict.
The crucial thing, he said, was to be sure that the free exercise of religion was not being infringed. In a public debate with Peter Steinfels,
the liberal Catholic "religion editor" of the *New York Times*, I was told
the same thing.

It happened to be election year in New York for the mayor, which
often explains a lot. But this pattern recurs in other denominations
and other states and cities, as well as in other countries. Across a wide
swath of animist and Muslim Africa, young girls are subjected to the
hell of circumcision and infibulation, which involves the slicing off of
the labia and the clitoris, often with a sharp stone, and then the stitch-
ing up of the vaginal opening with strong twine, not to be removed
until it is broken by male force on the bridal night. Compassion and
biology allow for a small aperture to be left, meanwhile, for the passage of menstrual blood. The resulting stench, pain, humiliation, and
misery exceed anything that can be easily imagined, and inevitably
result in infection, sterility, shame, and the death of many women
and babies in childbirth. No society would tolerate such an insult to its
womanhood and therefore to its survival if the foul practice was not
holy and sanctified. But then, no New Yorker would permit atrocities
against infants if not for the same consideration. Parents professing to

believe the nonsensical claims of "Christian Science" have been accused, but not always convicted, of denying urgent medical care to their offspring. Parents who imagine themselves to be "Jehovah's Witnesses" have refused permission for their children to receive blood transfusions. Parents who imagine that a man named Joseph Smith was led to a set of buried golden tablets have married their underage "Mormon" daughters to favored uncles and brothers-in-law, who sometimes have older wives already. The Shia fundamentalists in Iran lowered the age of "consent" to nine, perhaps in admiring emulation of the age of the youngest "wife" of the "Prophet" Muhammad. Hindu child brides in India are flogged, and sometimes burned alive, if the pathetic dowry they bring is judged to be too small. The Vatican, and its vast network of dioceses, has in the past decade alone been forced to admit complicity in a huge racket of child rape and child torture, mainly but by no means exclusively homosexual, in which known pederasts and sadists were shielded from the law and reassigned to parishes where the pickings of the innocent and defenseless were often richer. In Ireland alone—once an unquestioning disciple of Holy Mother Church—it is now estimated that the *un*molested children of religious schools were very probably the minority.

Now, religion professes a special role in the protection and instruction of children. "Woe to him," says the Grand Inquisitor in Dostoyevsky's *The Brothers Karamazov*, "who harms a child." The New Testament has Jesus informing us that one so guilty would be better off at the bottom of the sea, and with a millstone around his neck at that. But both in theory and in practice, religion uses the innocent and the defenseless for the purposes of experiment. By all means let an observant Jewish adult male have his raw-cut penis placed in the mouth of a rabbi. (That would be legal, at least in New York.) By all means let grown women who distrust their clitoris or their labia have them sawn away by some other wretched adult female. By all means let Abraham offer to commit suicide to prove his devotion to the Lord or his belief in the voices he was hearing in his head. By all means let devout parents deny themselves the succor of medicine when in acute pain and distress. By all means—for all I care—let a priest sworn to celibacy be a promiscuous homosexual. By all means let a congregation that believes in whipping out the devil choose a new grown-up sinner each week and lash him until he or she bleeds. By all means let anyone who believes in creationism instruct his fellows during lunch breaks. But the conscription of the unprotected child for these purposes is something that even the most dedicated secularist can safely describe as a sin.

I do not set myself up as a moral exemplar, and would be swiftly knocked down if I did, but if I was suspected of raping a child, or torturing a child, or infecting a child with venereal disease, or selling a child into sexual or any other kind of slavery, I might consider committing suicide whether I was guilty or not. If I had actually committed the offense, I would welcome death in any form that it might take. This revulsion is innate in any healthy person, and does not need to be taught. Since religion has proved itself uniquely delinquent on the one subject where moral and ethical authority might be counted as universal and absolute, I think we are entitled to at least three provisional conclusions. The first is that religion and the churches are manufactured, and that this salient fact is too obvious to ignore. The second is that ethics and morality are quite independent of faith, and cannot be derived from it. The third is that religion is—because it claims a special divine exemption for its practices and beliefs—not just amoral but immoral. The ignorant psychopath or brute who mistreats his children must be punished but can be understood. Those who claim a heavenly warrant for the cruelty have been tainted by evil, and also constitute far more of a danger.

IN THE CITY OF JERUSALEM, there is a special ward in the mental hospital for those who represent a special danger to themselves and others. These deluded patients are the sufferers from the "Jerusalem syndrome." Police and security officers are trained to recognize them, though their mania is often concealed behind a mask of deceptively beatific calm. They have come to the holy city in order to announce themselves as the Messiah or redeemer, or to proclaim the end of days. The connection between religious faith and mental disorder is, from the viewpoint of the tolerant and the "multicultural," both very obvious and highly unmentionable. If someone murders his children and then says that god ordered him to do it, we might find him not guilty by reason of insanity but he would be incarcerated nonetheless. If someone lives in a cave and claims to be seeing visions and experiencing prophetic dreams, we may leave him alone until he turns out to be planning, in a nonphantasmal way, the joy of suicide bombing. If someone announces himself to be god's anointed, and begins stockpiling Kool-Aid and weapons and helping himself to the wives and daughters of his acolytes, we raise a bit more than a skeptical eyebrow. But if these things can be preached under the protection of an established religion, we are expected to take them at face value. All three monotheisms, just to take the most salient example, praise Abraham for being willing to hear voices and then to take his son Isaac for a long and rather mad and gloomy walk. And then the caprice by which his murderous hand is finally stayed is written down as divine mercy.

The relationship between physical health and mental health is now well understood to have a strong connection to the sexual function, or dysfunction. Can it be a coincidence, then, that all religions claim the right to legislate in matters of sex? The principal way in which believers inflict on themselves, on each other, and on nonbelievers, has always been their claim to monopoly in this sphere. Most religions (with the exception of the few cults that actually permit or encourage it) do not have to bother much with enforcing the taboo on incest. Like murder and theft, this is usually found to be abhorrent to humans without any further explanation. But merely to survey the history of sexual dread and proscription, as codified by religion, is to be met with a very disturbing connection between extreme prurience and extreme repression. Almost every sexual impulse has been made the occasion for prohibition, guilt, and shame. Manual sex, oral sex, anal sex, non–missionary position sex: to name it is to discover a fearsome ban upon it. Even in modern and hedonistic America, several states legally define "sodomy" as that which is not directed at face-to-face heterosexual procreation.

This raises gigantic objections to the argument from "design," whether we choose to call that design "intelligent" or not. Clearly, the human species is designed to experiment with sex. No less clearly, this fact is well-known to the priesthoods. When Dr. Samuel Johnson had completed the first real dictionary of the English language, he was visited by a delegation of respectable old ladies who wished to congratulate him for not including any indecent words. His response—which was that he was interested to see that the ladies had been looking them up—contains almost all that needs to be said on this point. Orthodox Jews conduct congress by means of a hole in the sheet, and subject their women to ritual baths to cleanse the stain of menstruation. Muslims subject adulterers to public lashings with a whip. Christians used to lick their lips while examining women for signs of witchcraft. I need not go on in this vein: any reader of this book will know of a vivid example, or will simply guess my meaning.

A consistent proof that religion is man-made and anthropomorphic can also be found in the fact that it is usually "man" made, in the sense of masculine, as well. The holy book in the longest continuous use—the Talmud—commands the observant one to thank his maker every day that he was not born a woman. (This raises again the insistent question: who but a slave thanks his master for what his master has decided to do without bothering to consult him?) The Old Testament, as Christians condescendingly call it, has woman cloned from man for his use and comfort. The New Testament has Saint Paul expressing both fear and contempt for the female. Throughout all religious texts, there is a primitive fear that half the human race is simultaneously defiled and unclean, and yet is also a temptation to sin that is impossible to resist. Perhaps this explains the hysterical cult of virginity and of a Virgin, and the dread of the female form and of female reproductive functions? And there may be someone who can explain the sexual and other cruelties of the religious without any reference to the obsession with celibacy, but that someone will not be me. I simply laugh when I read the Koran, with its endless prohibitions on sex and its corrupt promise of infinite debauchery in the life to come: it is like seeing through the "let's pretend" of a child, but without the indulgence that comes from watching the innocent at play. The homicidal lunatics—rehearsing to be genocidal lunatics—of 9/11 were perhaps tempted by virgins, but it is far more revolting to contemplate that, like so many of their fellow jihadists, they *were* virgins. Like monks of old, the fanatics are taken early from their families, taught to despise their mothers and sisters, and come to adulthood without ever having had a normal conversation, let alone a normal relationship, with a woman. This is disease by definition. Christianity is too repressed to offer sex in paradise—indeed it has never been able to evolve a tempting heaven at all—but it has been lavish in its promise of sadistic and everlasting punishment for sexual backsliders, which is nearly as revealing in making the same point in a different way.

A SPECIAL SUBGENRE of modern literature is the memoir of a man or woman who once underwent a religious education. The modern world is now sufficiently secular for some of these authors to attempt to be funny about what they underwent, and what they were expected to believe. However, such books tend necessarily to be written by those with enough fortitude to have survived the experience. We have no way to quantify the damage done by telling tens of millions of children that masturbation will make them blind, or that impure thoughts will lead to an eternity of torment, or that members of other faiths including members of their own families will burn, or that venereal disease will result from kisses. Nor can we hope to quantify the damage done by holy instructors who rammed home these lies and accompanied them with floggings and rapes and public humiliations. Some of those who "rest in unvisited tombs" may have contributed to the good of the world, but those who preached hatred and fear and guilt and who ruined innumerable childhoods should have been thankful that the hell they preached was only one among their wicked falsifications, and that they were not sent to rot there.

Violent, irrational, intolerant, allied to racism and tribalism and bigotry, invested in ignorance and hostile to free inquiry, contemptuous of women and coercive toward children: organized religion ought to have a great deal on its conscience. There is one more charge to be added to the bill of indictment. With a necessary part of its collective mind, religion looks forward to the destruction of the world. By this I do not mean it "looks forward" in the purely eschatological sense of anticipating the end. I mean, rather, that it openly or covertly wishes that end to occur. Perhaps half aware that its unsupported arguments are not entirely persuasive, and perhaps uneasy about its own greedy accumulation of temporal power and wealth, religion has never ceased to proclaim the Apocalypse and the day of judgment. This has been a constant trope, ever since the first witch doctors and shamans learned to predict eclipses and to use their half-baked celestial knowledge to terrify the ignorant. It stretches from the epistles of Saint Paul, who clearly thought and hoped that time was running out for humanity, through the deranged fantasies of the book of Revelation, which were at least memorably written by the alleged Saint John the Divine on the Greek island of Patmos, to the best-selling pulp-fiction *Left Behind* series, which, ostensibly "authored" by Tim LaHaye and Jerry B. Jenkins, was apparently generated by the old expedient of letting two orangutans loose on a word processor:

The blood continued to rise. Millions of birds flocked into the area and feasted on the remains . . . and the winepress was trampled outside the city, and blood came out of the winepress, up to the horse's bridles, for one thousand six hundred furlongs.

This is sheer manic relish, larded with half-quotations. More reflectively, but hardly less regrettably, it can be found in Julia Ward Howe's "Battle Hymn of the Republic," which dwells on the same winepress, and in Robert Oppenheimer's murmur as he watched the first nuclear detonation at Alamagordo, New Mexico, and heard himself quoting the Hindu epic the Bhagavad Gita: "I am become Death, the destroyer of worlds." One of the very many connections between religious belief and the sinister, spoiled, selfish childhood of our species is the repressed desire to see everything smashed up and ruined and brought to naught. This tantrum-need is coupled with two other sorts of "guilty joy," or, as the Germans say, *schadenfreude*. First, one's own death is canceled—or perhaps repaid or compensated—by the obliteration of all others. Second, it can always be egotistically hoped that one will be personally spared, gathered contentedly to the bosom of the mass exterminator, and from a safe place observe the sufferings of those less fortunate. Tertullian, one of the many church fathers who found it difficult to give a persuasive account of paradise, was perhaps clever in going for the lowest possible common denominator and promising that one of the most intense pleasures of the afterlife would be endless contemplation of the tortures of the damned. He spoke more truly than he knew in evoking the man-made character of faith.

As in all cases, the findings of science are far more awe-inspiring than the rantings of the godly. The history of the cosmos begins, if we use the word "time" to mean anything at all, about twelve billion years ago. (If we use the word "time" wrongly, we shall end up with the infantile computation of the celebrated Archbishop James Ussher of Armagh, who calculated that the earth—"the earth" alone, mind you, not the cosmos—had its birthday on Saturday, October 22, in 4004 BC, at six in the afternoon. This dating was endorsed by William Jennings Bryan, a former American secretary of state and two-time Democratic presidential nominee, in courtroom testimony in the third decade of the twentieth century.) The true age of the sun and its orbiting planets—one of them destined to harbor life and all the others doomed to lifelessness—is perhaps four and a half billion years and subject to revision. This particular microscopic solar system most probably has at least that long again to run its fiery course: the life expectancy of our sun is a solid five billion more years. However, mark your calendar. At around that point, it will emulate millions of other suns and explosively mutate into a swollen "red giant," causing the earth's oceans to boil and extinguishing all possibility of life in any form. No description by any prophet or visionary has even begun to picture the awful intensity and irrevocability of that moment. One has at least some pitiful self-centered reason not to fear undergoing it: on current projections the biosphere will very probably have been destroyed by different and slower sorts of warming and heating in the meantime. As a species on earth, according to many sanguine experts, we do not have many more eons ahead of us.

With what contempt and suspicion, then, must one regard those who are not willing to wait, and who beguile themselves and terrify others—especially the children, as usual—with horrific visions of apocalypse, to be followed by stern judgment from the one who supposedly placed us in this inescapable dilemma to begin with. We may laugh now at the foam-flecked hell-and-damnation preachers who loved to shrivel young souls with pornographic depictions of eternal torture, but this phenomenon has reappeared in a more troubling form with the holy alliance between the believers and what they can borrow or steal from the world of science. Here is Professor Pervez Hoodbhoy, a distinguished professor of nuclear and high-energy physics at the University of Islamabad in Pakistan, writing about the frightening mentality which prevails in his country—one of the world's first states to define its very nationality by religion:

> In a public debate on the eve of the Pakistani nuclear tests, the former chief of the Pakistani army General Mirza Aslam Beg said: "We can make a first strike and a second and even a third." The prospect of nuclear war left him unmoved. "You can die crossing the street," he said, "or you could die in a nuclear war. You've got to die someday, anyway." . . . India and Pakistan are largely traditional societies, where the fundamental belief structure demands disempowerment and surrender to larger forces. A fatalistic Hindu belief that the stars above determine our destiny, or the equivalent Muslim belief in *kismet* certainly account for part of the problem.

I shall not disagree with the very brave Professor Hoodbhoy, who helped alert us to the fact that there were several secret bin Laden supporters among the bureaucrats of the Pakistani nuclear program, and who also exposed the wild fanatics within that system who hoped to harness the power of the mythical *djinns*, or desert devils, for military purposes. In his world, the enemies are mainly Muslims and Hindus. But within the "Judeo-Christian" world also, there are those who like to fantasize about a final conflict and embellish the vision with mushroom-shaped clouds. It is a tragic and potentially lethal irony that those who most despise science and the method of free inquiry should have been able to pilfer from it and annex its sophisticated products to their sick dreams.

The death wish, or something not unlike it, may be secretly present in all of us. At the turn of the year 1999 into 2000, many educated people talked and published infinite nonsense about a series of possible calamities and dramas. This was no better than primitive numerology: in fact it was slightly worse in that 2000 was only a number on Christian calendars and even the stoutest defenders of the Bible story now admit that if Jesus was ever born it wasn't until at least AD 4. The occasion was nothing more than an odometer for idiots, who sought the cheap thrill of impending doom. But religion makes such impulses legitimate, and claims the right to officiate at the end of life, just as it hopes to monopolize children at life's beginning. There can be no doubt that the cult of death and the insistence upon portents of the end proceed from a surreptitious desire to see it happen, and to put an end to the anxiety and doubt that always threaten the hold of faith. When the earthquake hits, or the tsunami inundates, or the twin towers ignite, you can see and hear the secret satisfaction of the faithful. Gleefully they strike up: "You see, this is what happens when you don't listen to us!" With an unctuous smile they offer a redemption that is not theirs to bestow and, when questioned, put on the menacing scowl that says, "Oh, so you reject our offer of paradise? Well, in that case we have quite another fate in store for you." Such love! Such care!

The element of the wish for obliteration can be seen without disguise in the millennial sects of our own day, who betray their selfishness as well as their nihilism by announcing how many will be "saved" from the ultimate catastrophe. Here the extreme Protestants are almost as much at fault as the most hysterical Muslims. In 1844, one of the greatest American religious "revivals" occurred, led by a semiliterate lunatic named George Miller. Mr. Miller managed to crowd the mountaintops of America with credulous fools who (having sold their belongings cheap) became persuaded that the world would end on October 22 that year. They removed themselves to high ground—what difference did they expect *that* to make?—or to the roofs of their hovels. When the ultimate failed to arrive, Miller's choice of terms was highly suggestive. It was, he announced, "The Great Disappointment." In our own time, Mr. Hal Lindsey, author of the best-selling *The Late Great Planet Earth*, has betrayed the same thirst for extinction. Indulged by senior American conservatives and respectfully interviewed on TV, Mr. Lindsey once dated the start of "The Tribulation"—a seven-year period of strife and terror—for 1988. This would have produced Armageddon itself (the closure of "The Tribulation") in 1995. Mr. Lindsey may be a charlatan, but it is a certainty that he and his followers suffer from a persistent feeling of anticlimax.

Antibodies to fatalism and suicide and masochism do exist, however, and are just as innate in our species. There is a celebrated story from Puritan Massachusetts in the late eighteenth century. During a session of the state legislature, the sky suddenly became leaden and overcast at midday. Its threatening aspect—a darkness at noon—convinced many legislators that the event so much on their clouded minds was imminent. They asked to suspend business and go home to die. The speaker of the assembly, Abraham Davenport, managed to keep his nerve and dignity. "Gentlemen," he said, "either the Day of Judgment is here or it is not. If it is not, there is no occasion for alarm and lamentation. If it is, however, I wish to be found doing my duty. I move, therefore, that candles be brought." In his own limited and superstitious day, this was the best that Mr. Davenport could do. Nonetheless, I second his motion.

Chapter Five

The Metaphysical Claims of Religion Are False

> I am a man of one book.
> —Thomas Aquinas

> We sacrifice the intellect to God.
> —Ignatius Loyola

> Reason is the Devil's harlot, who can do nought but
> slander and harm whatever God says and does.
> —Martin Luther

> Looking up at the stars, I know quite well
> That for all they care, I can go to hell.
> —W. H. Auden, "The More Loving One"

I wrote earlier that we would never again have to confront the impressive faith of an Aquinas or a Maimonides (as contrasted with the blind faith of millennial or absolutist sects, of which we have an apparently unlimited and infinitely renewable supply). This is for a simple reason. Faith of that sort—the sort that can stand up at least for a while in a confrontation with reason—is now plainly impossible. The early fathers of faith (they made very sure that there would be no

mothers) were living in a time of abysmal ignorance and fear. Maimonides did not include, in his *Guide to the Perplexed*, those whom
he described as not worth the effort: the "Turkish" and black and
nomadic peoples whose "nature is like the nature of mute animals."
Aquinas half believed in astrology, and was convinced that the fully
formed nucleus (not that he would have known the word as we do)
of a human being was contained inside each individual sperm. One
can only mourn over the dismal and stupid lectures on sexual con-
tinence that we might have been spared if this nonsense had been
exposed earlier than it was. Augustine was a self-centered fantasist
and an earth-centered ignoramus: he was guiltily convinced that god
cared about his trivial theft from some unimportant pear trees, and
quite persuaded—by an analogous solipsism—that the sun revolved
around the earth. He also fabricated the mad and cruel idea that the
souls of unbaptized children were sent to "limbo." Who can guess the
load of misery that this diseased "theory" has placed on millions of
Catholic parents down the years, until its shamefaced and only partial
revision by the church in our own time? Luther was terrified of demons and believed that the mentally afflicted were the devil's work.
Muhammad is claimed by his own followers to have thought, as did
Jesus, that the desert was pullulating with *djinns*, or evil spirits.

One must state it plainly. Religion comes from the period of
human prehistory where nobody—not even the mighty Democritus
who concluded that all matter was made from atoms—had the smallest idea what was going on. It comes from the bawling and fearful
infancy of our species, and is a babyish attempt to meet our inescapable demand for knowledge (as well as for comfort, reassurance, and
other infantile needs). Today the least educated of my children knows
much more about the natural order than any of the founders of religion, and one would like to think—though the connection is not a
fully demonstrable one—that this is why they seem so uninterested in
sending fellow humans to hell.

All attempts to reconcile faith with science and reason are consigned to failure and ridicule for precisely these reasons. I read, for example, of some ecumenical conference of Christians who desire to show their broad-mindedness and invite some physicists along. But I am compelled to remember what I know—which is that there would be no such churches in the first place if humanity had not been afraid of the weather, the dark, the plague, the eclipse, and all manner of other things now easily explicable. And also if humanity had not been compelled, on pain of extremely agonizing consequences, to pay the exorbitant tithes and taxes that raised the imposing edifices of religion.

It is true that scientists have sometimes been religious, or at any rate superstitious. Sir Isaac Newton, for example, was a spiritualist and alchemist of a particularly laughable kind. Fred Hoyle, an ex-agnostic who became infatuated with the idea of "design," was the Cambridge astronomer who coined the term "big bang." (He came up with that silly phrase, incidentally, as an attempt to discredit what is now the accepted theory of the origins of the universe. This was one of those lampoons that, so to speak, backfired, since like "Tory" and "impressionist" and "suffragette" it became adopted by those at whom it was directed.) Steven Hawking is not a believer, and when invited to Rome to meet the late Pope John Paul II asked to be shown the records of the trial of Galileo. But he does speak without embarrassment of the chance of physics "knowing the mind of God," and this now seems quite harmless as a metaphor, as for example when the Beach Boys sing, or I say, "God only knows . . ."

Before Charles Darwin revolutionized our entire concept of our origins, and Albert Einstein did the same for the beginnings of our cosmos, many scientists and philosophers and mathematicians took what might be called the default position and professed one or another version of "deism," which held that the order and predictability of the universe seemed indeed to imply a designer, if not necessarily a designer who took any active part in human affairs. This compromise was a logical and rational one for its time, and was especially influential among the Philadelphia and Virginia intellectuals, such as

Benjamin Franklin and Thomas Jefferson, who managed to seize a moment of crisis and use it to enshrine Enlightenment values in the founding documents of the United States of America.

Yet as Saint Paul so unforgettably said, when one is a child one speaks and thinks as a child. But when one becomes a man, one puts away childish things. It is not quite possible to locate the exact moment when men of learning stopped spinning the coin as between a creator and a long complex process, or ceased trying to split the "deistic" difference, but humanity began to grow up a little in the closing decades of the eighteenth century and the opening decades of the nineteenth. (Charles Darwin was born in 1809, on the very same day as Abraham Lincoln, and there is no doubt as to which of them has proved to be the greater "emancipator.") If one had to emulate the foolishness of Archbishop Ussher and try to come up with the exact date on which the conceptual coin came down solidly on one side, it would be the moment when Pierre-Simon de Laplace was invited to meet Napoleon Bonaparte.

Laplace (1749–1827) was the brilliant French scientist who took the work of Newton a stage further and showed by means of mathematical calculus how the operations of the solar system were those of bodies revolving systematically in a vacuum. When he later turned his attention to the stars and the nebulae, he postulated the idea of gravitational collapse and implosion, or what we now breezily term the "black hole." In a five-volume book entitled *Celestial Mechanics* he laid all this out, and like many men of his time was also intrigued by the orrery, a working model of the solar system as seen, for the first time, from the *outside*. These are now commonplace but were then revolutionary, and the emperor asked to meet Laplace in order to be given either a set of the books or (accounts differ) a version of the orrery. I personally suspect that the gravedigger of the French Revolution wanted the toy rather than the volumes: he was a man in a hurry and had managed to get the church to baptize his dictatorship with a crown. At any event, and in his childish and demanding and imperious fashion, he wanted to know why the figure of god did not appear in Laplace's mind-expanding calculations. And there came the cool, lofty, and considered response. *"Je n'ai pas besoin de cette hypothèse."* Laplace was to become a marquis and could perhaps more modestly have said, "It works well enough without that idea, Your Majesty." But he simply stated that he didn't need it.

And neither do we. The decay and collapse and discredit of god-worship does not begin at any dramatic moment, such as Nietzsche's histrionic and self-contradictory pronouncement that god was dead. Nietzsche could no more have known this, or made the assumption that god had ever been alive, than a priest or witch doctor could ever declare that he knew god's will. Rather, the end of god-worship discloses itself at the moment, which is somewhat more gradually revealed, when it becomes *optional*, or only one among many possible beliefs. For the greater part of human existence, it must always be stressed, this "option" did not really exist. We know, from the many fragments of their burned and mutilated texts and confessions, that there were always human beings who were unconvinced. But from the time of Socrates, who was condemned to death for spreading unwholesome skepticism, it was considered ill-advised to emulate his example. And for billions of people down the ages, the question simply did not come up. The votaries of Baron Samedi in Haiti enjoyed the same monopoly, founded upon the same brute coercion, as did those of John Calvin in Geneva or Massachusetts: I select these examples because they are yesterday in terms of human time. Many religions now come before us with ingratiating smirks and outspread hands, like an unctuous merchant in a bazaar. They offer consolation and solidarity and uplift, competing as they do in a marketplace. But we have a right to remember how barbarically they behaved when they were strong and were making an offer that people could not refuse. And if we chance to forget what that must have been like, we have only to look to those states and societies where the clergy still has the power to dictate its own terms. The pathetic vestiges of this can still be seen, in modern societies, in the efforts made by religion to secure control over education, or to exempt itself from tax, or to pass laws forbidding people to insult its omnipotent and omniscient deity, or even his prophet.

In our new semi-secular and mediocre condition, even the religious will speak with embarrassment of the time when theologians would dispute over futile propositions with fanatical intensity: measuring the length of angels' wings, for example, or debating how many such mythical creatures could dance on the head of a pin. Of course it is horrifying to remember how many people were tortured and killed, and how many sources of knowledge fed to the flames, in bogus arguments over the Trinity, or the Muslim hadith, or the arrival of a false Messiah. But it is better for us not to fall into relativism, or what E. P. Thompson called "the enormous condescension of posterity." The scholastic obsessives of the Middle Ages were doing the best they could on the basis of hopelessly limited information, ever-present fear of death and judgment, very low life expectancy, and an audience of illiterates. Living in often genuine fear of the consequences of error, they exerted their minds to the fullest extent then possible, and evolved quite impressive systems of logic and the dialectic. It is not the fault of men like Peter Abelard if they had to work with bits and pieces of Aristotle, many of whose writings were lost when the Christian emperor Justinian closed the schools of philosophy, but were preserved in Arabic translation in Baghdad and then retransmitted to a benighted Christian Europe by way of Jewish and Muslim Andalusia. When they got hold of the material and reluctantly conceded that there had been intelligent discussion of ethics and morality before the supposed advent of Jesus, they tried their hardest to square the circle. We have nothing much to learn from *what* they thought, but a great deal to learn from *how* they thought.

One medieval philosopher and theologian who continues to speak eloquently across the ages is William Ockham. Sometimes known as William of Ockham (or Occam) and presumably named after his native village in Surrey, England, that still boasts the name, he was born on a date unknown to us and died—probably in great agony and fear, and probably of the horrific Black Death—in Munich in 1349. He was a Franciscan (in other words, an acolyte of the afore-mentioned mammal who was said to have preached to birds) and thus conditioned to a radical approach to poverty, which brought him into collision with the papacy in Avignon in 1324. The quarrel between the papacy and the emperor over secular and ecclesiastical division of powers is irrelevant to us now (since both sides ultimately "lost"), but Ockham was forced to seek even the emperor's protection in face of the worldliness of the pope. Faced with charges of heresy and the threat of excommunication, he had the fortitude to respond that the pope himself was the heretic. Nonetheless, and because he always argued within the enclosed frame of Christian reference, he is admitted even by the most orthodox Christian authorities to have been an original and courageous thinker.

He was interested, for example, in the stars. He knew far less about the nebulae than we do, or than Laplace did. In fact, he knew nothing about them at all. But he employed them for an interesting speculation. *Assuming* that god can make us feel the presence of a nonexistent entity, and further *assuming* that he need not go to this trouble if the same effect can be produced in us by the actual presence of that entity, god could still if he wished cause us to believe in the existence of stars without their being actually present. "Every effect which God causes through the mediation of a secondary cause he can produce immediately by himself." However, this does not mean that we must believe in anything absurd, since "God cannot cause in us knowledge such that by it a thing is seen evidently to be present though it is absent, for that involves a contradiction." Before you begin to drum your fingers at the huge tautology that impends here, as it does in so much theology and theodicy, consider what Father Coplestone, the eminent Jesuit, has to say in commentary:

> If God had annihilated the stars, he could still cause in us the act of seeing what had once been, so far as the act is considered subjectively, just as he could give us a vision of what will be in the

future. Either act would be an immediate apprehension, in the first case of what has been and in the second case of what will be.

This is actually very impressive, and not just for its time. It has taken us several hundred years since Ockham to come to the realization that when we gaze up at the stars, we very often *are* seeing light from distant bodies that have long since ceased to exist. It doesn't particularly matter that the right to look through telescopes and speculate about the result was obstructed by the church: this is not Ockham's fault and there is no general law that obliges the church to be that stupid. And, moving from the unimaginable interstellar past which sends light across distances that overwhelm our brains, we have come to the realization that we also know something about the future of our system, including the rate of its expansion and the notion of its eventual terminus. However, and crucially, we can now do this while dropping (or even, if you insist, retaining) the idea of a god. But in either case, *the theory works without that assumption.* You can believe in a divine mover if you choose, but it makes no difference at all, and belief among astronomers and physicists has become private and fairly rare.

It was actually Ockham who prepared our minds for this unwelcome (to him) conclusion. He devised a "principle of economy," popularly known as "Ockham's razor," which relied for its effect on disposing of unnecessary assumptions and accepting the first sufficient explanation or cause. *"Do not multiply entities beyond necessity."* This principle extends itself. "Everything which is explained through positing something different from the act of understanding," he wrote, "can be explained without positing such a distinct thing." He was not afraid to follow his own logic wherever it might take him, and anticipated the coming of true science when he agreed that it was possible to know the nature of "created" things without any reference to their "creator." Indeed, Ockham stated that it cannot be strictly proved that god, if defined as a being who possesses the qualities of supremacy, perfection, uniqueness, and infinity, exists at all. However, if one intends to identify a first cause of the existence of the world, one may choose to call that "god" even if one does not know the precise nature of the first cause. And even the first cause has its difficulties, since a cause will itself need another cause. "It is difficult or impossible," he wrote, "to prove against the philosophers that there cannot be an infinite regress in causes of the same kind, of which one can exist without the other." Thus the postulate of a designer or creator only raises the unanswerable question of who designed the designer or created the creator. Religion and theology and theodicy (this is now me talking and not Ockham) have consistently failed to overcome this objection. Ockham himself simply had to fall back on the hopeless position that the existence of god can only be "demonstrated" by faith.

Credo quia absurdum, as the "church father" Tertullian put it, either disarmingly or annoyingly according to your taste. "I believe it because it is absurd." It is impossible to quarrel seriously with such a view. If one must have faith in order to believe something, or believe *in* something, then the likelihood of that something having any truth or value is considerably diminished. The harder work of inquiry, proof, and demonstration is infinitely more rewarding, and has confronted us with findings far more "miraculous" and "transcendent" than any theology.

Actually, the "leap of faith"—to give it the memorable name that Soren Kierkegaard bestowed upon it—is an imposture. As he himself pointed out, it is not a "leap" that can be made once and for all. It is a leap that has to go on and on being performed, in spite of mounting evidence to the contrary. This effort is actually too much for the human mind, and leads to delusions and manias. Religion understands perfectly well that the "leap" is subject to sharply diminishing returns, which is why it often doesn't in fact rely on "faith" at all but instead corrupts faith and insults reason by offering evidence and pointing to confected "proofs." This evidence and these proofs include arguments from design, revelations, punishments, and miracles. Now that religion's monopoly has been broken, it is within the compass of any human being to see these evidences and proofs as the feeble-minded inventions that they are.

Chapter Six

Arguments from Design

All my moral and intellectual being is penetrated by an invincible conviction that whatever falls under the dominion of our senses must be in nature and, however exceptional, cannot differ in its essence from all the other effects of the visible and tangible world of which we are a self-conscious part. The world of the living contains enough marvels and mysteries as it is—marvels and mysteries acting upon our emotions and intelligence in ways so inexplicable that it would almost justify the conception of life as an enchanted state. No, I am too firm in my consciousness of the marvelous to be ever fascinated by the mere supernatural which (take it any way you like) is but a manufactured article, the fabrication of minds insensitive to the intimate delicacies of our relation to the dead and to the living, in their countless multitudes; a desecration of our tenderest memories; an outrage on our dignity.

—JOSEPH CONRAD, AUTHOR'S NOTE TO *THE SHADOW-LINE*

There is a central paradox at the core of religion. The three great monotheisms teach people to think abjectly of themselves, as miserable and guilty sinners prostrate before an angry and jealous god who, according to discrepant accounts, fashioned them either out of dust and clay or a clot of blood. The positions for prayer are usually emulations of the supplicant serf before an ill-tempered monarch.

73

The message is one of continual submission, gratitude, and fear. Life itself is a poor thing: an interval in which to prepare for the hereafter or the coming—or second coming—of the Messiah.

On the other hand, and as if by way of compensation, religion teaches people to be extremely self-centered and conceited. It assures them that god cares for them individually, and it claims that the cosmos was created with them specifically in mind. This explains the supercilious expression on the faces of those who practice religion ostentatiously: pray excuse my modesty and humility but I happen to be busy on an errand for god.

Since human beings are naturally solipsistic, all forms of superstition enjoy what might be called a natural advantage. In the United States, we exert ourselves to improve high-rise buildings and high-speed jet aircraft (the two achievements that the murderers of September 11, 2001, put into hostile apposition) and then pathetically refuse to give them floors, or row numbers, that carry the unimportant number thirteen. I know that Pythagoras refuted astrology by the simple means of pointing out that identical twins do not have the same future, I further know that the zodiac was drawn up long before several of the planets in our solar system had been detected, and of course I understand that I could not be "shown" my immediate or long-term future without this disclosure altering the outcome. Thousands of people consult their "stars" in the newspapers every day, and then have unpredicted heart attacks or traffic accidents. (An astrologer of a London tabloid was once fired by means of a letter from his editor which began, "As you will no doubt have foreseen.") In his *Minima Moralia*, Theodor Adorno identified the interest in stargazing as the consummation of feeble-mindedness. However, happening to glance at the projected situation for Aries one morning, as I once did to be told that "a member of the opposite sex is interested and will show it," I found it hard to suppress a tiny surge of idiotic excitement, which in my memory has outlived the later disappointment. Then again, every time I leave my apartment there is no sign of a bus, whereas every time I return to it a bus is just drawing up. In bad moods I mutter "just my luck" to myself, even though a part of my small two- or three-pound brain reminds me that the mass-transit schedule of Washington, D.C., is drawn up and implemented without any refer- ence to my movements. (I mention this in case it might later become important: if I am hit by a bus on the day this book is published there will certainly be people who will say it was no accident.)

So why should I not be tempted to overrule W. H. Auden and believe that the firmament is in some mysterious way ordered for my benefit? Or, coming down by a few orders of magnitude, that fluctua- tions in my personal fortunes are of absorbing interest to a supreme being? One of the many faults in my design is my propensity to be- lieve or to wish this, and though like many people I have enough edu- cation to see through the fallacy, I have to admit that it is innate. In Sri Lanka once, I was traveling in a car with a group of Tamils, on a relief expedition to a Tamil area of the coastline that had been hard- hit by a cyclone. My companions were all members of the Sai Baba sect, which is very strong in South India and Sri Lanka. Sai Baba himself has claimed to raise the dead, and makes a special on-camera performance of producing holy ash from his bare palms. (Why ash? I used to wonder.)

Anyway, the trip began with my friends breaking some coconuts on a rock to ensure a safe journey. This evidently did not work, be- cause halfway across the island our driver plowed straight into a man who staggered out in front of us as we were racing, too fast, through a village. The man was horribly injured and—this being a Sinhala village—the crowd that instantly gathered was not well disposed to these Tamil intruders. It was a very sticky situation, but I was able to defuse it somewhat by being an Englishman wearing an off-white Graham Greene type suit, and by having press credentials that had been issued by the London Metropolitan Police. This impressed the local cop enough to have us temporarily released, and my compan- ions, who had been very scared indeed, were more than grateful for my presence and for my ability to talk fast. In fact, they telephoned their cult headquarters to announce that Sai Baba himself had been with us, in the temporary shape of my own person. From then on, I was treated literally with reverence, and not allowed to carry anything or fetch my own food. It did occur to me meanwhile to check on the man we had run over: he had died of his injuries in hospital. (I wonder what his horoscope had foreshadowed for that day.) Thus in miniature I saw how one mere human mammal—myself—can suddenly begin to attract shy glances of awe and wonder, and how another human mammal—our luckless victim—could be somehow irrelevant to Sai Baba's benign design.

"There but for the grace of God," said John Bradford in the sixteenth century, on seeing wretches led to execution, "go I." What this apparently compassionate observation really means—not that it really "means" anything—is, "There by the grace of God goes someone else." As I was writing this chapter, a heart-stopping accident took place in a coal mine in West Virginia. Thirteen miners survived the explosion but were trapped underground, compelling the nation's attention for a whole fraught news cycle until with huge relief it was announced that they had been located safe and sound. These glad tidings turned out to be premature, which was an impossible additional anguish for the families who had already begun celebrating and giving thanks before discovering that all but one of their menfolk had suffocated under the rock. It was also an embarrassment to the newpapers and news bulletins that had rushed out too soon with the false consolation. And can you guess what the headline on those newspapers and bulletins had been? Of course you can. "Miracle!"—with or without the exclamation point—was the invariable choice, surviving mockingly in print and in the memory to intensify the grief of the relatives. There doesn't seem to be a word to describe the absence of divine intervention in this case. But the human wish to credit good things as miraculous and to charge bad things to another account is apparently universal. In England the monarch is the hereditary head of the church as well as the hereditary head of the state: William Cobbett once pointed out that the English themselves colluded in this servile absurdity by referring to "The Royal Mint" but "The National Debt." Religion plays the same trick, and in the same way, and before our very eyes. On my first visit to the Sacré Coeur in Montmartre, a church that was built to celebrate the deliverance of Paris from the Prussians and the Commune of 1870–71, I saw a panel in bronze which showed the exact pattern in which a shower of Allied bombs, dropped in 1944, had missed the church and burst in the adjoining neighborhood . . .

Given this overwhelming tendency to stupidity and selfishness in myself and among our species, it is somewhat surprising to find the light of reason penetrating at all. The brilliant Schiller was wrong in his *Joan of Arc* when he said that "against stupidity the gods themselves contend in vain." It is actually by *means* of the gods that we make our stupidity and gullibility into something ineffable.

The "design" arguments, which are products of this same solipsism, take two forms: the macro and micro. They were most famously summarized by William Paley (1743–1805) in his book *Natural Philosophy*. Here we encounter the homespun example of the primitive human who stumbles across a ticking watch. He may not know what it is *for*, but he can discern that it is not a rock or a vegetable, and that it has been manufactured, and even manufactured for some purpose. Paley wanted to extend this analogy both to nature and to man. His complacency and wrongheadedness are well caught by J. G. Farrell in his portrayal of a Paley-trained Victorian divine in *The Siege of Krishnapur*:

> "How d'you explain the subtle mechanism of the eye, infinitely more complex than the mere telescope that miserable humanity has been able to invent? How d'you explain the eel's eye, which might be damaged by burrowing into mud and stones and is therefore protected by a transparent horny covering? How is it that the iris of a fish's eye does not contract? Ah,

poor, misguided youth, it is because the fish's eye has been designed by Him who is above all, to suit the dim light in which the fish makes his watery dwelling! How d'you explain the Indian Hog?" he cried. "How d'you account for its two bent teeth, more than a yard long, growing upwards from its upper jaw?"

"To defend itself?"

"No, young man, it has two tusks for that purpose issuing from the lower jaw like those of a common boar. . . . No, the answer is that the animal sleeps standing up and, in order to support its head, it hooks its upper tusks on the branches of the trees . . . for the Designer of the World has given thought even to the hog's slumbers!"

(Paley did not bother to explain how the Designer of the World came to command so many of his human creatures to treat the said hog as if it were a demon or a leper.) In fact, surveying the natural order, John Stuart Mill was far nearer the mark when he wrote:

If a tenth part of the pains taken in finding signs of an all-powerful benevolent god had been employed in collecting evidence to blacken the creator's character, what scope would not have been found in the animal kingdom? It is divided into devourers and devoured, most creatures being lavishly fitted with instruments to torment their prey.

Now that the courts have protected Americans (at least for the moment) from the inculcation of compulsory "creationist" stupidity in the classroom, we can echo that other great Victorian Lord Macaulay and say that "every schoolchild knows" that Paley had put his creaking, leaking cart in front of his wheezing and broken-down old horse. Fish do not have fins because they need them for the water, any more than birds are equipped with wings so that they can meet the dictionary definition of an "avian." (Apart from anything else, there are too many flightless species of birds.) It is exactly the other way about: a process of adaptation and selection. Let no one doubt the power of the original illusion. Whittaker Chambers in his seismic book *Witness* recounts the first moment when he abandoned historical materialism, mentally deserted the Communist cause, and embarked on the career which would undo Stalinism in America. It was on the morning when he glimpsed the ear of his baby daughter. The pretty whorls and folds of this external organ persuaded him in a flash of revelation that no coincidence could have created it. A fleshly flap of such utter beauty must be divine. Well, I too have marveled at the sweet little ears of my female offspring, but never without noticing that (a) they always need a bit of a clean-out, (b) that they look mass-produced even when set against the inferior ears of other people's daughters, (c) that as people get older their ears look more and more absurd from behind, and (d) that much lower animals, such as cats and bats, have much more fascinating and lovely and more potent ears. To echo Laplace, in fact, I would say that there are many, many persuasive arguments against Stalin-worship, but that the anti-Stalin case is fully valid without Mr. Chambers's ear-flap-based assumption.

Ears are predictable and uniform, and their flaps are every bit as adorable when the child has been born stone deaf. The same is not true, in the same sense, of the universe. Here there are anomalies and mysteries and imperfections—to use the most minimal terms—that do not even show adaptation, let alone selection. Thomas Jefferson in old age was fond of the analogy of the timepiece in his own case, and would write to friends who inquired after his health that the odd spring was breaking and the occasional wheel wearing out. This of course raises the uncomfortable (for believers) idea of the built-in fault that no repairman can fix. Should this be counted as part of the "design" as well? (As usual, those who take the credit for the one will fall silent and start shuffling when it comes to the other side of the ledger.) But when it comes to the whirling, howling wilderness of outer space,

with its red giants and white dwarfs and black holes, its titanic ex-
plosions and extinctions, we can only dimly and shiveringly conclude
that the "design" hasn't been imposed quite yet, and wonder if this is
how dinosaurs "felt" when the meteors came smashing through the
earth's atmosphere and put an end to the pointless bellowing rivalry
across primeval swamps.

Even what was first known about the comparatively consoling
symmetry of the solar system, with its nonetheless evident tendency
to instability and entropy, upset Sir Isaac Newton enough to make
him propose that god intervened every now and then to put the or-
bits back on an even keel. This exposed him to teasing from Leibniz,
who asked why god couldn't have got it working right the first time
around. It is, indeed, only because of the frightening emptiness elsewhere that we are bound to be impressed by the apparently unique
and beautiful conditions that have allowed intelligent life to occur on
earth. But then, vain as we are, we would be impressed, wouldn't we?
This vanity allows us to overlook the implacable fact that, of the other
bodies in our own solar system alone, the rest are all either far too cold
to support anything recognizable as life, or far too hot. The same, as it
happens, is true of our own blue and rounded planetary home, where
heat contends with cold to make large tracts of it into useless wasteland, and where we have come to learn that we live, and have always
lived, on a climatic knife edge. Meanwhile, the sun is getting ready to
explode and devour its dependent planets like some jealous chief or
tribal deity. Some design!

So much for the macro-dimension. What of the micro? Ever since
they were forced to take part in this argument, which they were with
great reluctance, the religious have tried to echo Hamlet's admonition
to Horatio that there are more things in heaven and earth than are
dreamed of by mere humans. Our side willingly concedes this point:
we are prepared for discoveries in the future that will stagger our
faculties even more than the vast advances in knowledge that have
come to us since Darwin and Einstein. However, these discoveries

will come to us in the same way—by means of patient and scrupulous and (this time, we hope) unfettered inquiry. In the meanwhile, we also have to improve our minds by the laborious exercise of refuting the latest foolishness contrived by the faithful. When the bones of prehistoric animals began to be discovered and scrutinized in the nineteenth century, there were those who said that the fossils had been placed in the rock by god, in order to test our faith. This cannot be disproved. Nor can my own pet theory that, from the patterns of behavior that are observable, we may infer a design that makes planet earth, all unknown to us, a prison colony and lunatic asylum that is employed as a dumping ground by far-off and superior civilizations. However, I was educated by Sir Karl Popper to believe that a theory that is unfalsifiable is to that extent a weak one.

Now we are being told that astonishing features, such as the human eye, cannot be the result of, so to speak, "blind" chance. As it happens, the "design" faction have chosen an example that could not be bettered. We now know a great deal about the eye, and about which creatures have it and which do not, and why. I must here for a moment give way to my friend Dr. Michael Shermer:

Evolution also posits that *modern organisms should show a variety of structures from simple to complex, reflecting an evolutionary history rather than an instantaneous creation*. The human eye, for example, is the result of a long and complex pathway that goes back hundreds of millions of years. Initially a simple eyespot with a handful of light-sensitive cells that provided information to the organism about an important source of the light; it developed into a recessed eyespot, where a small surface indentation filled with light-sensitive cells provided additional data on the direction of light; then into a deep recession eyespot, where additional cells at greater depth provide more accurate information about the environment; then into a pinhole camera eye that is able to focus an image on the back of a deeply-recessed layer of light-sensitive cells; then into a pinhole lens eye that is able to focus the image; then into a complex eye found in such modern mammals as humans.

All the intermediate stages of this process have been located in other creatures, and sophisticated computer models have been developed which have tested the theory and shown that it actually "works." There is a further proof of the evolution of the eye, as Shermer points out. This is the ineptitude of its "design":

> The anatomy of the human eye, in fact, shows anything but "intelligence" in its design. It is built upside down and backwards, requiring photons of light to travel through the cornea, lens, aquaeous fluid, blood vessels, ganglion cells, amacrine cells, horizontal cells, and bipolar cells before they reach the light-sensitive rods and cones that transduce the light signal into neural impulses—which are then sent to the visual cortex at the back of the brain for processing into meaningful patterns. For optimal vision, why would an intelligent designer have built an eye upside down and backwards?

It is because we evolved from sightless bacteria, now found to share our DNA, that we are so myopic. These are the same ill-designed optics, complete with deliberately "designed" retinal blind spot, through which earlier humans claimed to have "seen" miracles "with their own eyes." The problem in those cases was located elsewhere in the cortex, but we must never forget Charles Darwin's injunction that even the most highly evolved of us will continue to carry "the indelible stamp of their lowly origin."

I would add to Shermer that, though it is true we are the highest and smartest animals, ospreys have eyes we have calculated to be sixty times more powerful and sophisticated than our own and that blindness, often caused by microscopic parasites that are themselves miracles of ingenuity, is one of the oldest and most tragic disorders known to man. And why award the superior eye (or in the case of the cat or bat, also the ear) to the inferior species? The osprey can swoop accurately on a fast-moving fish that it has detected underwater from many, many feet above, all the while maneuvering with its extraordinary wings. Ospreys have almost been exterminated by man, while you yourself can be born as blind as a worm and still become a pious and observant Methodist, for example.

"To suppose that the eye," wrote Charles Darwin,

> with all its inimitable contrivances for adjusting the focus to different distances, for admitting different amounts of light, and for the correction of spherical and chromatic aberration, could have been formed by natural selection, seems, I freely confess, absurd in the highest possible degree.

He wrote this in an essay titled "Organs of Extreme Perfection and Complication." Since that time, the evolution of the eye has become almost a separate department of study. And why should it not? It is immensely fascinating and rewarding to know that at least forty different sets of eyes, and possibly sixty different sets, have evolved in quite distinct and parallel, if comparable, ways. Dr. Daniel Nilsson, perhaps the foremost authority on the subject, has found among other things that three entirely different groups of fish have independently developed *four* eyes. One of these sea creatures, *Bathylychnops exilis*, possesses a pair of eyes that look outward, and another pair of eyes (set in the wall of the main two) that direct their gaze straight downward. This would be an encumbrance to most animals, but it has some obvious advantages for an aquatic one. And it is highly important to notice that the embryological development of the second set of eyes is not a copy or a miniature of the first set, but an entirely different evolution. As Dr. Nilsson puts it in a letter to Richard Dawkins: "This species has reinvented the lens despite the fact that it already had one. It serves as a good support for the view that lenses are not difficult to evolve." A creative deity, of course, would have been more likely to double the complement of optics in the first place, which would have left us with nothing to wonder about, or to discover. Or as Darwin went on to say, in the same essay:

> When it was first said that the sun stood still and the world turned round, the common sense of mankind declared the doctrine false; but the old saying of *vox populi, vox Dei*, as every philosopher knows, cannot be trusted in science. Reason tells me, that if numerous gradations from an imperfect and simple eye to one perfect and complex, each grade being useful to its possessor, can be shown to exist, as is certainly the case; if further, the eye ever slightly varies, and the variations be inherited, as is likewise certainly the case; and if such variations should ever be useful to any animal under changing conditions of life, then the difficulty of believing that a perfect and complex eye could be formed by natural selection, though insuperable by our imagination, cannot be considered real.

We may smile slightly when we notice that Darwin wrote of the sun standing still, and when we notice that he spoke of the eye's "perfection," but only because we are fortunate enough to know more than he did. What is worth noting, and retaining, is his proper use of the sense of what is wondrous.

The real "miracle" is that we, who share genes with the original bacteria that began life on the planet, have evolved as much as we have. Other creatures did not develop eyes at all, or developed extremely weak ones. There is an intriguing paradox here: evolution does not have eyes but it can create them. The brilliant Professor Francis Crick, one of the discoverers of the double helix, had a colleague named Leslie Orgel who encapsulated this paradox more elegantly than I can. "Evolution," he said, "is smarter than you are." But this compliment

to the "intelligence" of natural selection is not by any means a concession to the stupid notion of "intelligent design." Some of the results
are extremely impressive, as we are bound to think in our own case.
("What a piece of work is a man!" as Hamlet exclaims, before going
on to contradict himself somewhat by describing the result as a "quin-
tessence of dust"; both statements having the merit of being true.) But
the process by which the results are attained is slow and infinitely
laborious, and has given us a DNA "string" which is crowded with
useless junk and which has much in common with much lower creatures. The stamp of the lowly origin is to be found in our appendix, in
the now needless coat of hair that we still grow (and then shed) after
five months in the womb, in our easily worn-out knees, our vestigial
tails, and the many caprices of our urinogenital arrangements. Why
do people keep saying, "God is in the details"? He isn't in ours, unless
his yokel creationist fans wish to take credit for his clumsiness, failure,
and incompetence.

Those who have yielded, not without a struggle, to the overwhelming evidence of evolution are now trying to award themselves a medal
for their own acceptance of defeat. The very magnificence and variety
of the process, they now wish to say, argues for a directing and origi-
nating mind. In this way they choose to make a fumbling fool of their
pretended god, and make him out to be a tinkerer, an approximator,
and a blunderer, who took eons of time to fashion a few serviceable
figures and heaped up a junkyard of scrap and failure meanwhile.
Have they no more respect for the deity than that? They unwisely say
that evolutionary biology is "only a theory," which betrays their ignorance of the meaning of the word "theory" as well as of the meaning
of the word "design." A "theory" is something evolved—if you forgive
the expression—to fit the known facts. It is a successful theory if it
survives the introduction of hitherto unknown facts. And it becomes
an accepted theory if it can make accurate predictions about things
or events that have not yet been discovered, or have not yet occurred.
This can take time, and is also subject to a version of Ockham's pro-

cedure: Pharaonic astronomers in Egypt could predict eclipses even though they believed the earth to be flat: it just took them a great deal more unnecessary work. Einstein's prediction of the precise angular deflection of starlight due to gravity—verified during an eclipse off the west coast of Africa that occured in 1913—was more elegant, and was held to vindicate his "theory" of relativity.

There are many disputes between evolutionists as to *how* the complex process occurred, and indeed as to how it began. Francis Crick even allowed himself to flirt with the theory that life was "inseminated" on earth by bacteria spread from a passing comet. However, all these disputes, when or if they are resolved, will be resolved by using the scientific and experimental methods that have proven themselves so far. By contrast, creationism, or "intelligent design" (its only cleverness being found in this underhanded rebranding of itself) is *not even a theory*. In all its well-financed propaganda, it has never even attempted to show how one single piece of the natural world is explained better by "design" than by evolutionary competition. Instead, it dissolves into puerile tautology. One of the creationists' "questionnaires" purports to be a "yes/no" interrogation of the following:

> *Do you know of any building that didn't have a builder?*
> *Do you know of any painting that didn't have a painter?*
> *Do you know of any car that didn't have a maker?*
> *If you answered YES for any of the above, give details.*

We know the answer in all cases: these were painstaking inventions (also by trial and error) of mankind, and were the work of many hands, and are still "evolving." This is what makes piffle out of the ignorant creationist sneer, which compares evolution to a whirlwind blowing through a junkyard of parts and coming up with a jumbo jet. For a start, there are no "parts" lying around waiting to be assembled. For another thing, the process of acquisition and discarding of "parts" (most especially wings) is as far from a whirlwind as could conceivably be. The time involved is more like that of a glacier than a storm. For still another thing, jumbo jets are not riddled with nonworking or superfluous "parts" lamely inherited from less successful aircraft. Why have we agreed so easily to call this exploded old nontheory by its cunningly chosen new disguise of "intelligent design"? There is nothing at all "intelligent" about it. It is the same old mumbo-jumbo (or in this instance, jumbo-mumbo).

Airplanes are, in their human-designed way, "evolving." And so, in a quite different way, are we. In early April 2006 a long study at the University of Oregon was published in the journal *Science*. Based on the reconstruction of ancient genes from extinct animals, the researchers were able to show how the nontheory of "irreducible complexity" is a joke. Protein molecules, they found, slowly employed trial and error, reusing and modifying existing parts, to act in a key-and-lock manner and switch discrepant hormones "on" and "off." This genetic march was blindly inaugurated 450 million years ago, before life left the ocean and before the evolution of bones. We now know things about our nature that the founders of religion could not even begin to guess at, and that would have stilled their overconfident tongues if they had known of them. Yet again, once one has disposed of superfluous assumptions, speculation about who designed us to be designers becomes as fruitless and irrelevant as the question of who designed that designer. Aristotle, whose reasoning about the unmoved mover and the uncaused cause is the beginning of this argument, concluded that the logic would necessitate forty-seven or fifty-five gods. Surely even a monotheist would be grateful for Ockham's razor at this point? From a plurality of prime movers, the monotheists have bargained it down to a single one. They are getting ever nearer to the true, round figure.

WE MUST ALSO CONFRONT the fact that evolution is, as well as smarter than we are, infinitely more callous and cruel, and also capricious.

Investigation of the fossil record and the record of molecular biology shows us that approximately 98 percent of all the species that have ever appeared on earth have lapsed into extinction. There have been extraordinary periods of life explosion, invariably succeeded by great "dyings out." In order for life to take hold at all on a cooling planet, it had first to occur with fantastic profusion. We have a micro-glimpse of this in our little human lives: men produce infinitely more seminal fluid than is required to build a human family, and are tortured—not completely unpleasantly—by the urgent need to spread it all over the place or otherwise get rid of it. (Religions have needlessly added to the torture by condemning various simple means of relieving this presumably "designed" pressure.) The exuberant teeming variety of insect life, or sparrow or salmon or codfish life, is a titanic waste that ensures, in some but not all cases, that there will be enough survivors.

The higher animals are hardly exempt from this process. The religions that we know of have—for self-evident reasons—also emerged from peoples that we know of. And in Asia and the Mediterranean and the Middle East, the human record is traceable back for an impressively long and continuous period of time. However, even the religious myths mention periods of darkness and plague and calamity, when it seemed that nature had turned against human existence. The folk memory, now confirmed by archaeology, makes it seem highly probable that huge inundations occurred when the Black Sea and the Mediterranean were formed, and that these forbidding and terrifying events continued to impress the storytellers of Mesopotamia and elsewhere. Every year, Christian fundamentalists renew their expeditions to Mount Ararat in modern Armenia, convinced that one day they will discover the wreckage of Noah's Ark. This effort is futile and would prove nothing even if it were successful, but if these people should chance to read the reconstructions of what really did happen, they would find themselves confronted with something far more memorable than the banal account of Noah's flood: a sudden massive wall of dark water roaring across a thickly populated plain. This

"Atlantis" event would have adhered to the prehistoric memory, all right, as indeed it does to ours.

However, we do not even possess a buried or ill-chronicled memory of what happened to most of our fellow humans in the Americas. When the Catholic Christian conquistadores arrived in the Western Hemisphere in the early sixteenth century AD, they behaved with such indiscriminate cruelty and destructiveness that one of their number, Bartolemeo de las Casas, actually proposed a formal renunciation and apology, and an acknowledgment that the whole enterprise had been a mistake. Well-intentioned as he may have been, he based his bad conscience on the idea that the "Indians" had been living in an undisturbed Eden, and that Spain and Portugal had missed their chance of rediscovering the innocence that had pre-dated the fall of Adam and Eve. This was wishful piffle and also extreme condescension: the Olmec and other tribes had gods of their own—mainly propitiated by human sacrifice—and had also developed elaborate systems of writing, astronomy, agriculture, and trade. They wrote down their history and had discovered a 365-day calendar that was more accurate than its European counterparts. One particular society—the Mayan—had also managed to come up with that beautiful concept of zero to which I alluded earlier, and without which mathematical computation is very difficult. It may be significant that the papacy of the Middle Ages always resisted the idea of "zero" as alien and heretical, perhaps because of its supposedly Arab (in fact Sanskrit) origin but perhaps also because it contained a frightening possibility.

Something is known of the civilizations of the American isthmus, but until very recently we were unaware of the vast cities and networks that once stretched across the Amazon basin and some regions of the Andes. Serious work has only just begun on the study of these impressive societies, which grew and flourished when Moses and Abraham and Jesus and Muhammad and Buddha were being revered, but which took no part at all in those arguments and were not included in the calculations of the monotheistic faithful. It is a certainty that these people, too, had their creation myths and their revelations of the divine will, for all the good it did them. But they suffered and triumphed and expired without ever being in "our" prayers. And they died out in the bitter awareness that there would be nobody to remember them as they had been, or even *as if* they had been. All their "promised lands" and prophecies and cherished legends and ceremonies might as well have occurred on another planet. This is how arbitrary human history actually is.

There seems to be little or no doubt that these peoples were annihilated not just by human conquerors but by microorganisms of which neither they nor their invaders had any knowledge. These germs may have been indigenous or they may have been imported, but the effect was the same. Here again one sees the gigantic manmade fallacy that informs our "Genesis" story. How can it be proven in one paragraph that this book was written by ignorant men and not by any god? Because man is given "dominion" over all beasts, fowl and fish. But no dinosaurs or plesiosaurs or pterodactyls are specified, because the authors did not know of their existence, let alone of their supposedly special and immediate creation. Nor are any marsupials mentioned, because Australia—the next candidate after Mesoamerica for a new "Eden"—was not on any known map. Most important, in Genesis man is not awarded dominion over germs and bacteria because the existence of these necessary yet dangerous fellow creatures was not known or understood. And if it had been known or understood, it would at once have become apparent that these forms of life had "dominion" *over us*, and would continue to enjoy it uncontested until the priests had been elbowed aside and medical research at last given an opportunity. Even today, the balance between *Homo sapiens* and Louis Pasteur's "invisible army" of microbes is by no means decided, but DNA has at least enabled us to sequence the genome of our lethal rivals, like the avian flu virus, and to elucidate what we have in common.

Probably the most daunting task that we face, as partly rational animals with adrenal glands that are too big and prefrontal lobes that are too small, is the contemplation of our own relative weight in the scheme of things. Our place in the cosmos is so unimaginably small that we cannot, with our miserly endowment of cranial matter, contemplate it for long at all. No less difficult is the realization that we may also be quite random as presences on earth. We may have learned about our modest position on the scale, about how to prolong our lives, cure ourselves of disease, learn to respect and profit from other tribes and other animals, and employ rockets and satellites for ease of communication; but then, the awareness that our death is coming and will be succeeded by the death of the species and the heat death of the universe is scant comfort. Still, at least we are not in the position of those humans who died without ever having the chance to tell their story, or who are dying today at this moment after a few bare, squirming minutes of painful and fearful existence.

In 1909, a discovery of immense importance was made in the Canadian Rockies, on the border of British Columbia. It is known as the Burgess shale, and though it is a natural formation and has no magical properties, it is almost like a time machine or a key that enables us to visit the past. The very remote past: this limestone quarry came into existence about 570 million years ago and records what palaeontologists familiarly call "the Cambrian explosion." Just as there have been great " dyings" and extinctions during evolutionary time, so there have been energetic moments when life was suddenly profuse and various again. (An intelligent "designer" might have managed without these chaotic episodes of boom and bust.)

Most of the surviving modern animals have their origins in this grand Cambrian burgeoning, but until 1909 we were unable to view them in anything like their original habitat. Until then, also, we had to rely upon the evidence mainly of bones and shells, whereas the Burgess shale contains much fossilized "soft anatomy," including the contents of digestive systems. It is a sort of Rosetta Stone for the decoding of life forms.

Our own solipsism, often expressed in diagram or cartoon form, usually represents evolution as a kind of ladder or progression, with a fish gasping on the shore in the first frame, hunched and prognathous figures in the succeeding ones, and then, by slow degrees, an erect man in a suit waving his umbrella and shouting "Taxi!" Even those who have observed the "sawtooth" pattern of fluctuation between emergence and destruction, further emergence and still further destruction, and who have already charted the eventual end of the universe, are half agreed that there is a stubborn tendency toward an upward progression. This is no great surprise: inefficient creatures will either die out or be destroyed by more successful ones. But progress does not negate the idea of randomness, and when he came to examine the Burgess shale, the great paleontologist Stephen Jay Gould arrived at the most disquieting and unsettling conclusion of all. He examined the fossils and their development with minute care and realized that if this tree could be replanted or this soup set boiling again, it would very probably not reproduce the same results that we now "know."

It may be worth mentioning that this conclusion was no more welcome to Gould than it is to you or to me: in his youth he had imbibed a version of Marxism and the concept of "progress" was real to him. But he was too scrupulous a scholar to deny the evidence that was so plainly displayed, and while some evolutionary biologists are willing to say that the millimetrical and pitiless process had a "direction" toward our form of intelligent life, Gould subtracted himself from their company. If the numberless evolutions from the Cambrian period could be recorded and "rewound," as it were, and the tape then played again, he established there was no certainty that it would come out the same way. Several branches of the tree (a better analogy would be with small twigs on an extremely dense bush) end up going nowhere, but given another "start" they might have blossomed and flourished, just as some that did blossom and flourish might equally well have withered and died. We all appreciate that our nature and existence is based upon our being vertebrate. The earliest known vertebrate (or "chordate") located in the Burgess shale is a two-inch and rather elegant creature named, after an adjoining mountain and also for its sinuous beauty, *Pikaia gracilens*. It was originally and wrongly classified as a worm (one must never forget how recent most of our knowledge really is), but in its segments, muscularity, and dorsal-rod flexibility it is a necessary ancestor that yet demands no worship. Millions of other life forms perished before the Cambrian period was over, but this little prototype survived. To quote Gould:

> Wind the tape of time back to Burgess times, and let it play again. If *Pikaia* does not survive in the replay, we are wiped out of future history—all of us, from shark to robin to orangutan. And I don't think that any handicapper, given Burgess evidence as known today, would have granted very favorable odds for the persistence of *Pikaia*.
>
> And so, if you wish to ask the question of the ages—why do humans exist?—a major part of the answer, touching those aspects of the issue that science can treat at all, must be: because *Pikaia* survived the Burgess decimation. This response does not cite a single law of nature; it embodies no statement about predictable evolutionary pathways, no calculation of probabilities based on general rules of anatomy or ecology. The survival of *Pikaia* was a contingency of "just history." I do not think that any "higher" answer can be given, and I cannot imagine that any resolution could be more fascinating. We are the offspring of history, and must establish our own paths in this most diverse and interesting of conceivable universes—one indifferent to our suffering, and therefore offering us maximum freedom to thrive, or to fail, in our own chosen way.

A way "chosen," one must add, within very strictly defined limits. Here is the cool, authentic voice of a dedicated scientist and humanist. In a dim way, we knew all this already. Chaos theory has familiarized us with the idea of the unscripted butterfly wing-flap that, stirring a tiny zephyr, eventuates in a raging typhoon. Saul Bellow's Augie March shrewdly observed the fritillary corollary that "if you hold down one thing, you hold down the adjoining." And Gould's mind-stunning but mind-opening book on the Burgess shale is entitled *Wonderful Life,* a double entendre with an echo of the best-loved of all American sentimental movies. At the climax of this engaging but abysmal film, Jimmy Stewart wishes he had never been born but is then shown by an angel what the world would be like if his wish had been granted. A middlebrow audience is thus given a vicarious glimpse of a version of Heisenberg's principle of uncertainty: any attempt to measure something will have the effect of minutely altering that which is being measured. We have only recently established that a cow is closer in family to a whale than to a horse: other wonders certainly await us. If our presence here, in our present form, is indeed random and contingent, then at least we can consciously look forward to the further evolution of our poor brains, and to stupendous advances in medicine and life extension, derived from work on our elementary stem cells and umbilical-cord blood cells.

In the steps of Darwin, Peter and Rosemary Grant of Princeton University have gone for the past thirty years to the Galápagos Islands, lived in the arduous conditions of the tiny island of Daphne Major, and actually watched and measured the way that finches evolved and adapted as their surroundings changed. They have shown conclusively that the size and shape of the finches' beaks would adjust themselves to drought and scarcity, by adaption to the size and character of different seeds and beetles. Not only could the three-million-year-old original flock change in one way, but if the beetle and seed situation changed back, their beaks could follow suit. The Grants took care, and they *saw* it happening, and could publish their findings and proofs for all to see. We are in their debt. Their lives were harsh, but who could wish that they had mortified themselves in a holy cave or on top of a sacred pillar instead?

In 2005, a team of researchers at the University of Chicago conducted serious work on two genes, known as microcephalin and ASPM, that when disabled are the cause of microcephaly. Babies born with this condition have a shrunken cerebral cortex, quite probably an occasional reminder of the period when the human brain was very much smaller than it is now. The evolution of humans has been generally thought to have completed itself about fifty to sixty thousand years ago (an instant in evolutionary time), yet those two genes have apparently been evolving faster in the past thirty-seven thousand years, raising the possibility that the human brain is a work in progress. In March 2006, further work at the same university revealed that there are some seven hundred regions of the human genome where genes have been reshaped by natural selection within the past five thousand to fifteen thousand years. These genes include some of those responsible for our "senses of taste and smell, digestion, bone structure, skin color and brain function." (One of the great emancipating results of genomics is to show that all "racial" and color differences are recent, superficial, and misleading.) It is a moral certainty that between the time I finish writing this book and the time that it is published, several more fascinating and enlightening discoveries will be made in this burgeoning field. It may be too soon to say that all the progress is positive or "upward," but human development is still under way. It shows in the manner in which we acquire immunities, and also in the way in which we do not. Genome studies have identified early groups of northern Europeans who learned to domesticate cattle and acquired a distinct gene for "lactose tolerance," while some people of more recent African descent (we all originate from Africa) are prone to a form of sickle-cell anemia which, while upsetting in and of itself, results from an earlier mutation that gave protection against malaria. And all this will be further clarified if we are modest and patient enough to understand the building blocks of nature and the lowly stamp of our origins. No divine plan, let alone angelic intervention, is required. *Everything works without that assumption.*

Thus, though I dislike to differ with such a great man, Voltaire was simply ludicrous when he said that if god did not exist it would be necessary to invent him. The human invention of god is the problem to begin with. Our evolution has been examined "backward," with life temporarily outpacing extinction, and knowledge now at last capable of reviewing and explaining ignorance. Religion, it is true, still possesses the huge if cumbersome and unwieldy advantage of having come "first." But as Sam Harris states rather pointedly in *The End of Faith*, if we lost all our hard-won knowledge and all our archives, and all our ethics and morals, in some Márquez-like fit of collective amnesia, and had to reconstruct everything essential from scratch, it is difficult to imagine at what point we would need to remind or reassure ourselves that Jesus was born of a virgin.

Thoughtful believers can take some consolation, too. Skepticism and discovery have freed them from the burden of having to defend their god as a footling, clumsy, straws-in-the-hair mad scientist, and also from having to answer distressing questions about who inflicted the syphilis bacillus or mandated the leper or the idiot child, or devised the torments of Job. The faithful stand acquitted on that charge: we no longer have any need of a god to explain what is no longer mysterious. What believers will do, now that their faith is optional and private and irrelevant, is a matter for them. We should not care, as long as they make no further attempt to inculcate religion by any form of coercion.

Chapter Seven

Revelation: The Nightmare of the "Old" Testament

Another way in which religion betrays itself, and attempts to escape mere reliance on faith and instead offer "evidence" in the sense normally understood, is by the argument from revelation. On certain very special occasions, it is asserted, the divine will was made known by direct contact with randomly selected human beings, who were supposedly vouchsafed unalterable laws that could then be passed on to those less favored.

There are some very obvious objections to be made to this. In the first place, several such disclosures have been claimed to occur, at different times and places, to hugely discrepant prophets or mediums. In some cases—most notably the Christian—one revelation is apparently not sufficient, and needs to be reinforced by successive apparitions, with the promise of a further but ultimate one to come. In other cases, the opposite difficulty occurs and the divine instruction is delivered, only once, and for the final time, to an obscure personage whose lightest word then becomes law. Since all of these revelations, many of them hopelessly inconsistent, cannot by definition be simultaneously true, it must follow that some of them are false and illusory. It could also follow that only one of them is authentic, but in the first place this seems dubious and in the second place it appears to necessitate religious war in order to decide whose revelation is the true one. A further difficulty is the apparent tendency of the Almighty to reveal himself only to unlettered and quasi-historical individuals, in regions of Middle Eastern wasteland that were long the home of idol worship and superstition, and in many instances already littered with existing prophecies.

The syncretic tendencies of monotheism, and the common ancestry of the tales, mean in effect that a rebuttal to one is a rebuttal to all. Horribly and hatefully though they may have fought with one another, the three monotheisms claim to share a descent at least from the Pentateuch of Moses, and the Koran certifies Jews as "people of the book," Jesus as a prophet, and a virgin as his mother. (Interestingly, the Koran does not blame the Jews for the murder of Jesus, as one book of the Christian New Testament does, but this is only because it makes the bizarre claim that someone else was crucified by the Jews in his place.)

The foundation story of all three faiths concerns the purported meeting between Moses and god, at the summit of Mount Sinai. This in turn led to the handing down of the Decalogue, or Ten Commandments. The tale is told in the second book of Moses, known as the book of Exodus, in chapters 20–40. Most attention has been concentrated on chapter 20 itself, where the actual commandments are given. It should not perhaps be necessary to summarize and expose these, but the effort is actually worthwhile.

In the first place (I am using the King James or "Authorized" Version: one among many rival texts laboriously translated by mortals either from Hebrew or Greek or Latin), the so-called commandments do not appear as a neat list of ten orders and prohibitions. The first three are all variations of the same one, in which god insists on his own primacy and exclusivity, forbids the making of graven images, and prohibits the taking of his own name in vain. This prolonged throat-clearing is accompanied by some very serious admonitions, including a dire warning that the sins of the fathers will be visited on their children "even unto the third and fourth generation." This negates the moral and reasonable idea that children are innocent of their parents' offenses. The fourth commandment insists on the observance of a holy Sabbath day, and forbids all believers—and their slaves and domestic servants—to perform any work in the course of it. It is added that, as was said in the book of Genesis, god made all the world in six days and rested on the seventh (leaving room for speculation as to what he did on the eighth day). The dictation then becomes more terse. "Honor thy father and thy mother" (this not for its own sake but in order "that thy days may be long upon the land which the Lord thy God giveth thee"). Only then come the four famous "shalt nots," which flatly prohibit killing, adultery, theft, and false witness. Finally, there is a ban on covetousness, forbidding the desire for "thy neighbor's" house, manservant, maidservant, ox, ass, wife, and other chattel.

It would be harder to find an easier proof that religion is manmade. There is, first, the monarchical growling about respect and fear, accompanied by a stern reminder of omnipotence and limitless revenge, of the sort with which a Babylonian or Assyrian emperor might have ordered the scribes to begin a proclamation. There is then a sharp reminder to keep working and only to relax when the absolutist says so. A few crisp legalistic reminders follow, one of which is commonly misrendered because the original Hebrew actually says "thou shalt do no murder." But however little one thinks of the Jewish tradition, it is surely insulting to the people of Moses to imagine that they had come this far under the impression that murder, adultery, theft, and perjury were permissible. (The same unanswerable point can be made in a different way about the alleged later preachings of Jesus: when he tells the story of the Good Samaritan on that Jericho road he is speaking of a man who acted in a humane and generous manner without, obviously, ever having heard of Christianity, let alone having followed the pitiless teachings of the god of Moses, who never mentions human solidarity and compassion at all.) No society ever discovered has failed to protect itself from self-evident crimes like those supposedly stipulated at Mount Sinai. Finally, instead of the condemnation of evil actions, there is an oddly phrased condemnation of impure thoughts. One can tell that this, too, is a man-made product of the alleged time and place, because it throws in "wife" along with the other property, animal, human, and material, of the neighbor. More important, it demands the impossible: a recurrent problem with all religious edicts. One may be forcibly restrained from wicked actions, or barred from committing them, but to forbid people from *contemplating* them is too much. In particular, it is absurd to hope to banish envy of other people's possessions or fortunes, if only because the spirit of envy can lead to emulation and ambition and have positive consequences. (It seems improbable that the American fundamentalists, who desire to see the Ten Commandments emblazoned in every schoolroom and courtroom—almost like a graven image—are so hostile to the spirit of capitalism.) If god really wanted people to be free of such thoughts, he should have taken more care to invent a different species.

Then there is the very salient question of what the commandments do *not* say. Is it too modern to notice that there is nothing about the protection of children from cruelty, nothing about rape, nothing about slavery, and nothing about genocide? Or is it too exactingly "in context" to notice that some of these very offenses are about to be positively recommended? In verse 2 of the immediately following chapter, god tells Moses to instruct his followers about the conditions under which they may buy or sell slaves (or bore their ears through with an awl) and the rules governing the sale of their daughters. This is succeeded by the insanely detailed regulations governing oxes that gore and are gored, and including the notorious verses forfeiting "life for life, eye for eye, tooth for tooth." Micromanagement of agricultural disputes breaks off for a moment, with the abrupt verse (22:18)

"Thou shalt not suffer a witch to live." This was, for centuries, the warrant for the Christian torture and burning of women who did not conform. Occasionally, there are injunctions that are moral, and also (at least in the lovely King James version) memorably phrased: "Thou shalt not follow a multitude to do evil" was taught to Bertrand Russell by his grandmother, and stayed with the old heretic all his life. However, one mutters a few sympathetic words for the forgotten and obliterated Hivites, Canaanites, and Hittites, also presumably part of the Lord's original creation, who are to be pitilessly driven out of their homes to make room for the ungrateful and mutinous children of Israel. (This supposed "covenant" is the basis for a nineteenth-century irredentist claim to Palestine that has brought us endless trouble up to the present day.)

Seventy-four of the elders, including Moses and Aaron, then meet god face-to-face. Several whole chapters are given over to the minutest stipulations about the lavish, immense ceremonies of sacrifice and propitiation that the Lord expects of his newly adopted people, but this all ends in tears and with collapsing scenery to boot: Moses returns from his private session on the mountaintop to discover that the effect of a close encounter with god has worn off, at least on Aaron, and that the children of Israel have made an idol out of their jewelry and trinkets. At this, he impetuously smashes the two Sinai tablets (which appear therefore to have been man-made and not god-made, and which have to be redone hastily in a later chapter) and orders the following:

> "Put every man his sword by his side, and go in and out from gate
> to gate throughout the camp, and slay every man his brother, and
> every man his companion, and every man his neighbor."
>
> And the children of Levi did according to the word of Moses,
> and there fell of the people that day about three thousand men.

A small number when compared to the Egyptian infants already massacred by god in order for things to have proceeded even this far, but it helps to make the case for "antitheism." By this I mean the view that we ought to be glad that none of the religious myths has any truth to it, or in it. The Bible may, indeed does, contain a warrant for trafficking in humans, for ethnic cleansing, for slavery, for bride-price, and for indiscriminate massacre, but we are not bound by any of it because it was put together by crude, uncultured human mammals.

It goes without saying that none of the gruesome, disordered events described in Exodus ever took place. Israeli archaeologists are among the most professional in the world, even if their scholarship has sometimes been inflected with a wish to prove that the "covenant" between god and Moses was founded on some basis in fact. No group of diggers and scholars has ever worked harder, or with greater expectations, than the Israelis who sifted through the sands of Sinai and Canaan. The first of them was Yigael Yadin, whose best-known work was at Masada and who had been charged by David Ben-Gurion to dig up "the title deeds" that would prove the Israeli claim to the Holy Land. Until a short time ago, his evidently politicized efforts were allowed a certain superficial plausibility. But then much more extensive and objective work was undertaken, presented most notably by Israel Finkelstein of the Institute of Archaeology at Tel Aviv University, and his colleague Neil Asher Silberman. These men regard the "Hebrew Bible" or Pentateuch as beautiful, and the story of modern Israel as an all-around inspiration, in which respects I humbly beg to differ. But their conclusion is final, and the more creditable for asserting evidence over self-interest. There was no flight from Egypt, no wandering in the desert (let alone for the incredible four-decade length of time mentioned in the Pentateuch), and no dramatic conquest of the Promised Land. It was all, quite simply and very ineptly, made up at a much later date. No Egyptian chronicle mentions this episode either, even in passing, and Egypt was the garrison power in Canaan as well as the Nilotic region at all the material times. Indeed, much of the evidence is the other way. Archaeology *does* confirm the presence of Jewish communities in Palestine from many thousands of years ago (this can be deduced, among other things, from the absence of those pig bones in the middens and dumps), and it does show that there was a "kingdom of David," albeit rather a modest one, but all the Mosaic myths can be safely and easily discarded. I do not think that this is what the sour critics of faith sometimes call a "reductionist" conclusion. There is great pleasure to be had from the study of archaeology and of ancient texts, and great instruction, too. And it brings us ever nearer to some approximation of the truth. On the other hand, it also raises the question of antitheism once more. In *The Future of an Illusion*, Freud made the obvious point that religion suffered from one incurable deficiency: it was too clearly derived from our own desire to escape from or survive death. This critique of wish-thinking is strong and unanswerable, but it does not really deal with the horrors and cruelties and madnesses of the Old Testament. Who—except for an ancient priest seeking to exert power by the tried and tested means of fear—could possibly *wish* that this hopelessly knotted skein of fable had any veracity?

Well, the Christians had been at work on the same wishful attempt at "proof" long before the Zionist school of archaeology began to turn a spade. Saint Paul's Epistle to the Galatians had transmitted god's promise to the Jewish patriarchs, as an unbroken patrimony, to the Christians, and in the nineteenth and early twentieth centuries you could hardly throw away an orange peel in the Holy Land without hitting a fervent excavator. General Gordon, the biblical fanatic later slain by the Mahdi at Khartoum, was very much to the fore. William Albright of Baltimore was continually vindicating Joshua's Jericho and other myths. Some of these diggers, even given the primitive techniques of the period, counted as serious rather than merely opportunistic. Morally serious too: the French Dominican archaeologist Roland de Vaux gave a hostage to fortune by saying that "if the historical faith of Israel is not founded in history, such faith is erroneous, and therefore, our faith is also." A most admirable and honest point, on which the good father may now be taken up.

Long before modern inquiry and painstaking translation and ex-cavation had helped enlighten us, it was well within the compass of a thinking person to see that the "revelation" at Sinai and the rest of the Pentateuch was an ill-carpentered fiction, bolted into place well after the nonevents that it fails to describe convincingly or even plausibly. Intel-ligent schoolchildren have been upsetting their teachers with innocent but unanswerable questions ever since Bible study was instituted. The self-taught Thomas Paine has never been refuted since he wrote, while suffering dire persecution by French Jacobin antireligionists, to show

> that these books are spurious, and that Moses is not the author of them; and still further, that they were not written in the time of Moses, nor till several hundred years afterwards, that they are an attempted history of the life of Moses, and of the times in which he is said to have lived; and also of the times prior thereto, written by some very ignorant and stupid pretenders several hun-dred years after the death of Moses; as men now write histories of things that happened, or are supposed to have happened, several hundred or several thousand years ago.

In the first place, the middle books of the Pentateuch (Exodus, Le-viticus, and Numbers: Genesis contains no mention of him) allude to Moses in the third person, as in "the Lord spake unto Moses." It could be argued that he preferred to speak of himself in the third person, though this habit is now well associated with megalomania, but this would make laughable such citations as Numbers 12:3 in which we read, "Now the man Moses was *very meek* above all the men which were on the face of the earth." Apart from the absurdity of claiming to be meek in such a way as to assert superiority in meekness over all others, we have to remember the commandingly authoritarian and bloody manner in which Moses is described, in almost every other chapter, as having behaved. This gives us a choice between raving so-lipsism and the falsest of modesty.

But perhaps Moses himself can be acquitted on these two charges, since he could hardly have managed the contortions of Deuteronomy. In this book there is an introduction of the subject, then an introduction of Moses himself in mid-speech, then a resumption of narrative by whoever is writing, then another speech by Moses, and then an account of the death, burial, and magnificence of Moses himself. (It is to be presumed that the account of the funeral was not written by the man whose funeral it was, though this problem does not seem to have occurred to whoever fabricated the text.)

That whoever wrote the account was writing many years later seems to be very clear. We are told that Moses reached the age of one hundred and ten, with "his eye not dim nor his natural force abated," and then ascended to the summit of Mount Nebo, from which he could obtain a clear view of the Promised Land that he would never actually enter. The prophet, his natural force all of a sudden abated, then dies in the land of Moab and is interred there. No one knows, says the author, *"unto this day,"* where the sepulcher of Moses lies. It is added that there has *since* been no comparable prophet in Israel. These two expressions have no effect if they do not denote the passage of a considerable time. We are then expected to believe that an unspecified "he" buried Moses: if this was Moses himself in the third person again it seems distinctly implausible, and if it was god himself who performed the obsequy then there is no way for the writer of Deuteronomy to have known it. Indeed, the author seems very unclear about all the details of this event, as would be expected if he was reconstructing something half-forgotten. The same is self-evidently true of innumerable other anachronisms, where Moses speaks of events (the consumption of "manna" in Canaan; the capture of the huge bedstead of the "giant" Og, king of Bashan) which may never have occurred at all but which are not even claimed to have occurred until well after his death.

The strong likelihood that this interpretation is the correct one is reinforced in Deuteronomy's fourth and fifth chapters, where Moses assembles his followers and gives them the Lord's commandments all over again. (This is not such a surprise: the Pentateuch contains two discrepant accounts of the Creation, two different genealogies of the seed of Adam, and two narratives of the Flood.) One of these chapters has Moses talking about himself at great length, and the other has him in reported speech. In the fourth chapter, the commandment against making graven images is extended to prohibiting any "similitude" or "likeness" of any figure, whether human or animal, for any purpose. In the fifth chapter, the contents of the two stone tablets are repeated roughly in the same form as in Exodus, but with a significant difference. This time, the writer forgets that the Sabbath day is holy because god made heaven and earth in six days and then rested on the seventh. Suddenly, the Sabbath is holy because god brought his people out of the land of Egypt.

Then we must come to those things which probably did not happen and which we must be glad did not. In Deuteronomy Moses gives orders for parents to have their children stoned to death for indiscipline (which seems to violate at least one of the commandments) and continually makes demented pronouncements ("He that is wounded in the stones, or hath his privy member cut off, shall not enter into the congregation of the Lord"). In Numbers, he addresses his generals after a battle and rages at them for sparing so many civilians:

> Now, therefore, kill every male among the little ones, and kill every woman that hath known a man by lying with him. But all the women-children that hath not known a man by lying with him, keep alive for yourselves.

This is certainly not the worst of the genocidal incitements that occur in the Old Testament (Israeli rabbis solemnly debate to this very day whether the demand to exterminate the Amalekites is a coded commandment to do away with the Palestinians), but it has an element of lasciviousness that makes it slightly too obvious what the rewards of a freebooting soldier could be. At least so I think and so thought Thomas Paine, who wrote not to disprove religion but rather to vindicate deism against what he considered to be foul accretions in the holy books. He said that this was "an order to butcher the boys, to massacre the mothers, and debauch the daughters," which drew him a hurt reply from one of the celebrated divines of the day, the bishop of Llandaff. The stout Welsh bishop indignantly claimed that it was not at all clear from the context that the young females were being preserved for immoral purposes rather than for unpaid labor. Against dumb innocence like this it might be heartless to object, if it were not for the venerable clergyman's sublime indifference to the fate of the boy-children and indeed their mothers.

One could go through the Old Testament book by book, here pausing to notice a lapidary phrase ("Man is born to trouble," as the book of Job says, "as the sparks fly upward") and there a fine verse, but always encountering the same difficulties. People attain impossible ages and yet conceive children. Mediocre individuals engage in single combat or one-on-one argument with god or his emissaries, raising afresh the whole question of divine omnipotence or even divine common sense, and the ground is forever soaked with the blood of the innocent. Moreover, the context is oppressively confined and *local*. None of these provincials, or their deity, seems to have any idea of a world beyond the desert, the flocks and herds, and the imperatives of nomadic subsistence. This is forgivable on the part of the provincial yokels, obviously, but then what of their supreme guide and wrathful tyrant? Perhaps he was made in their image, even if not graven?

Chapter Eight

The "New" Testament Exceeds the Evil of the "Old" One

The work of rereading the Old Testament is sometimes tiring but always necessary, because as one proceeds there begin to occur some sinister premonitions. Abraham—another ancestor of all monotheism—is ready to make a human sacrifice of his own first-born. And a rumor comes that "a virgin shall conceive, and bear a son." Gradually, these two myths begin to converge. It's needful to bear this in mind when coming to the New Testament, because if you pick up any of the four Gospels and read them at random, it will not be long before you learn that such and such an action or saying, attributed to Jesus, was done so that an ancient prophecy should come true. (Speaking of the arrival of Jesus in Jerusalem, riding astride a donkey, Matthew says in his chapter 21, verse 4, "All of this was done, that it might be fulfilled which was spoken by the prophet." The reference is probably to Zechariah 9:9, where it is said that when the Messiah comes he will be riding on an ass. The Jews are still awaiting this arrival and the Christians claim it has already taken place!) If it should seem odd that an action should be deliberately performed in order that a foretelling be vindicated, that is because it *is* odd. And it is necessarily odd because, just like the Old Testament, the "New" one is also a work of crude carpentry, hammered together long after its purported events, and full of improvised attempts to make things come out right. For concision, I shall again defer to a finer writer than myself and quote what H. L. Mencken irrefutably says in his *Treatise on the Gods*:

> The simple fact is that the New Testament, as we know it, is a helter-skelter accumulation of more or less discordant documents, some of them probably of respectable origin but others palpably apocryphal, and that most of them, the good along with the bad, show unmistakable signs of having been tampered with.

Both Paine and Mencken, who put themselves for different reasons to an honest effort to read the texts, have been borne out by later biblical scholarship, much of it first embarked upon to show that the texts were still relevant. But this argument takes place over the heads of those to whom the "Good Book" is all that is required. (One recalls the governor of Texas who, asked if the Bible should also be taught in Spanish, replied that "if English was good enough for Jesus, then it's good enough for me." Rightly are the simple so called.)

In 2004, a soap-opera film about the death of Jesus was produced by an Australian fascist and ham actor named Mel Gibson. Mr. Gibson adheres to a crackpot and schismatic Catholic sect consisting mainly of himself and of his even more thuggish father, and has stated that it is a pity that his own dear wife is going to hell because she does not accept the correct sacraments. (This foul doom he calmly describes as "a statement from the chair.") The doctrine of his own sect is explicitly anti-Semitic, and the movie sought tirelessly to lay the blame for the Crucifixion upon the Jews. In spite of this obvious bigotry, which did lead to criticism from some more cautious Christians, *The Passion of the Christ* was opportunistically employed by many "mainstream" churches as a box-office recruiting tool. At one of the ecumenical prepublicity events which he sponsored, Mr. Gibson defended his filmic farrago—which is also an exercise in sadomasochistic homoeroticism starring a talentless lead actor who was apparently born in Iceland or Minnesota—as being based on the reports of "eyewitnesses." At the time, I thought it extraordinary that a multimillion-dollar hit could be openly based on such a patently fraudulent claim, but nobody seemed to turn a hair. Even Jewish authorities were largely silent. But then, some of them wanted to dampen down this old argument, which for centuries had led to Easter pogroms against the "Christ-killing Jews." (It was not until two decades after the Second World War that the Vatican formally withdrew the charge of "deicide" against the Jewish people as a whole.) And the truth is that the Jews used to claim credit for the Crucifixion. Maimonides described the punishment of the detestable Nazarene heretic as one of the greatest achievements of the Jewish elders, insisted that the name Jesus never be mentioned except when accompanied by a curse, and announced that his punishment was to be boiled in excrement for all eternity. What a good Catholic Maimonides would have made!

However, he fell into the same error as do the Christians, in assuming that the four Gospels were in any sense a historical record. Their multiple authors—none of whom published anything until many decades after the Crucifixion—cannot agree on anything of importance. Matthew and Luke cannot concur on the Virgin Birth or the genealogy of Jesus. They flatly contradict each other on the "Flight into Egypt," Matthew saying that Joseph was "warned in a dream" to make an immediate escape and Luke saying that all three stayed in Bethlehem until Mary's "purification according to the laws of Moses," which would make it forty days, and then went back to Nazareth via Jerusalem. (Incidentally, if the dash to Egypt to conceal a child from Herod's infanticide campaign has any truth to it, then Hollywood and many, many Christian iconographers have been deceiving us. It would have been very difficult to take a blond, blue-eyed baby to the Nile delta without attracting rather than avoiding attention.)

The Gospel according to Luke states that the miraculous birth occurred in a year when the Emperor Caesar Augustus ordered a census for the purpose of taxation, and that this happened at a time when Herod reigned in Judaea and Quirinius was governor of Syria. That is the closest to a triangulation of historical dating that any biblical writer even attempts. But Herod died four years "BC," and during his rulership the governor of Syria was not Quirinius. There is no mention of any Augustan census by any Roman historian, but the Jewish chronicler Josephus mentions one that did occur—without the onerous requirement for people to return to their places of birth, and six years after the birth of Jesus is supposed to have taken place. This is, all of it, quite evidently a garbled and oral-based reconstruction undertaken some considerable time after the "fact." The scribes cannot even agree on the mythical elements: they disagree wildly about the Sermon on the Mount, the anointing of Jesus, the treachery of Judas, and Peter's haunting "denial." Most astonishingly, they cannot converge on a common account of the Crucifixion or the Resurrection. Thus, the one interpretation that we simply have to discard is the one that claims divine warrant for all four of them. The book on which all four may possibly have been based, known speculatively to scholars as "Q," has been lost forever, which seems distinctly careless on the part of the god who is claimed to have "inspired" it.

Sixty years ago, at Nag Hammadi in Egypt, a trove of neglected "Gospels" was discovered near a very ancient Coptic Christian site. These scrolls were of the same period and provenance as many of the subsequently canonical and "authorized" Gospels, and have long gone under the collective name of "Gnostic." This was the title given them by a certain Irenaeus, an early church father who placed them under a ban as heretical. They include the "Gospels" or narratives of marginal but significant figures in the accepted "New" Testament, such as "Doubting Thomas" and Mary Magdalene. They now also include the Gospel of Judas, known for centuries to have existed but now brought to light and published by the National Geographic Society in the spring of 2006.

The book is chiefly spiritualist drivel, as one might expect, but it offers a version of "events" that is fractionally more credible than the official account. For one thing, it maintains as do its partner texts that the supposed god of the "Old" Testament is the one to be avoided, a ghastly emanation from sick minds. (This makes it easy to see why it was so firmly banned and denounced: orthodox Christianity is nothing if it is not a vindication and completion of that evil story.) Judas attends the final Passover meal, as usual, but departs from the customary script. When Jesus appears to pity his other disciples for knowing so little about what is at stake, his rogue follower boldly says that he believes he knows what the difficulty is. "I know who you are and where you have come from," he tells the leader. "You are from the immortal realm of Barbelo." This "Barbelo" is not a god but a heavenly destination, a motherland beyond the stars. Jesus comes from this celestial realm, but is not the son of any Mosaic god. Instead, he is an avatar of Seth, the third and little-known son of Adam. He is the one who will show the Sethians the way home. Recognizing that Judas is at least a minor adept of this cult, Jesus takes him to one side and awards him the special mission of helping him shed his fleshly form and thus return heavenward. He also promises to show him the stars that will enable Judas to follow on.

Deranged science fiction though this is, it makes infinitely more sense than the everlasting curse placed on Judas for doing what somebody had to do, in this otherwise pedantically arranged chronicle of a death foretold. It also makes infinitely more sense than blaming the Jews for all eternity. For a long time, there was incandescent debate over which of the "Gospels" should be regarded as divinely inspired. Some argued for these and some for others, and many a life was horribly lost on the proposition. Nobody dared say that they were all man-inscribed long after the supposed drama was over, and the "Revelation" of Saint John seems to have squeezed into the canon because of its author's (rather ordinary) name. But as Jorge Luis Borges put it, had the Alexandrian Gnostics won the day, some later Dante would have drawn us a hypnotically beautiful word-picture of the wonders of "Barbelo." This concept I might choose to call "the Borges shale": the verve and imagination needed to visualize a cross section of evolutionary branches and bushes, with the extraordinary but real possibility that a different stem or line (or tune or poem) had predominated in the labyrinth. Great ceilings and steeples and hymns, he might have added, would have consecrated it, and skilled torturers would have worked for days on those who doubted the truth of Barbelo: beginning with the fingernails and working their way ingeniously toward the testicles, the vagina, the eyes, and the viscera. Nonbelief in Barbelo would, correspondingly, have been an unfailing sign that one had no morals at all.

The best argument I know for the highly questionable existence of Jesus is this. His illiterate living disciples left us no record and in any event could not have been "Christians," since they were never to read those later books in which Christians must affirm belief, and in any case had no idea that anyone would ever found a church on their master's announcements. (There is scarcely a word in any of the later-assembled Gospels to suggest that Jesus wanted to be the founder of a church, either.)

Notwithstanding all that, the jumbled "Old" Testament prophecies indicate that the Messiah will be born in the city of David, which seems indeed to have been Bethlehem. However, Jesus's parents were apparently from Nazareth and if they had a child he was most probably delivered in that town. Thus a huge amount of fabrication—concerning Augustus, Herod, and Quirinius—is involved in confecting the census tale and moving the nativity scene to Bethlehem (where, by the way, no "stable" is ever mentioned). But why do this at all, since a much easier fabrication would have had him born in Bethlehem in the first place, without any needless to-do? The very attempts to bend and stretch the story may be inverse proof that someone of later significance *was* indeed born, so that in retrospect, and to fulfill the prophecies, the evidence had to be massaged to some extent. But then even my attempt to be fair and open-minded in this case is subverted by the Gospel of John, which seems to suggest that Jesus was neither born in Bethlehem nor descended from King David. If the apostles do not know or cannot agree, of what use is my analysis? In any case, if his royal lineage is something to brag and prophesy about, why the insistence elsewhere on apparently lowly birth? Almost all religions from Buddhism to Islam feature either a humble prophet or a prince who comes to identify with the poor, but what is this if not populism? It is hardly a surprise if religions choose to address themselves first to the majority who are poor and bewildered and uneducated.

The contradictions and illiteracies of the New Testament have filled up many books by eminent scholars, and have never been explained by any Christian authority except in the feeblest terms of "metaphor" and "a Christ of faith." This feebleness derives from the fact that until recently, Christians could simply burn or silence anybody who asked any inconvenient questions. The Gospels are useful, however, in re-demonstrating the same point as their predecessor volumes, which is that religion is man-made. "The law was given by Moses," says Saint John, "but grace and truth came by Jesus Christ." Saint Matthew tries for the same effect, basing everything on a verse or two from the prophet Isaiah which told King Ahaz, almost eight centuries before the still unfixed date of the birth of Jesus, that "the Lord shall give you a sign; a virgin will conceive and bear a son." This encouraged Ahaz to believe that he would be given victory over his enemies (which in the result, even if you take his story as historical narrative, he was not). The picture is even further altered when we know that the word translated as "virgin," namely *almah*, means only "a young woman." In any case, parthenogenesis is not possible for human mammals, and even if this law were to be relaxed in just one case, it would not prove that the resulting infant had any divine power. Thus, and as usual, religion arouses suspicion by trying to prove too much. By reverse analogy, the Sermon on the Mount replicates Moses on Mount Sinai, and the nondescript disciples stand in for the Jews who followed Moses wherever he went, and thus prophecy is fulfilled for anyone who doesn't notice or doesn't care that the story is being "reverse-engineered," as we might now say. In a short passage of only one Gospel (seized upon by the Jew-baiting Mel Gibson) the rabbis are made to echo god on Sinai and actually to *call* for the guilt in the blood of Jesus to descend upon all their subsequent generations: a demand that, even if it were to be made, lay well beyond their right, or their power.

But the case of the Virgin Birth is the easiest possible proof that humans were involved in the manufacture of a legend. Jesus makes large claims for his heavenly father but never mentions that his mother is or was a virgin, and is repeatedly very rude and coarse to her when she makes an appearance, as Jewish mothers will, to ask or to see how he is getting on. She herself appears to have no memory of the Archangel Gabriel's visitation, or of the swarm of angels, both telling her that she is the mother of god. In all accounts, everything that her son does comes to her as a complete surprise, if not a shock. What can he be doing talking to rabbis in the temple? What's he saying when he curtly reminds her that he's on his father's business? One might have expected a stronger maternal memory, especially from someone who had undergone the experience, alone among all women, of discovering herself pregnant without having undergone the notorious preconditions for that happy state. Luke even makes a telling slip at one point, speaking of the "parents of Jesus" when he refers only to Joseph and Mary as they visit the temple for her purification and are hailed by the old man Simeon who pronounces his wonderful *Nunc dimittis*, which (another of my old chapel favorites) may also be an intended echo of Moses glimpsing the Promised Land only in extreme old age.

Then there is the extraordinary matter of Mary's large brood. Matthew informs us (13:55–57) that there were four brothers of Jesus, and some sisters also. In the Gospel of James, which is not canonical but not disowned either, we have the account by Jesus's brother of that same name, who was evidently very active in religious circles at the same period. Arguably, Mary could have "conceived" as a *virgo intacta* and delivered a baby, which would certainly have made her to that extent less intact. But how did she go on producing children, by the man Joseph who only exists in reported speech, and thus make the holy family so large that "eyewitnesses" kept remarking on it?

In order to resolve this near-unmentionable and near-sexual dilemma, reverse-engineering is again applied, this time much more recently than the frantic early church councils that decided which Gospels were "synoptic" and which were "apocryphal." It is determined that Mary herself (of whose birth there is absolutely no account in any holy book) must have had a prior "Immaculate Conception" that rendered her essentially stainless. And it is further determined that, since the wage of sin is death and she cannot possibly have sinned, she cannot have died. Hence the dogma of the "Assumption," which asserts out of thin air that thin air is the medium through which she went to heaven while avoiding the grave. It is of interest to note the dates of these magnificently ingenious edicts. The doctrine of the Immaculate Conception was announced or discovered by Rome in 1852, and the dogma of the Assumption in 1951. To say that something is "man-made" is not always to say that it is stupid. These heroic rescue attempts deserve some credit, even as we watch the leaky original vessel sink without trace. But, "inspired" though the church's resolution may be, it would insult the deity to claim that such inspiration was in any way divine.

JUST AS THE SCRIPT of the Old Testament is riddled with dreams and with astrology (the sun standing still so that Joshua can complete his massacre at a site that has never been located), so the Christian bible is full of star-predictions (notably the one over Bethlehem) and witch doctors and sorcerers. Many of the sayings and deeds of Jesus are innocuous, most especially the "beatitudes" which express such fanciful wish-thinking about the meek and the peacemakers. But many are unintelligible and show a belief in magic, several are absurd and show a primitive attitude to agriculture (this extends to all mentions of plowing and sowing, and all allusions to mustard or fig trees), and many are on the face of it flat-out immoral. The analogy of humans to lilies, for instance, suggests—along with many other injunctions—that things like thrift, innovation, family life, and so forth are a sheer waste of time. ("Take no thought for the morrow.") This is why some of the Gospels, synoptic and apocryphal, report people (including his family members) saying at the time that they thought Jesus must be mad. There were also those who noticed that he was often a rather rigid Jewish sectarian: in Matthew 15:21–28 we read of his contempt for a Canaanite woman who implored his aid for an exorcism and was brusquely told that he would not waste his energy on a non-Jew. (His disciples, and the persistence of the woman, eventually persuaded him to unbend, and to cast out the non-devil.) In my opinion, an idiosyncratic story like this is another oblique reason for thinking that some such personality may at some time have lived. There were many deranged prophets roaming Palestine at the time, but this one reportedly believed himself, at least some of the time, to be god or the son of god. And that has made all the difference. Make just two assumptions: that he believed this and that he also promised his followers that he would reveal his kingdom before they came to the end of their own lives, and all but one or two of his gnomic remarks make some kind of sense. This point was never put more frankly than by C. S. Lewis (who has recently reemerged as the most popular Christian apologist) in his *Mere Christianity*. He happens to be speaking about the claim of Jesus to take sins on himself:

> Now, unless the speaker is God, this is really so preposterous as to be comic. We can all understand how a man forgives offenses against himself. You tread on my toes and I forgive you, you steal my money and I forgive you. But what should we make of a man, himself unrobbed and untrodden-on, who announced

that he forgave you for treading on other men's toes and stealing other men's money? Asinine fatuity is the kindest description we should give of his conduct. Yet this is what Jesus did. He told people that their sins were forgiven, and never waited to consult all the other people whom their sins had undoubtedly injured. He unhesitatingly behaved as if He was the party chiefly concerned, the person chiefly offended in all offenses. This makes sense only if he really was the God whose laws are broken and whose love is wounded in every sin. In the mouth of any speaker who is not God, these words would imply what I can only regard as a silliness and conceit unrivalled by any other character in history.

It will be noticed that Lewis assumes on no firm evidence whatever that Jesus actually *was* a "character in history," but let that pass. He deserves some credit for accepting the logic and morality of what he has just stated. To those who argue that Jesus may have been a great moral teacher without being divine (of whom the deist Thomas Jefferson incidentally claimed to be one), Lewis has this stinging riposte:

That is the one thing we must not say. A man who was merely a man and said the sort of things Jesus said would not be a great moral teacher. He would either be a lunatic—on a level with the man who says he is a poached egg—or else he would be the Devil of Hell. You must make your choice. Either this man was, and is, the Son of God: or else a madman and something worse. You can shut Him up for a fool, you can spit at Him and kill Him as a demon; or you can fall at His feet and call Him Lord and God. But let us not come with any patronizing nonsense about His being a great human teacher. He has not left that open to us. He did not intend to.

I am not choosing a straw man here: Lewis is the main chosen propaganda vehicle for Christianity in our time. And nor am I accepting his rather wild supernatural categories, such as devil and demon. Least of all do I accept his reasoning, which is so pathetic as to defy description and which takes his two false alternatives as exclusive antitheses, and then uses them to fashion a crude non sequitur ("Now it seems to me obvious that He was neither a lunatic nor a fiend: and consequently, however strange or terrifying or unlikely it may seem, I have to accept the view that He was and is God."). However, I do credit him with honesty and with some courage. Either the Gospels are in some sense literal truth, or the whole thing is essentially a fraud and perhaps an immoral one at that. Well, it can be stated with certainty, and on their own evidence, that the Gospels are most certainly not literal truth. This means that many of the "sayings" and teachings of Jesus are hearsay upon hearsay upon hearsay, which helps explain their garbled and contradictory nature. The most glaring of these, at least in retrospect and certainly from the believers' point of view, concern the imminence of his second coming and his complete indifference to the founding of any temporal church. The *logia* or reported speeches are repeatedly cited, by bishops of the early church who wished that they had been present at the time but were not, as eagerly solicited thirdhand commentaries. Let me give a conspicuous example. Many years after C. S. Lewis had gone to his reward, a very serious young man named Barton Ehrman began to examine his own fundamentalist assumptions. He had attended the two most eminent Christian fundamentalist academies in the United States, and was considered by the faithful to be among their champions. Fluent in Greek and Hebrew (he is now holder of a chair in religious studies), he eventually could not quite reconcile his faith with his scholarship. He was astonished to find that some of the best-known Jesus stories were scribbled into the canon long after the fact, and that this was true of perhaps the best-known of them all.

This story is the celebrated one about the woman taken in adultery (John 8:3–11). Who has not heard or read of how the Jewish Pharisees, skilled in casuistry, dragged this poor woman before Jesus and demanded to know if he agreed with the Mosaic punishment of stoning her to death? If he did not, he violated the law. If he did, he made nonsense of his own preachings. One easily pictures the squalid zeal with which they pounced upon the woman. And the calm reply (after writing upon the ground)—"He that is without sin among you, let him first cast a stone at her"—has entered our literature and our consciousness.

This episode is even celebrated on celluloid. It makes a flashback appearance in Mel Gibson's travesty, and it is a lovely moment in David Lean's *Dr. Zhivago*, where Lara goes to the priest in her extremity and is asked what Jesus said to the fallen woman. "Go, and sin no more," is her reply. "And did she, child?" asks the priest fiercely. "I don't know, Father." "Nobody knows," responds the priest, unhelpfully in the circumstances.

Nobody, indeed, does know. Long before I read Ehrman, I had some questions of my own. If the New Testament is supposed to vindicate Moses, why are the gruesome laws of the Pentateuch to be undermined? An eye for an eye and a tooth for a tooth and the killing of witches may seem brutish and stupid, but if only non-sinners have the right to punish, then how could an imperfect society ever determine how to prosecute offenders? We should all be hypocrites. And what authority did Jesus have to "forgive"? Presumably, at least one wife or husband somewhere in the city felt cheated and outraged. Is Christianity, then, sheer sexual permissiveness? If so, it has been gravely misunderstood ever since. And what was being written on the ground? Nobody knows, again. Furthermore, the story says that after the Pharisees and the crowd had melted away (presumably from embarrassment), nobody was left except Jesus and the woman. In that case, who is the narrator of what he said to her? For all that, I thought it a fine enough story.

Professor Ehrman goes further. He asks some more obvious questions. If the woman was "taken in adultery," which means in flagrante delicto, then where is her male partner? Mosaic law, adumbrated in

Leviticus, makes it clear that both must undergo the stoning. I suddenly realized that the core of the story's charm is that of the shivering lonely girl, hissed at and dragged away by a crowd of sex-starved fanatics, and finally encountering a friendly face. As to the writing in the dust, Ehrman mentions an old tradition which postulates that Jesus was scrawling the known transgressions of others present, thus leading to blushing and shuffling and eventually to hasty departure. I find I love this idea, even if it would mean a level of worldly curiosity and prurience (and foresight) on his part that raises its own difficulties.

Overarching all this is the shocking fact that, as Ehrman concedes:

The story is not found in our oldest and best manuscripts of the Gospel of John; its writing style is very different from what we find in the rest of John (including the stories immediately before and after); and it includes a large number of words and phrases that are otherwise alien to the Gospel. The conclusion is unavoidable: this passage was not originally part of the Gospel.

I have again selected my source on the basis of "evidence against interest": in other words from someone whose original scholarly and intellectual journey was not at all intended to challenge holy writ. The case for biblical consistency or authenticity or "inspiration" has been in tatters for some time, and the rents and tears only become more obvious with better research, and thus no "revelation" can be derived from that quarter. So, then, let the advocates and partisans of religion rely on faith alone, and let them be brave enough to admit that this is what they are doing.

Chapter Nine

The Koran Is Borrowed from Both Jewish and Christian Myths

The doings and "sayings" of Moses and Abraham and Jesus being so ill-founded and so inconsistent, as well as so often immoral, one must proceed in the same spirit of inquiry to what many believe is the last revelation: that of the Prophet Muhammad and his Koran or "recitation." Here again, the Angel (or Archangel) Gabriel is found at work, dictating suras, or verses, to a person of little or no learning. Here again are stories of a Noah-like flood, and injunctions against idol worship. Here again the Jews are the first recipients of the message and the first both to hear it and to discard it. And here again there is a vast commentary of doubtful anecdote about the actual doings and sayings of the Prophet, this time known as the hadith.

Islam is at once the most and the least interesting of the world's monotheisms. It builds upon its primitive Jewish and Christian predecessors, selecting a chunk here and a shard there, and thus if these fall, it partly falls also. Its founding narrative likewise takes place within an astonishingly small compass, and relates facts about extremely tedious local quarrels. None of the original documents, such as they are, can be contrasted with any Hebrew or Greek or Latin texts. Almost all of the tradition is oral, and all of it is in Arabic. Indeed, many authorities agree that the Koran is only intelligible in that tongue, which is itself subject to innumerable idiomatic and regional inflections. This would leave us, on the face of it, with the absurd and potentially dangerous conclusion that god was a monoglot. Before me is a book, *Introducing Muhammad*, written by two extremely unctuous British Muslims who are hoping to present a friendly version of Islam to the West. Ingratiating and selective as their text may be, they insist that "as the literal Word of God, the Koran is the Koran only in the original revealed text. A translation can never be the Koran, that inimitable symphony, 'the very sound of which moves men and women to tears.' A translation can only be an attempt to give the barest suggestion of the meaning of words contained in the Koran. This is why all Muslims, whatever their mother tongue, always recite the Koran in its original Arabic." The authors go on to make some highly disobliging observations about the Penguin translation by N. J. Dawood, which makes me glad that I have always employed the Pickthall version but no likelier to be convinced that if I wish to become a convert I must master another language. In my own country of birth, I am sadly aware that there is a beautiful poetic tradition, unavailable to me because I will never know the marvelous tongue called Gaelic. Even if god is or was an Arab (an unsafe assumption), how could he expect to "reveal" himself by way of an illiterate person who in turn could not possibly hope to pass on the unaltered (let alone unalterable) words?

The point may seem minor but it is not. To Muslims, the annunciation of the divine to a person of extreme unlettered simplicity has something of the same value as the humble vessel of the Virgin Mary has to Christians. It also possesses the same useful merit of being entirely unverifiable, and unfalsifiable. Since Mary must be presumed to have spoken Aramaic and Muhammad Arabic, it can I suppose be granted that god is in fact multilingual and can speak any language he chooses. (He opted in both cases to use the Archangel Gabriel as the intermediate deliverer of his message.) However, the impressive fact remains that all religions have staunchly resisted any attempt to translate their sacred texts into languages "understood of the people," as the Cranmer prayer book phrases it. There would have been no Protestant Reformation if it were not for the long struggle to have the Bible rendered into "the Vulgate" and the priestly monopoly therefore broken. Devout men like Wycliffe, Coverdale, and Tyndale were burned alive for even attempting early translations. The Catholic Church has never recovered from its abandonment of the mystifying Latin ritual, and the Protestant mainstream has suffered hugely from rendering its own Bibles into more everyday speech. Some mystical Jewish sects still insist on Hebrew and play Kabbalistic word games even with the spaces between letters, but among most Jews, too, the supposedly unchangeable rituals of antiquity have been abandoned. The spell of the clerical class has been broken. Only in Islam has there been no reformation, and to this day any vernacular version of the Koran must still be printed with an Arabic parallel text. This ought to arouse suspicion even in the slowest mind.

Later Muslim conquests, impressive in their speed and scope and decisiveness, have lent point to the idea that these Arabic incantations must have had something to them. But if you allow this cheap earthly victory as a proof, you allow the same to Joshua's blood-soaked tribes-men or to the Christian crusaders and conquistadores. There is a fur-ther objection. All religions take care to silence or to execute those who question them (and I choose to regard this recurrent tendency as a sign of their weakness rather than their strength). It has, however, been some time since Judaism and Christianity resorted openly to torture and censorship. Not only did Islam begin by condemning all doubters to eternal fire, but it still claims the right to do so in almost all of its dominions, and still preaches that these same dominions can and must be extended by war. There has never been an attempt in any age to challenge or even investigate the claims of Islam that has not been met with extremely harsh and swift repression. Provisionally, then, one is entitled to conclude that the apparent unity and confidence of the faith is a mask for a very deep and probably justifiable insecurity. That there are and always have been sanguinary feuds *between* different schools of Islam, resulting in strictly inter-Muslim accusations of heresy and profanity and in terrible acts of violence, naturally goes without saying.

I have tried my best with this religion, which is as foreign to me as it is to the many millions who will always doubt that god entrusted a nonreader (through an intermediary) with the demanding call to "read." As I said, I long ago acquired a copy of the Marmaduke Pickthall translation of the Koran, which has been certified by senior sources in the ulema, or Islamic religious authority, to be the nearest to an approximate rendition into English. I have been to innumerable gatherings, from Friday prayers in Tehran to mosques in Damascus and Jerusalem and Doha and Istanbul and Washington, D.C., and I can attest that "the recitation" in Arabic does indeed have the apparent power to create bliss and also rage among those who hear it. (I have also attended prayers in Malaysia and Indonesia and Bosnia where there is resentment, among non-Arabic-speaking Muslims, at the privilege granted to Arabs and to Arabic, and to Arab movements and regimes, in a religion that purports to be universal.) I have in my own home received Sayed Hossein Khomeini, grandson of the ayatollah and a cleric from the holy city of Qum, and carefully handed him my own copy of the Koran. He kissed it, discussed it at length and with reverence, and for my instruction wrote in the back-flap the verses which he thought had disproved his grandfather's claim to clerical authority in this world, as well as overthrown his grandfather's claim to take the life of Salman Rushdie. Who am I to adjudicate in such a dispute? However, the idea that the identical text can yield different commandments to different people is quite familiar to me for other reasons. There is no need to overstate the difficulty of understanding Islam's alleged profundities. If one comprehends the fallacies of any "revealed" religion, one comprehends them all.

I have only once, in twenty-five years of often heated arguments in Washington, D.C., been threatened with actual violence. This was when I was at dinner with some staffers and supporters of the Clinton White House. One of those present, a then well-known Democratic pollster and fund-raiser, questioned me about my most recent trip to the Middle East. He wanted my opinion as to why the Muslims were so "all-fired, god-damn *fundamentalist*." I ran through my repertoire of explanations, adding that it was often forgotten that Islam was a relatively young faith, and still in the heat of its self-confidence. Not for Muslims the crisis of self-doubt that had overtaken Western Christianity. I added that, for example, while there was little or no evidence for the life of Jesus, the figure of the Prophet Muhammad was by contrast a person in ascertainable history. The man changed color faster than anyone I have ever seen. After shrieking that Jesus Christ had meant more to more people than I could ever imagine, and that I was disgusting beyond words for speaking so casually, he drew back his foot and aimed a kick which only his decency—conceivably his Christianity—prevented him from landing on my shin. He then ordered his wife to join him in leaving.

I now feel that I owe him an apology, or at least half of one. Although we do know that a person named Muhammad almost certainly existed within a fairly small bracket of time and space, we have the same problem as we do in all the precedent cases. The accounts that relate his deeds and words were assembled many years later and are hopelessly corrupted into incoherence by self-interest, rumor, and illiteracy.

The tale is familiar enough even if it is new to you. Some Meccans of the seventh century followed an Abrahamic tradition and even believed that their temple, the Kaaba, had been built by Abraham. The temple itself—most of its original furnishings having been destroyed by later fundamentalists, notably the Wahhabis—is said to have become depraved by idolatry. Muhammad the son of Abdullah became one of those *Hunafa* who "turned away" to seek solace elsewhere.

(The book of Isaiah also enjoins true believers to "come out" from the ungodly and be separate.) Retiring to a desert cave on Mount Hira for the month of heat, or Ramadan, he was "asleep or in a trance" (I am quoting Pickthall's commentary) when he heard a voice commanding him to read. He replied twice that he was unable to read and was thrice commanded to do so. Eventually asking what he should read, he was further commanded in the name of a lord who "created man from a clot of blood." After the Angel Gabriel (who so identified himself) had told Muhammad that he was to be Allah's messenger, and had departed, Muhammad confided in his wife Khadijah. On their return to Mecca she took him to meet her cousin, an elderly man named Waraqa ibn Naufal, "who knew the Scriptures of the Jews and Christians." This whiskered veteran declared that the divine envoy who once visited Moses had come again to Mount Hira. From then on, Muhammad adopted the modest title of "Slave of Allah," the latter word being simply the Arabic for "god."

The only people who at first took the smallest interest in Muhammad's claim were the greedy guardians of the temple at Mecca, who saw it as a threat to their pilgrimage business, and the studious Jews of Yathrib, a town two hundred miles distant, who had been for some time proclaiming the advent of the Messiah. The first group became more threatening and the second more friendly, as a result of which Muhammad made the journey, or hejira, to Yathrib, which is now known as Medina. The date of the flight counts as the inauguration of the Muslim era. But as with the arrival of the Nazarene in Jewish Palestine, which began with so many cheerful heavenly auguries, this was all to end very badly with a realization on the part of the Arabian Jews that they were faced with yet another disappointment, if not indeed another impostor.

According to Karen Armstrong, one of the most sympathetic—not to say apologetic—analysts of Islam, the Arabs of the time had a wounded feeling that they had been left out of history. God had appeared to Christians and Jews, "but he had sent the Arabs no prophet and no scripture in their own language." Thus, though she does not put it this way, the time for someone to have a local revelation was long overdue. And, once having had it, Muhammad was not inclined to let it be criticized as secondhand by adherents of older faiths. The record of his seventh-century career, like the books of the Old Testament, swiftly becomes an account of vicious quarrels between a few hundred or sometimes a few thousand unlearned villagers and townspeople, in which the finger of god was supposed to settle and determine the outcome of parochial disputes. As with the primeval bloodlettings of the Sinai and Canaan, which are likewise unattested by any independent evidence, millions of people have been held hostage ever since by the supposedly providential character of these ugly squabbles.

There is some question as to whether Islam is a separate religion at all. It initially fulfilled a need among Arabs for a distinctive or special creed, and is forever identified with their language and their impressive later conquests, which, while not as striking as those of the young Alexander of Macedonia, certainly conveyed an idea of being backed by a divine will until they petered out at the fringes of the Balkans and the Mediterranean. But Islam when examined is not much more than a rather obvious and ill-arranged set of plagiarisms, helping itself from earlier books and traditions as occasion appeared to require. Thus, far from being "born in the clear light of history," as Ernest Renan so generously phrased it, Islam in its origins is just as shady and approximate as those from which it took its borrowings. It makes immense claims for itself, invokes prostrate submission or "surrender" as a maxim to its adherents, and demands deference and respect from nonbelievers into the bargain. There is nothing—absolutely nothing—in its teachings that can even begin to justify such arrogance and presumption.

The prophet died in the year 632 of our own approximate calendar. The first account of his life was set down a full hundred and twenty years later by Ibn Ishaq, whose original was lost and can only be consulted through its reworked form, authored by Ibn Hisham, who died in 834. Adding to this hearsay and obscurity, there is no agreed-upon account of how the Prophet's followers assembled the Koran, or of how his various sayings (some of them written down by secretaries) became codified. And this familiar problem is further complicated—even more than in the Christian case—by the matter of succession. Unlike Jesus, who apparently undertook to return to earth very soon and who (*pace* the absurd Dan Brown) left no known descendants, Muhammad was a general and a politician and—though unlike Alexander of Macedonia a prolific father—left no instruction as to who was to take up his mantle. Quarrels over the leadership began almost as soon as he died, and so Islam had its first major schism—between the Sunni and the Shia—before it had even established itself as a system. We need take no side in the schism, except to point out that one at least of the schools of interpretation must be quite mistaken. And the initial identification of Islam with an earthly caliphate, made up of disputatious contenders for the said mantle, marked it from the very beginning as man-made.

It is said by some Muslim authorities that during the first caliphate of Abu Bakr, immediately after Muhammad's death, concern arose that his orally transmitted words might be forgotten. So many Muslim soldiers had been killed in battle that the number who had the Koran safely lodged in their memories had become alarmingly small. It was therefore decided to assemble every living witness, together with "pieces of paper, stones, palm leaves, shoulder-blades, ribs and bits of leather" on which sayings had been scribbled, and give them to Zaid ibn Thabit, one of the Prophet's former secretaries, for an authoritative collation. Once this had been done, the believers had something like an authorized version.

If true, this would date the Koran to a time fairly close to Muhammad's own life. But we swiftly discover that there is no certainty or agreement about the truth of the story. Some say that it was Ali—the fourth and not the first caliph, and the founder of Shiism—who had the idea. Many others—the Sunni majority—assert that it was Caliph Uthman, who reigned from 644 to 656, who made the finalized decision. Told by one of his generals that soldiers from different provinces were fighting over discrepant accounts of the Koran, Uthman ordered Zaid ibn Thabit to bring together the various texts, unify them, and have them transcribed into one. When this task was complete, Uthman ordered standard copies to be sent to Kufa, Basra, Damascus, and elsewhere, with a master copy retained in Medina. Uthman thus played the canonical role that had been taken, in the standardization and purging and censorship of the Christian Bible, by Irenaeus and by Bishop Athanasius of Alexandria. The roll was called, and some texts were declared sacred and inerrant while others became "apocryphal." Outdoing Athanasius, Uthman ordered that all earlier and rival editions be destroyed.

Even supposing this version of events to be correct, which would mean that no chance existed for scholars ever to determine or even dispute what really happened in Muhammad's time, Uthman's attempt to abolish disagreement was a vain one. The written Arabic language has two features that make it difficult for an outsider to learn: it uses dots to distinguish consonants like "b" and "t," and in its original form it had no sign or symbol for short vowels, which could be rendered by various dashes or comma-type marks. Vastly different readings even of Uthman's version were enabled by these variations. Arabic script itself was not standardized until the later part of the ninth century, and in the meantime the undotted and oddly voweled Koran was generating wildly different explanations of itself, as it still does. This might not matter in the case of the *Iliad*, but remember that we are supposed to be talking about the unalterable (and *final*) word of god. There is obviously a connection between the sheer feebleness of this claim and the absolutely fanatical certainty with which it is advanced. To take one instance that can hardly be called negligible, the Arabic words written on the outside of the Dome of the Rock in Jerusalem are different from any version that appears in the Koran.

The situation is even more shaky and deplorable when we come to the hadith, or that vast orally generated secondary literature which supposedly conveys the sayings and actions of Muhammad, the tale of the Koran's compilation, and the sayings of "the companions of the Prophet." Each hadith, in order to be considered authentic, must be supported in turn by an *isnad*, or chain, of supposedly reliable witnesses. Many Muslims allow their attitude to everyday life to be determined by these anecdotes: regarding dogs as unclean, for example, on the sole ground that Muhammad is said to have done so. (My own favorite tale goes the other way: the Prophet is said to have cut off the long sleeve of his garment rather than disturb a cat that was slumbering on it. Cats in Muslim lands have been generally spared the awful treatment visited on them by Christians, who have often regarded them as satanic familiars of witches.)

As one might expect, the six authorized collections of hadith, which pile hearsay upon hearsay through the unwinding of the long spool of isnads ("A told B, who had it from C, who learned it from D"), were put together centuries after the events they purport to describe. One of the most famous of the six compilers, Bukhari, died 238 years after the death of Muhammad. Bukhari is deemed unusually reliable and honest by Muslims, and seems to have deserved his reputation in that, of the *three hundred thousand* attestations he accumulated in a lifetime devoted to the project, he ruled that *two hundred thousand* of them were entirely valueless and unsupported. Further exclusion of dubious traditions and questionable isnads reduced his grand total to ten thousand hadith. You are free to believe, if you so choose, that out of this formless mass of illiterate and half-remembered witnessing the pious Bukhari, more than two centuries later, managed to select only the pure and undefiled ones that would bear examination.

Some of these candidates for authenticity might have been easier to sift out than others. The Hungarian scholar Ignaz Goldziher, to quote a recent study by Reza Aslan, was among the first to show that many of the hadith were no more than "verses from the Torah and the Gospels, bits of Rabbinic sayings, ancient Persian maxims, passages of Greek philosophy, Indian proverbs, and even an almost word-for-word reproduction of the Lord's Prayer." Great chunks of more or less straight biblical quotation can be found in the hadith, including the parable of the workers hired at the last moment, and the injunction "Let not thy left hand know what thy right hand doeth," the last example meaning that this piece of pointless pseudoprofundity has a place in two sets of revealed scripture. Aslan notes that by the time of the ninth century, when Muslim legal scholars were attempting to formulate and codify Islamic law through the process known as *ijtihad*, they were obliged to separate many hadith into the following categories: "lies told for material gain and lies told for ideological advantage." Quite rightly, Islam effectively disowns the idea that it is a new faith, let alone a cancellation of the earlier ones, and it uses the prophecies of the Old Testament and the Gospels of the New like a perpetual crutch or fund, to be leaned on or drawn upon. In return for this derivative modesty, all it asks is to be accepted as the absolute and final revelation.

As might be expected, it contains many internal contradictions. It is often cited as saying that "there is no compulsion in religion," and as making reassuring noises about those of other faiths being peoples "of the book" or "followers of an earlier revelation." The idea of being "tolerated" by a Muslim is as repulsive to me as the other condescensions whereby Catholic and Protestant Christians agreed to "tolerate" one another, or extend "toleration" to Jews. The Christian world was so awful in this respect, and for so long, that many Jews preferred to live under Ottoman rule and submit to special taxes and other such distinctions. However, the actual Koranic reference to Islam's benign tolerance is qualified, because some of these same "peoples" and "followers" may be "such of them as are bent on evil-doing." And it takes only a short acquaintance with the Koran and the hadith to discover other imperatives, such as the following:

Nobody who dies and finds good from Allah (in the hereafter) would wish to come back to this world even if he were given the whole world and whatever is in it, except the martyr who, on

seeing the superiority of martyrdom, would like to come back to
the world and be killed again.

Or:

God will not forgive those who serve other gods beside Him; but
he will forgive whom He will for other sins. He that serves other
gods besides God is guilty of a heinous sin.

I chose the first of these two violent excerpts (from a whole the-
saurus of unsavory possible ones) because it so perfectly negates what
Socrates is reported to have said in Plato's *Apology* (to which I am
coming). And I chose the second because it is such a patent and abject
borrowing from the "Ten Commandments."

The likelihood that any of this humanly derived rhetoric is "inerrant," let alone "final," is conclusively disproved not just by its innumerable contradictions and incoherencies but by the famous episode
of the Koran's alleged "satanic verses," out of which Salman Rushdie
was later to make a literary project. On this much-discussed occasion,
Muhammad was seeking to conciliate some leading Meccan poly-
theists and in due course experienced a "revelation" that allowed them
after all to continue worshipping some of the older local deities. It
struck him later that this could not be right and that he must have
inadvertently been "channeled" by the devil, who for some reason had
briefly chosen to relax his habit of combating monotheists on their
own ground. (Muhammad believed devoutly not just in the devil
himself but in minor desert devils, or *djinns*, as well.) It was noticed
even by some of his wives that the Prophet was capable of having a
"revelation" that happened to suit his short-term needs, and he was
sometimes teased about it. We are further told—on no authority that
need be believed—that when he experienced revelation in public he
would sometimes be gripped by pain and experience loud ringing in
his ears. Beads of sweat would burst out on him, even on the chilliest

of days. Some heartless Christian critics have suggested that he was an epileptic (though they fail to notice the same symptoms in the seizure experienced by Paul on the road to Damascus), but there is no need for us to speculate in this way. It is enough to rephrase David Hume's unavoidable question. Which is more likely—that a man should be used as a transmitter by god to deliver some already existing revelations, or that he should utter some already existing revelations and believe himself to be, or claim to be, ordered by god to do so? As for the pains and the noises in the head, or the sweat, one can only regret the seeming fact that direct communication with god is not an experience of calm, beauty, and lucidity.

The physical existence of Muhammad, however poorly attested by the hadith, is a source of both strength and weakness for Islam. It appears to put it squarely in the world, and provides us with plausible physical descriptions of the man himself, but it also makes the whole story earthy, material, and gross. We may flinch a little at this mammal's betrothal to a nine-year-old girl, and at the keen interest he took in the pleasures of the dining table and the division of the spoils after his many battles and numerous massacres. Above all—and here is a trap that Christianity has mostly avoided by awarding its prophet a human body but a nonhuman nature—he was blessed with numerous descendants and thus placed his religious posterity in a position where it was hostage to his physical one. Nothing is more human and fallible than the dynastic or hereditary principle, and Islam has been racked from its birth by squabbles between princelings and pretenders, all claiming the relevant drop of original blood. If the total of those claiming descent from the founder was added up, it would probably exceed the number of holy nails and splinters that went to make up the thousand-foot cross on which, judging by the number of splinter-shaped relics, Jesus was evidently martyred. As with the lineage of the isnads, a direct kinship line with the Prophet can be established if one happens to know, and be able to pay, the right local imam.

In the same way, Muslims still make a certain obeisance to those same "satanic verses," and tread the pagan polytheistic path that was laid out long before their Prophet was born. Every year at the hajj, or annual pilgrimage, one can see them circling the cuboid Kaaba shrine in the center of Mecca, taking care to do so seven times ("following the direction of the sun around the earth," as Karen Armstrong weirdly and no doubt multiculturally puts it) before kissing the black stone set in the Kaaba's wall. This probable meteorite, which no doubt impressed the yokels when it first fell to earth ("the gods must be crazy: no, make that *god* must be crazy"), is a stop on the way to other ancient pre-Islamic propitiations, during which pebbles must be hurled defiantly at a rock that represents the Evil One. Animal sacrifices complete the picture. Like many but not all of Islam's principal sites, Mecca is closed to unbelievers, which somewhat contradicts its claim to universality.

It is often said that Islam differs from other monotheisms in not having had a "reformation." This is both correct and incorrect. There are versions of Islam—most notably the Sufi, much detested by the devout—which are principally spiritual rather than literal and which have taken on some accretions from other faiths. And, since Islam has avoided the mistake of having an absolute papacy capable of uttering binding edicts (hence the proliferation of conflicting fatwas from conflicting authorities) its adherents cannot be told to cease believing what they once held as dogma. This might be to the good, but the fact remains that Islam's core claim—to be unimprovable and final—is at once absurd and unalterable. Its many warring and discrepant sects, from Ismaili to Ahmadi, all agree on this indissoluble claim.

"Reformation" has meant, for Jews and Christians, a minimal willingness to reconsider holy writ as if it were (as Salman Rushdie so daringly proposed in his turn) something that can be subjected to literary and textual scrutiny. The number of possible "Bibles" is now admitted to be immense, and we know for example that the portentous Christian term "Jehovah" is a mistranslation of the unuttered spaces between the letters of the Hebrew "Yahweh." Yet no comparable project has ever been undertaken in Koranic scholarship. No serious attempt has been made to catalog the discrepancies between its various editions and manuscripts, and even the most tentative efforts to do so have been met with almost Inquisitional rage. A critical case in point is the work of Christoph Luxenburg, *The Syriac-Aramaic Version of the Koran*, published in Berlin in the year 2000. Luxenburg coolly proposes that, far from being a monoglot screed, the Koran is far better understood once it is conceded that many of its words are Syriac-Aramaic rather than Arabic. (His most celebrated example concerns the rewards of a "martyr" in paradise: when retranslated and redacted the heavenly offering consists of sweet white raisins rather than virgins.) This is the same language, and the same region, from which much of Judaism and Christianity emerged: there can be no doubt that unfettered research would result in the dispelling of much obscurantism. But, at the very point when Islam ought to be joining its predecessors in subjecting itself to rereadings, there is a "soft" consensus among almost all the religious that, because of the supposed duty of respect that we owe the faithful, this is the very time to allow Islam to assert its claims at their own face value. Once again, faith is helping to choke free inquiry and the emancipating consequences that it might bring.

Chapter Ten

The Tawdriness of the Miraculous and the Decline of Hell

The daughters of the high priest Anius changed whatever they chose into wheat, wine or oil. Athalida, daughter of Mercury, was resuscitated several times. Aesculapius resuscitated Hippolytus. Hercules dragged Alcestis back from death. Heres returned to the world after passing a fortnight in hell. The parents of Romulus and Remus were a god and a vestal virgin. The Palladium fell from heaven in the city of Troy. The hair of Berenice became a constellation. . . . Give me the name of one people among whom incredible prodigies were not performed, especially when few knew how to read and write.

—Voltaire, *Miracles and Idolatry*

An old fable concerns the comeuppance of a braggart who was forever retelling the story of a truly stupendous leap that he had once made on the island of Rhodes. Never, it seemed, had there ever been witnessed such a heroic long-jump. Though the teller never grew tired of the tale, the same could not be said of his audience. Finally, as he again drew breath to relate the story of the great feat, one of those present silenced him by saying gruffly, *"Hic Rhodus, hic salta!"* (Here is Rhodes, jump here!)

In much the same way as prophets and seers and great theologians seem to have died out, so the age of miracles seems to lie somewhere in our past. If the religious were wise, or had the confidence of their convictions, they ought to welcome the eclipse of this age of fraud and conjuring. But faith, yet again, discredits itself by proving to be insufficient to satisfy the faithful. Actual events are still required to impress the credulous. We have no difficulty in seeing this when we study the witch doctors and magicians and soothsayers of earlier or more remote cultures: obviously it was a clever person who first learned to predict an eclipse and then to use this planetary event to impress and cow his audience. Ancient kings in Cambodia worked out the day on which the Mekong and the Bassac rivers would annually suddenly start to flood and conjoin and, under terrific water pressure, appear to actually reverse their flow back into the great lake at Tonle Sap. Relatively soon, there was a ceremony at which the divinely appointed leader would duly appear and seem to order the waters to flow backward. Moses on the shore of the Red Sea could only have gaped at such a thing. (In more modern times, the showman King Sihanouk of Cambodia exploited this natural miracle to considerable effect.)

Given all that, it is surprising how petty some of the "supernatural" miracles now seem. As with spiritualist séances, which cynically offer burblings from the beyond to relatives of the late deceased, nothing truly interesting is ever said or done. To the story of Muhammad's "night flight" to Jerusalem (the hoofprint of his horse Borak is still allegedly to be seen on the site of the Al-Aqsa Mosque) it would be unkind to make the obvious riposte that horses cannot and do not fly. It is more pertinent to notice that people, ever since the beginning of their long and exhausting journeys across the earth's surface, gazing for days at the rear end of a mule, have fantasized about speeding up the tedious process. Folkloric seven-league boots can give the wearer a spring in his step, but this is only tinkering with the problem. The real dream, for thousands of years, involved envy of the birds (feathered descendants of the dinosaurs, as we now know) and the yearning to fly. Chariots in the sky, angels that could glide freely on the thermals . . . it is only too easy to see the root of the wish. Thus the Prophet speaks to the longing of every peasant who wishes that his beast could take wing and get on with it. But given infinite power, one might have thought that a more striking or less simpleminded miracle could have been confected. Levitation plays a vast role in Christian fantasy as well, as the stories of the Ascension and the Assumption confirm. At that epoch, the sky was thought to be a bowl, and its ordinary weather a source of portent or intervention. Given this pathetically limited view of the cosmos, the most trivial event could appear miraculous while an event that would truly astonish us—such as the sun ceasing to move—could yet appear as a local phenomenon.

Assuming that a miracle is a *favorable* change in the natural order, the last word on the subject was written by the Scottish philosopher David Hume, who granted us free will in the matter. A miracle is a disturbance or interruption in the expected and established course of things. This could involve anything from the sun rising in the west to an animal suddenly bursting into the recitation of verse. Very well, then, free will also involves decision. If you seem to witness such a thing, there are two possibilities. The first is that the laws of nature have been suspended (in your favor). The second is that you are under a misapprehension, or suffering from a delusion. Thus the likelihood of the second must be weighed against the likelihood of the first.

If you only hear a report of the miracle from a second or third party, the odds must be adjusted accordingly before you can decide to credit a witness who claims to have seen something that you did not see. And if you are separated from the "sighting" by many generations, and have no independent corroboration, the odds must be adjusted still more drastically. Again we might call upon the trusty Ockham, who warned us not to multiply unnecessary contingencies. Thus, let me give one ancient and one modern example: the first being bodily resurrection and the second being UFOs.

Miracles have declined, in their wondrous impact, since ancient times. Moreover, the more recent ones that have been offered us have been slightly tawdry. The notorious annual liquefaction of the blood of San Gennaro in Naples, for example, is a phenomenon that can easily be (and has been) repeated by any competent conjuror. Great secular "magicians" like Harry Houdini and James Randi have demonstrated with ease that levitation, fire-walking, water-divining, and spoon-bending can all be performed, under laboratory conditions, in order to expose the fraud and to safeguard the unwary customer from a fleecing. Miracles in any case do not vindicate the truth of the religion that practices them: Aaron supposedly vanquished Pharoah's magicians in an open competition but did not deny that they could perform wonders as well. However, there has not been a claimed resurrection for some time and no shaman who purports to do it has ever agreed to reproduce his trick in such a way as to stand a challenge. Thus we must ask ourselves: Has the art of resurrection died out? Or are we relying on dubious sources?

The New Testament is itself a highly dubious source. (One of Professor Barton Ehrman's more astonishing findings is that the account of Jesus's resurrection in the Gospel of Mark was only added many years later.) But according to the New Testament, the thing could be done in an almost commonplace way. Jesus managed it twice in other people's cases, by raising both Lazarus and the daughter of Jairus, and nobody seems to have thought it worthwhile to interview either survivor to ask about their extraordinary experiences. Nor does anyone seem to have kept a record of whether or not, or how, these two individuals "died" again. If they stayed immortal, then they joined the ancient company of the "Wandering Jew," who was condemned by early Christianity to keep walking forever after he met Jesus on the Via Dolorosa, this misery being inflicted upon a mere bystander in order to fulfill the otherwise unfulfilled prophecy that Jesus would come again in the lifetime of at least one person who had seen him the first time around. On the same day that Jesus met that luckless vagrant, he was himself put to death with revolting cruelty, at which time, according to the Gospel of Matthew 27:52–53, "the graves were opened; and many bodies of the saints which slept arose, and came out of the graves after his resurrection, and went into the holy city, and appeared unto many." This seems incoherent, since the corpses apparently rose both at the time of the death on the cross *and* of the Resurrection, but it is narrated in the same matter-of-fact way as the earthquake, the rending of the veil of the temple (two other events that did not attract the attention of any historian), and the reverent comments of the Roman centurion.

This supposed frequency of resurrection can only undermine the uniqueness of the one by which mankind purchased forgiveness of sins. And there is no cult or religion before or since, from Osiris to vampirism to voodoo, that does not rely on some innate belief in the "undead." To this day, Christians disagree as to whether the day of judgment will give you back the old wreck of a body that has already died on you, or will reequip you in some other form. For now, and on a review even of the claims made by the faithful, one can say that resurrection would not prove the truth of the dead man's doctrine, nor his paternity, nor the probability of still another return in fleshly or recognizable form. Yet again, also, too much is being "proved." The action of a man who volunteers to die for his fellow creatures is universally regarded as noble. The extra claim not to have "really" died makes the whole sacrifice tricky and meretricious. (Thus, those who say "Christ died for my sins," when he did not really "die" at all, are making a statement that is false in its own terms.) Having no reliable or consistent witnesses, in anything like the time period needed to certify such an extraordinary claim, we are finally entitled to say that we have a right, if not an obligation, to respect ourselves enough to disbelieve the whole thing. That is, unless or until superior evidence is presented, which it has not been. And exceptional claims demand exceptional evidence.

I have spent much of my life as a correspondent and long ago became used to reading firsthand accounts of the very same events I had witnessed, written by people I otherwise trusted, which did not accord with my own. (In my days as a Fleet Street correspondent, I even read stories in print under my *own* name which were not recognizable to me once the sub-editors had finished with them.) And I have interviewed some of the hundreds of thousands of people who claim to have had direct encounters with spacecraft, or the crew of spacecraft, from another galaxy. Some of these are so vivid and detailed (and so comparable with other depositions from other people who cannot have compared notes) that a few impressionable academics have proposed that we grant them the presumption of truth. But here is the obvious Ockhamist reason why it would be utterly wrong to do so. If the huge number of "contacts" and abductees are telling even a particle of truth, then it follows that their alien friends are not attempting to keep their own existence a secret. Well, in that case, why do they never stay still for anything more than a single-shot photo? There has never been an uncut roll of film offered, let alone a small piece of a metal unavailable on earth, or a tiny sample of tissue. And sketches of the beings have a consistent anthropomorphic resemblance to those offered in science-fiction comics. Since travel from Alpha Centauri (the preferred origin) would involve some bending of the laws of physics, even the smallest particle of matter would be of enormous use, and would have a literally earth-shattering effect. Instead of which—nothing. Nothing, that is, except the growth of a huge new superstition, based upon a belief in occult texts and shards that are available only to a favored few. Well, I have seen *that* happen before. The only responsible decision is to suspend or withhold judgment until the votaries have come up with something that is not merely childish.

Extend this to the present day, where the statues of virgins or saints are sometimes said to weep or bleed. Even if I could not easily introduce you to people who can produce this identical effect in their spare time, using pig fat or other materials, I would still ask myself why a deity should be content to produce such a paltry effect. As it happens, I am one of the very few people who has ever taken part in the examination of a sainthood "cause," as the Roman Catholic Church calls it. In June of 2001 I was invited by the Vatican to testify at a hearing on the beatification of Agnes Bojaxhiu, an ambitious Albanian nun who had become well-known under the nom de guerre of "Mother Teresa." Although the then pope had abolished the famous office of "Devil's Advocate," the better to confirm and canonize an enormous number of new "saints," the church was still obliged to seek testimony from critics, and thus I found myself representing the devil, as it were, pro bono.

I had already helped expose one of the "miracles" connected with the work of this woman. The man who originally made her famous was a distinguished if rather silly British evangelist (later a Catholic) named Malcolm Muggeridge. It was his BBC documentary, *Something Beautiful for God*, which launched the "Mother Teresa" brand on the world in 1969. The cameraman for this film was a man named Ken Macmillan, who had won high praise for his work on Lord Clark's great art history series, *Civilisation*. His understanding of color and lighting was of a high order. Here is the story as Muggeridge told it, in the book that accompanied the film:

> [Mother Teresa's] Home for the Dying is dimly lit by small windows high up in the walls, and Ken [Macmillan] was adamant that filming was quite impossible there. We only had one small light with us, and to get the place adequately lighted in the time at our disposal was quite impossible. It was decided that, nonetheless, Ken should have a go, but by way of insurance he took, as well, some film in an outside courtyard where some of the inmates were sitting in the sun. In the processed film, the part taken inside was bathed in a particularly beautiful soft light, whereas the part taken outside was rather dim and confused. . . . I myself am absolutely convinced that the technically unaccountable light is, in fact, the Kindly Light that Cardinal Newman refers to in his well-known exquisite hymn.

He concluded that

> This is precisely what miracles are for—to reveal the inner real-
> ity of God's outward creation. I am personally persuaded that
> Ken recorded the first authentic photographic miracle. . . . I fear
> I talked and wrote about it to the point of tedium.

He was certainly correct in that last sentence: by the time he
had finished he had made Mother Teresa into a world-famous figure. My contribution was to check out and put into print the direct
verbal testimony of Ken Macmillan, the cameraman himself. Here
it is:

> During *Something Beautiful for God*, there was an episode where
> we were taken to a building that Mother Teresa called the
> House of the Dying. Peter Chafer, the director, said, "Ah well,
> it's very dark in here. Do you think we can get something?"
> And we had just taken delivery at the BBC of some new film
> made by Kodak, which we hadn't had time to test before we
> left, so I said to Peter, "Well, we may as well have a go." So we
> shot it. And when we got back several weeks later, a month or
> two later, we are sitting in the rushes theater at Ealing Studios
> and eventually up come the shots of the House of the Dying.
> And it was surprising. You could see every detail. And I said,
> "That's amazing. That's extraordinary." And I was going to
> go on to say, you know, three cheers for Kodak. I didn't get a
> chance to say that though, because Malcolm, sitting in the front
> row, spun around and said: "It's divine light! It's Mother Teresa.
> You'll find that it's divine light, old boy." And three or four days
> later I found that I was being phoned by journalists from Lon-
> don newspapers who were saying things like: "We hear you've
> just come back from India with Malcolm Muggeridge and you
> were the witness of a miracle."

So a star was born . . . For these and for my other criticisms I was invited by the Vatican into a closed room containing a Bible, a tape recorder, a monsignor, a deacon, and a priest, and asked if I could throw any light of my own on the matter of "the Servant of God, Mother Teresa." But, even as they appeared to be asking me this in good faith, their colleagues on the other side of the world were certifying the necessary "miracle" that would allow the beatification (prelude to full canonization) to go forward. Mother Teresa died in 1997. On the first anniversary of her death, two nuns in the Bengali village of Raigunj claim to have strapped an aluminum medal of the departed (a medal that had supposedly been in contact with her dead body) to the abdomen of a woman named Monica Besra. This woman, who was said to be suffering from a large uterine tumor, was thereupon quite cured of it. It will be noticed that Monica is a Catholic girl's name not very common in Bengal, and thus that probably the patient and certainly the nuns were already Mother Teresa fans. This definition would not cover Dr. Manju Murshed, the superintendent of the local hospital, nor Dr. T. K. Biswas and his gynecologist colleague Dr. Ranjan Mustafi. All three came forward to say that Mrs. Besra had been suffering from tuberculosis and an ovarian growth, and had been successfully treated for both afflictions. Dr. Murshed was particularly annoyed at the numerous calls he had received from Mother Teresa's order, the "Missionaries of Charity," pressing him to say that the cure had been miraculous. The patient herself did not make a very impressive interview subject, talking at high speed because, as she put it, she "might otherwise forget" and begging to be excused questions because she might have to "remember." Her own husband, a man named Selku Murmu, broke silence after a while to say that his wife had been cured by ordinary, regular medical treatment.

Any hospital supervisor in any country will tell you that patients sometimes make astonishing recoveries (just as apparently healthy people often fall inexplicably and gravely ill). Those who desire to certify miracles may wish to say that such recoveries have no "natural" explanation. But this does not at all mean that there is therefore a "supernatural" one. In this case, however, there was nothing even remotely surprising in Mrs. Besra's return to health. Some familiar disorders had been treated with well-known methods. Extraordinary claims were being made without even ordinary evidence. Yet there will soon come a day in Rome when a vast and solemn ceremony will proclaim the sainthood of Mother Teresa, as one whose intercession can improve upon medicine, to the entire world. Not only is this a scandal in itself, but it will further postpone the day when Indian villagers cease to trust quacks and fakirs. In other words, many people will die needlessly as a result of this phony and contemptible "miracle." If this is the best the church can do in a time when its claims can be checked by physicians and reporters, it isn't difficult to imagine what was rigged in past times of ignorance and fear, when the priests faced less doubt or opposition.

Once again the razor of Ockham is clean and decisive. When two explanations are offered, one must discard the one that explains the least, or explains nothing at all, or raises more questions than it answers.

The same goes for those occasions when the laws of nature are apparently suspended in a way that does *not* offer joy or apparent consolation. Natural disasters are actually not violations of the laws of nature, but rather are part of the inevitable fluctuations within them, but they have always been used to overawe the gullible with the mightiness of god's disapproval. Early Christians, operating in zones of Asia Minor where earthquakes were and are frequent, would rally crowds when a pagan temple fell down, and urge them to convert while there was still time. The colossal volcanic explosion at Krakatoa in the late nineteenth century provoked an enormous swing toward Islam among the terrified population of Indonesia. All the holy books talk excitedly of floods, hurricanes, lightning, and other portents. After the terrible Asian tsunami of 2005, and after the inundation of New Orleans in 2006, quite serious and learned men such as the archbishop of Canterbury were reduced to the level of stupefied peasants when they publicly agonized over how to interpret god's will in the matter. But if one makes the simple assumption, based on absolutely certain knowledge, that we live on a planet that is still cooling, has a molten core, faults and cracks in its crust, and a turbulent weather system, then there is simply no need for any such anxiety. Everything is already explained. I fail to see why the religious are so reluctant to admit this: it would free them from all the futile questions about why god permits so much suffering. But apparently this annoyance is a small price to pay in order to keep alive the myth of divine intervention.

The suspicion that a calamity might also be a punishment is further useful in that it allows an infinity of speculation. After New Orleans, which suffered from a lethal combination of being built below sea level and neglected by the Bush administration, I learned from a senior rabbi in Israel that it was revenge for the evacuation of Jewish settlers from the Gaza Strip, and from the mayor of New Orleans (who had not performed his own job with exceptional prowess) that it was god's verdict on the invasion of Iraq. You can nominate your own favorite sin here, as did the "reverends" Pat Robertson and Jerry Falwell after the immolation of the World Trade Center. In that instance, the proximate cause was to be sought and found in America's surrender to homosexuality and abortion. (Some ancient Egyptians believed that sodomy was the cause of earthquakes: I expect this interpretation to revive with especial force when the San Andreas Fault next gives a shudder under the Gomorrah of San Francisco.) When the debris had eventually settled on Ground Zero, it was found that two pieces of mangled girder still stood in the shape of a cross, and much wondering comment resulted. Since all architecture has always involved crossbeams, it would be surprising only if such a feature did *not* emerge. I admit that I would have been impressed if the wreckage had formed itself into a Star of David or a star and crescent, but there is no record of this ever having occurred anywhere, even in places where local people might be impressed by it. And remember, miracles are supposed to occur at the behest of a being who is omnipotent as well as omniscient and omnipresent. One might hope for more magnificent performances than ever seem to occur.

The "evidence" for faith, then, seems to leave faith looking even weaker than it would if it stood, alone and unsupported, all by itself. What can be asserted without evidence can also be dismissed without evidence. This is even more true when the "evidence" eventually offered is so shoddy and self-interested.

THE "ARGUMENT FROM AUTHORITY" is the weakest of all arguments. It is weak when it is asserted at second or third hand ("the Good Book says"), and it is even weaker when asserted at first hand, as every child knows who has heard a parent say "because I say so" (and as every parent knows who has heard himself reduced to uttering words he once found so unconvincing). Nonetheless, it takes a certain "leap" of another kind to find oneself asserting that all religion is made up by ordinary mammals and has no secret or mystery to it. Behind the veil of Oz, there is nothing but bluff. Can this really be true? As one who has always been impressed by the weight of history and culture, I do keep asking myself this question. Was it all in vain, then: the great struggle of the theologians and scholars, and the stupendous efforts of painters and architects and musicians to create something lasting and marvelous that would testify to the glory of god?

Not at all. It does not matter to me whether Homer was one person or many, or whether Shakespeare was a secret Catholic or a closet agnostic. I should not feel my own world destroyed if the greatest writer about love and tragedy and comedy and morals was finally revealed to have been the Earl of Oxford all along, though I must add that sole authorship is important to me and I would be saddened and diminished to learn that Bacon had been the man. Shakespeare has much more moral salience than the Talmud or the Koran or any account of the fearful squabbles of Iron Age tribes. But there is a great deal to be learned and appreciated from the scrutiny of religion, and one often finds oneself standing atop the shoulders of distinguished writers and thinkers who were certainly one's intellectual and sometimes even one's moral superiors. Many of them, in their own time, had ripped away the disguise of idolatry and paganism, and even risked martyrdom for the sake of disputes with their own coreligionists. However, a moment in history has now arrived when even a pygmy such as myself can claim to know more—through no merit of his own—and to see that the final ripping of the whole disguise is overdue. Between them, the sciences of textual criticism, archaeology, physics, and molecular biology have shown religious myths to be false and man-made and have also succeeded in evolving better and more enlightened explanations. The loss of faith can be compensated by the newer and finer wonders that we have before us, as well as by immersion in the near-miraculous work of Homer and Shakespeare and Milton and Tolstoy and Proust, all of which was also "man-made" (though one sometimes wonders, as in the case of Mozart). I can say this as one whose own secular faith has been shaken and discarded, not without pain.

When I was a Marxist, I did not hold my opinions as a matter of faith but I did have the conviction that a sort of unified field theory might have been discovered. The concept of historical and dialectical materialism was not an absolute and it did not have any supernatural element, but it did have its messianic element in the idea that an ultimate moment might arrive, and it most certainly had its martyrs and saints and doctrinaires and (after a while) its mutually excommunicating rival papacies. It also had its schisms and inquisitions and heresy hunts. I was a member of a dissident sect that admired Rosa Luxemburg and Leon Trotsky, and I can say definitely that we also had our prophets. Rosa Luxemburg seemed almost like a combination of Cassandra and Jeremiah when she thundered about the consequences of the First World War, and the great three-volume biography of Leon Trotsky by Isaac Deutscher was actually entitled *The Prophet* (in his three stages of being armed, unarmed, and outcast). As a young man Deutscher had been trained for the rabbinate, and would have made a brilliant Talmudist—as would Trotsky. Here is what Trotsky says—anticipating the gnostic Gospel of Judas—about the way that Stalin took over the Bolshevik Party:

> Of Christ's twelve Apostles Judas alone proved to be traitor. But if he had acquired power, he would have represented the other eleven Apostles as traitors, and also all the lesser Apostles whom Luke numbers as seventy.

And here, in Deutscher's chilling words, is what happened when the pro-Nazi forces in Norway forced the government to deny Trotsky asylum and deport him once again, to wander the world until he met death. The old man met with the Norwegian foreign minister Trygve Lie and others, and then:

> Trotsky raised his voice so that it resounded through the halls and corridors of the Ministry: "This is your first act of surrender to Nazism in your own country. You will pay for this. You think yourselves free and secure to deal with a political exile as you please. But the day is near—remember this!—the day is near when the Nazis will drive you from your country, all of you . . ." Trygve Lie shrugged at this odd piece of sooth-saying. Yet after less than four years the same government had indeed to flee from Norway before the Nazi invasion; and as the Ministers and their aged King Haakon stood on the coast, huddled together and waiting anxiously for a boat that was to take them to England, they recalled with awe Trotsky's words as a prophet's curse come true.

Trotsky had a sound materialist critique that enabled him to be prescient, not all of the time by any means, but impressively so on some occasions. And he certainly had a sense—expressed in his emotional essay *Literature and Revolution*—of the unquenchable yearning of the poor and oppressed to rise above the strictly material world and to achieve something transcendent. For a good part of my life, I had a share in this idea that I have not yet quite abandoned. But there came a time when I could not protect myself, and indeed did not wish to protect myself, from the onslaught of reality. Marxism, I conceded, had its intellectual and philosophical and ethical glories, but they were in the past. Something of the heroic period might perhaps be retained, but the fact had to be faced: there was no longer any guide to the future. In addition, the very concept of a total solution had led to the most appalling human sacrifices, and to the invention of excuses for them. Those of us who had sought a rational alternative to religion had reached a terminus that was comparably dogmatic. What else was to be expected of something that was produced by the close cousins of chimpanzees? Infallibility? Thus, dear reader, if you have come this far and found your own faith undermined—as I hope—I am willing to say that to some extent I know what you are going through. There are days when I miss my old convictions as if they were an amputated limb. But in general I feel better, and no less radical, and you will feel better too, I guarantee, once you leave hold of the doctrinaire and allow your chainless mind to do its own thinking.

Chapter Eleven

"The Lowly Stamp of Their Origin": Religion's Corrupt Beginnings

Where questions of religion are concerned, people are guilty of every possible sort of dishonesty and intellectual misdemeanor.
— Sigmund Freud, *The Future of an Illusion*

The various forms of worship, which prevailed in the Roman world, were all considered by the people to be equally true, by the philosopher as equally false, and by the magistrate as equally useful.
— Edward Gibbon, *Decline and Fall of the Roman Empire*

An old popular saying from Chicago has it that if you want to maintain your respect for city aldermen, or your appetite for sausages, you should take care not to be present when the former are being groomed or the latter are being manufactured. It is the anatomy of man, said Engels, that is the key to the anatomy of the ape. Thus, if we watch the process of a religion in its formation, we can make some assumptions about the origins of those religions that were put together before most people could read. From a wide selection of openly manufactured sausage religions, I shall pick the Melanesian "cargo cult," the Pentecostal superstar

Marjoe, and the Church of Jesus Christ of Latter-day Saints, commonly known as the Mormons.

The thought has surely occurred to many people throughout the ages: what if there is an afterlife but no god? What if there is a god but no afterlife? As far as I know, the clearest writer to give expression to this problem was Thomas Hobbes in his 1651 masterwork *Leviathan*. I strongly recommend that you read part III, chapter 38, and part IV, chapter 44, for yourselves, because Hobbes's command of both holy scripture and the English language is quite breathtaking. He also reminds us how perilous it was, and always has been, even to think about these things. His brisk and ironic throat-clearing is eloquent in itself. Reflecting on the nonsense story of Adam's "Fall" (the original instance of someone being created free and then loaded with impossible-to-obey prohibitions), Hobbes opined—not forgetting fearfully to add that he did so "with submission nevertheless both in this, and in all questions, whereof the determination dependeth on the Scriptures"—that if Adam was condemned to death by sinning, his death must have been postponed, since he contrived to raise a large posterity before actually dying.

Having planted the subversive thought—that forbidding Adam to eat from one tree lest he die, and from another lest he live forever, is absurd and contradictory—Hobbes was forced to imagine alternative scriptures and even alternative punishments and alternative eternities. His point was that people might not obey the rule of men if they were more afraid of divine retribution than of horrible death in the here and now, but he had acknowledged the process whereby people are always free to make up a religion that suits or gratifies or flatters them. Samuel Butler was to adapt this idea in his *Erewhon Revisited*. In the original *Erewhon*, Mr. Higgs pays a visit to a remote country from which he eventually makes his escape in a balloon. Returning two decades later, he finds that in his absence he has become a god named the "Sun Child," worshipped on the day he ascended into heaven. Two high priests are on hand to celebrate the ascension, and when Higgs threatens to expose them and reveal himself as a mere mortal he is told, "You must not do that, because all the morals of this country are bound around this myth, and if they once know that you did not ascend into heaven they will all become wicked."

In 1964 there appeared a celebrated documentary movie called *Mondo Cane*, or "the world of the dog," in which the directors captured numerous human cruelties and illusions. This was the first occasion on which one could see a new religion being assembled, in plain view, on camera. The inhabitants of the Pacific islands may have been separated for centuries from the more economically developed world, but when visited by the fatal impact many of them were shrewd enough to get the point immediately. Here were great vessels with billowing sails, bearing treasures and weapons and devices that were beyond any compare. Some of the more untutored islanders did what many people do when confronted with a new phenomenon, and tried to translate it into a discourse that they could themselves understand (not unlike those fearful Aztecs who, first seeing mounted Spanish soldiers in Mesoamerica, concluded that they had a centaur for an enemy). These poor souls decided that the westerners were their long-mourned ancestors, come back at last with goods from beyond the grave. That illusion cannot long have survived the encounter with the colonists, but later it was observed in several places that the brighter islanders had a better idea. Docks and jetties were built, they noticed, after which more ships came and unloaded more goods. Acting by analogy and mimesis, the locals constructed their own jetties and waited for these, too, to attract some ships. Futile as this proceeding was, it badly retarded the advance of later Christian missionaries. When they made their appearance, they were asked where the gifts were (and soon came up with some trinkets).

In the twentieth century the "cargo cult" revived in an even more impressive and touching form. Units of the United States armed forces, arriving in the Pacific to build airfields for the war on Japan, found that they were the objects of slavish emulation. Local enthusiasts abandoned their lightly worn Christian observances and devoted all their energies to the construction of landing strips that might attract loaded airplanes. They made simulated antennae out of bamboo. They built and lit fires, to simulate the flares that guided the American planes to land. This still goes on, which is the saddest bit of the *Mondo Cane* sequence. On the island of Tana, an American GI was declared to be the redeemer. His name, John Frum, seems to have been an invention too. But even after the last serviceman flew or sailed away after 1945, the eventual return of the savior Frum was preached and predicted, and an annual ceremony still bears his name. On another island named New Britain, adjacent to Papua New Guinea, the cult is even more strikingly analogous. It has ten commandments (the "Ten Laws"), a trinity that has one presence in heaven and another on earth, and a ritual system of paying tributes in the hope of propitiating these authorities. If the ritual is performed with sufficient purity and fervor, so its adherents believe, then an age of milk and honey will be ushered in. This radiant future, sad to say, is known as the "Period of the Companies," and will cause New Britain to flourish and prosper as if it were a multinational corporation.

Some people may be insulted at even the suggestion of a comparison here, but are not the holy books of official monotheism absolutely dripping with material yearning and with admiring—almost mouth-watering—descriptions of Solomon's wealth, the thriving flocks and herds of the faithful, the rewards for a good Muslim in paradise, to say nothing of many, many lurid tales of plunder and spoils? Jesus, it is true, shows no personal interest in gain, but he does speak of treasure in heaven and even of "mansions" as an inducement to follow him. Is it not further true that all religions down the ages have shown a keen interest in the amassment of material goods in the real world?

The thirst for money and worldly comfort is only a subtext of the mind-numbing story of Marjoe Gortner, the "infant phenomenon" of American evangelical hucksterism. Grotesquely christened "Marjoe" (a cretinous lumping together of the names Mary and Joseph) by his parents, young Master Gortner was thrust into the pulpit at the age of four, dressed in a revolting Little Lord Fauntleroy suit, and told to say that he had been divinely commanded to preach. If he complained or cried, his mother would hold him under the water tap or press a cushion on his face, always being careful, as he relates it, to leave no marks. Trained like a seal, he soon attracted the cameras and by the age of six was officiating at the weddings of grown-ups. His celebrity spread, and many flocked to see the miraculous child. His best guess is that he raised three million dollars in "contributions," none of which was earmarked for his education or his own future. At the age of seventeen he rebelled against his pitiless and cynical parents and "dropped out" into the early sixties California counterculture.

In the immortal children's Christmas pantomime *Peter Pan*, there comes a climactic moment when the little angel Tinkerbell seems to be dying. The glowing light that represents her on the stage begins to dim, and there is only one possible way to save the dire situation. An actor steps up to the front of the house and asks all the children, "Do you believe in fairies?" If they keep confidently answering "YES!" then the tiny light will start to brighten again. Who can object to this? One wants not to spoil children's belief in magic—there will be plenty of time later for disillusionment—and nobody is waiting at the exit asking them hoarsely to contribute their piggy banks to the Tinkerbell Salvation Church. The events at which Marjoe was exploited had all the intellectual content of the Tinkerbell scene, nastily combined with the ethics of Captain Hook.

A decade or so later, Mr. Gortner exacted the best possible revenge for his stolen and empty childhood, and decided to do the general public a favor in order to make up for his conscious fraudulence. He invited a film crew to follow him as he ostensibly "returned" to preach the gospel, and took the trouble to explain how all the tricks are pulled. This is how you induce motherly women (he was a handsome lad) to part with their savings. This is how you time the music to create an ecstatic effect. This is when you speak of how Jesus visited you personally.

Here is how you put invisible ink on your forehead, in the shape of a cross, so that it will suddenly show up when you start perspiring. This is when you really move in for the kill. He keeps all his promises, telling the film's director in advance what he can and will do and then going out into the auditorium to enact it with absolute conviction. People weep and yell, and collapse in spasms and fits, shrieking their savior's name. Cynical, coarse, brutish old men and women wait for the psychological moment to demand money, and start counting it gleefully before the charade of the "service" is even over. Occasionally one sees the face of a small child, dragged to the tent and looking wretched and uncomfortable as its parents writhe and moan and give away their hard-won pay. One knew, of course, that the whole racket of American evangelism was just that: a heartless con run by the second-string characters from Chaucer's "Pardoner's Tale." (You saps keep the faith. We'll just keep the money.) And this is what it must have been like when indulgences were openly sold in Rome, and when a nail or a splinter from the Crucifixion could fetch a nice price in any flea market in Christendom. But to see the crime exposed by someone who is both a victim and a profiteer is nonetheless quite shocking even to a hardened unbeliever. After such knowledge, what forgiveness? The film *Marjoe* won an Academy Award in 1972, and has made absolutely no difference at all. The mills of the TV preachers continue to grind, and the poor continue to finance the rich, just as if the glittering temples and palaces of Las Vegas had been built by the money of those who won rather than those who lost.

In his bewitching novel *The Child in Time*, Ian McEwan gives us a desolate character and narrator who is reduced by tragedy to a near-inert state in which he vacantly watches a great deal of daytime TV. Observing the way in which his fellow creatures allow themselves—volunteer themselves—to be manipulated and humiliated, he coins the phrase for those who indulge themselves in witnessing the spectacle. It is, he decides, "the democrat's pornography." It is not snobbish to notice the way in which people show their gullibility and their herd instinct, and their wish, or perhaps their need, to be credulous and to be fooled. This is an ancient problem. Credulity may be a form of innocence, and even innocuous in itself, but it provides a standing invitation for the wicked and the clever to exploit their brothers and sisters, and is thus one of humanity's great vulnerabilities. No honest account of the growth and persistence of religion, or the reception of miracles and revelations, is possible without reference to this stubborn fact.

If the followers of the prophet Muhammad hoped to put an end to any future "revelations" after the immaculate conception of the Koran, they reckoned without the founder of what is now one of the world's fastest-growing faiths. And they did not foresee (how could they, mammals as they were?) that the prophet of this ridiculous cult would model himself on theirs. The Church of Jesus Christ of Latter-day Saints—hereafter known as the Mormons—was founded by a gifted opportunist who, despite couching his text in openly plagiarized Christian terms, announced that "I shall be to this generation a new Muhammad" and adopted as his fighting slogan the words, which he thought he had learned from Islam, "Either the Al-Koran or the sword." He was too ignorant to know that if you use the word *al* you do not need another definite article, but then he did resemble Muhammad in being able only to make a borrowing out of other people's bibles.

In March 1826 a court in Bainbridge, New York, convicted a twenty-one-year-old man of being "a disorderly person and an impostor." That ought to have been all we ever heard of Joseph Smith, who at trial admitted to defrauding citizens by organizing mad gold-digging expeditions and also to claiming to possess dark or "necromantic" powers. However, within four years he was back in the local newspapers (all of which one may still read) as the discoverer of the "Book of Mormon." He had two huge local advantages which most mountebanks and charlatans do not possess. First, he was operating in the same hectically pious district that gave us the Shakers, the previously mentioned George Miller who repeatedly predicted the end of the world, and several other self-proclaimed American prophets. So notorious did this local tendency become that the region became known as the "Burned-Over District," in honor of the way in which it had surrendered to one religious craze after another. Second, he was operating in an area which, unlike large tracts of the newly opening North America, did possess the signs of an ancient history.

A vanished and vanquished Indian civilization had bequeathed a considerable number of burial mounds, which when randomly and amateurishly desecrated were found to contain not merely bones but also quite advanced artifacts of stone, copper, and beaten silver. There were eight of these sites within twelve miles of the underperforming farm which the Smith family called home. There were two equally stupid schools or factions who took a fascinated interest in such matters: the first were the gold-diggers and treasure-diviners who brought their magic sticks and crystals and stuffed toads to bear in the search for lucre, and the second those who hoped to find the resting place of a lost tribe of Israel. Smith's cleverness was to be a member of both groups, and to unite cupidity with half-baked anthropology.

The actual story of the imposture is almost embarrassing to read, and almost embarrassingly easy to uncover. (It has been best told by Dr. Fawn Brodie, whose 1945 book *No Man Knows My History* was a good-faith attempt by a professional historian to put the kindest possible interpretation on the relevant "events.") In brief, Joseph Smith announced that he had been visited (three times, as is customary) by an angel named Moroni. The said angel informed him of a book, "written upon gold plates," which explained the origins of those living on the North American continent as well as the truths of the gospel. There were, further, two magic stones, set in the twin breast-plates Urim and Thummim of the Old Testament, that would enable Smith himself to translate the aforesaid book. After many wrestlings, he brought this buried apparatus home with him on September 21, 1827, about eighteen months after his conviction for fraud. He then set about producing a translation.

The resulting "books" turned out to be a record set down by ancient prophets, beginning with Nephi, son of Lephi, who had fled Jerusalem in approximately 600 BC and come to America. Many battles, curses, and afflictions accompanied their subsequent wanderings and those of their numerous progeny. How did the books turn out to be this way? Smith refused to show the golden plates to anybody, claiming that for other eyes to view them would mean death. But he encountered a problem that will be familiar to students of Islam. He was extremely glib and fluent as a debater and story-weaver, as many accounts attest. But he was illiterate, at least in the sense that while he could read a little, he could not write. A scribe was therefore necessary to take his inspired dictation. This scribe was at first his wife Emma and then, when more hands were necessary, a luckless neighbor named Martin Harris. Hearing Smith cite the words of Isaiah 29, verses 11–12, concerning the repeated injunction to "Read," Harris mortgaged his farm to help in the task and moved in with the Smiths. He sat on one side of a blanket hung across the kitchen, and Smith sat on the other with his translation stones, intoning through the blanket. As if to make this an even happier scene, Harris was warned that if he tried to glimpse the plates, or look at the prophet, he would be struck dead.

Mrs. Harris was having none of this, and was already furious with the fecklessness of her husband. She stole the first hundred and sixteen pages and challenged Smith to reproduce them, as presumably—given his power of revelation—he could. (Determined women like this appear far too seldom in the history of religion.) After a very bad few weeks, the ingenious Smith countered with another revelation. He could not replicate the original, which might be in the devil's hands by now and open to a "satanic verses" interpretation. But the all-foreseeing Lord had meanwhile furnished some smaller plates, indeed the very plates of Nephi, which told a fairly similar tale. With infinite labor, the translation was resumed, with new scriveners behind the blanket as occasion demanded, and when it was completed all the original golden plates were transported to heaven, where apparently they remain to this day.

Mormon partisans sometimes say, as do Muslims, that this cannot have been fraudulent because the work of deception would have been too much for one poor and illiterate man. They have on their side two useful points: if Muhammad was ever convicted in public of fraud and attempted necromancy we have no record of the fact, and Arabic is a language that is somewhat opaque even to the fairly fluent outsider. However, we know the Koran to be made up in part of earlier books and stories, and in the case of Smith it is likewise a simple if tedious task to discover that twenty-five thousand words of the Book of Mormon are taken directly from the Old Testament. These words can mainly be found in the chapters of Isaiah available in Ethan Smith's *View of the Hebrews*: *The Ten Tribes of Israel in America*. This then popular work by a pious loony, claiming that the American Indians originated in the Middle East, seems to have started the other Smith on his gold-digging in the first place. A further two thousand words of the Book of Mormon are taken from the New Testament. Of the three hundred and fifty "names" in the book, more than one hundred come straight from the Bible and a hundred more are as near stolen as makes no difference. (The great Mark Twain famously referred to it as "chloroform in print," but I accuse him of hitting too soft a target, since the book does actually contain "The Book of Ether.") The words "and it came to pass" can be found at least two thousand times, which does admittedly have a soporific effect. Quite recent scholarship has exposed every single other Mormon "document" as at best a scrawny compromise and at worst a pitiful fake, as Dr. Brodie was obliged to notice when she reissued and updated her remarkable book in 1973.

Like Muhammad, Smith could produce divine revelations at short notice and often simply to suit himself (especially, and like Muhammad, when he wanted a new girl and wished to take her as another wife). As a result, he overreached himself and came to a violent end, having meanwhile excommunicated almost all the poor men who had been his first disciples and who had been browbeaten into taking his dictation. Still, this story raises some very absorbing questions, concerning what happens when a plain racket turns into a serious religion before our eyes.

Professor Daniel Dennett and his supporters have attracted a great deal of criticism for their "natural science" explanation of religion. Never mind the supernatural, argues Dennett, we may discard that while accepting that there have always been those for whom "belief in belief" is a good thing in itself. Phenomena can be explained in biological terms. In primitive times, is it not possible that those who believed in the shaman's cure had a better morale as a result, and thus a slightly but significantly higher chance of actually *being* cured? "Miracles" and similar nonsense to one side, not even modern medicine rejects this thought. And it seems possible, moving to the psychological arena, that people can be better off believing in something than in nothing, however untrue that something may be.

Some of this will always be disputed among anthropologists and other scientists, but what interests me and always has is this: Do the preachers and prophets also believe, or do they too just "believe in belief"? Do they ever think to themselves, this is too easy? And do they then rationalize the trick by saying that either (a) if these wretches weren't listening to me they'd be in even worse shape; or (b) that if it doesn't do them any good then it still can't be doing them much harm? Sir James Frazer, in his famous study of religion and magic *The Golden Bough*, suggests that the novice witch doctor is better off if he does *not* share the illusions of the ignorant congregation. For one thing, if he does take the magic literally he is much more likely to make a career-ending mistake. Better by far to be a cynic, and to rehearse the conjury, and to tell himself that everybody is better off in the end. Smith obviously seems like a mere cynic, in that he was never happier than when using his "revelation" to claim supreme authority, or to justify the idea that the flock should make over their property to him, or to sleep with every available woman. There are gurus and cult leaders of that kind born every day. Smith must certainly have thought it was too easy to get innocent wretches like Martin Harris to believe everything he told them, especially when they were thirsty for just a glimpse of that mouthwatering golden trove. But was there a moment when he also believed that he did have a destiny, and was ready to die to prove it? In other words, was he a huckster all the time, or was there a pulse inside him somewhere? The study of religion suggests to me that, while it cannot possibly get along without great fraud and also minor fraud, this remains a fascinating and somewhat open question.

There were dozens of part-educated, unscrupulous, ambitious, fanatical men like Smith in the Palmyra, New York, area at that epoch, but only one of them achieved "takeoff." This is for two probable reasons. First, and by all accounts, including those of his enemies, Smith had great natural charm and authority and fluency: what Max Weber called the "charismatic" part of leadership. Second, there were at that time a great number of people hungry for soil and a new start in the West, constituting a huge latent force behind the notion of a new leader (let alone a new holy book) that could augur a "Promised Land." The wanderings of the Mormons in Missouri and Illinois and Utah, and the massacres that they both suffered and inflicted on the way, gave body and sinew to the idea of martyrdom and exile—and to the idea of the "Gentiles," as they scornfully called the unbelievers. It is a great historical story and (unlike its origin in a piece of vulgar fabrication) can be read with respect. It does, however, have two indelible stains. The first is the sheer obviousness and crudity of its "revelations," which were opportunistically improvised by Smith and later by his successors as they went along. And the second is its revoltingly crude racism. Christian preachers of all kinds had justified slavery until the American Civil War and even afterwards, on the supposed biblical warrant that of the three sons of Noah (Shem, Ham, and Japhet), Ham had been cursed and cast into servitude. But Joseph Smith took this nasty fable even further, fulminating in his "Book of Abraham" that the swarthy races of Egypt had inherited this very curse. Also, at the made-up battle of "Cumora," a site located conveniently near his own birthplace, the "Nephites"—described as fair-skinned and "handsome"—contended against the "Lamanites," whose descendants were punished with dark pigment for turning away from god. As the crisis over American slavery mounted, Smith and his even more dubious disciples preached against the abolitionists in antebellum Missouri. They solemnly said that there had been a third group in heaven during the ultimate battle between God and Lucifer. This group, as it was explained, had tried to remain neutral. But after Lucifer's defeat they had been forced into the world, compelled "to take bodies in the accursed lineage of Canaan; and hence the negro or African race." Thus, when Dr. Brodie first wrote her book, no black American was allowed to hold even the lowly position of deacon, let alone a priesthood, in the Mormon Church. Nor were the descendants of Ham admitted to the sacred rites of the temple.

If anything proves the human manufacture of religion, it is the way that the Mormon elders resolved this difficulty. Confronted by the plain words of one of their holy books and the increasing contempt and isolation that it imposed upon them, they did as they had done when their fondness for polygamy would have brought federal retribution upon god's own Utah. They had still another "revelation" and, more or less in time for the passage of the Civil Rights Act of 1965, had it divinely disclosed to them that black people were human after all.

It must be said for the "Latter-day Saints" (these conceited words were added to Smith's original "Church of Jesus Christ" in 1833) that they have squarely faced one of the great difficulties of revealed religion. This is the problem of what to do about those who were born before the exclusive "revelation," or who died without ever having the opportunity to share in its wonders. Christians used to resolve this problem by saying that Jesus descended into hell after his crucifixion, where it is thought that he saved or converted the dead. There is indeed a fine passage in Dante's *Inferno* where he comes to rescue the spirits of great men like Aristotle, who had presumably been boiling away for centuries until he got around to them. (In another less ecumenical scene from the same book, the Prophet Muhammad is found being disemboweled in revolting detail.) The Mormons have improved on this rather backdated solution with something very literal-minded. They have assembled a gigantic genealogical database at a huge repository in Utah, and are busy filling it with the names of all people whose births, marriages, and deaths have been tabulated since records began. This is very useful if you want to look up your own family tree, and as long as you do not object to having your ancestors becoming Mormons. Every week, at special ceremonies in Mormon temples, the congregations meet and are given a certain quota of names of the departed to "pray in" to their church. This retrospective baptism of the dead seems harmless enough to me, but the American Jewish Committee became incensed when it was discovered that the Mormons had acquired the records of the Nazi "final solution," and were industriously baptizing what for once could truly be called a "lost tribe": the murdered Jews of Europe. For all its touching inefficacy, this exercise seemed in poor taste. I sympathize with the American Jewish Committee, but I nonetheless think that the followers of Mr. Smith should be congratulated for hitting upon even the most simpleminded technological solution to a problem that has defied solution ever since man first invented religion.

Chapter Twelve

A Coda: How Religions End

I t can be equally useful and instructive to take a glimpse at the closing of religions, or religious movements. The Millerites, for example, are no more. And we shall not hear again, in any but the most vestigial and nostalgic way, of Pan or Osiris or any of the thousands of gods who once held people in utter thrall. But I have to confess to a slight sympathy, that I have tried and failed to repress, for Sabbatai Sevi, the most imposing of the "false Messiahs." In the mid-seventeenth century, he galvanized whole Jewish communities across the Mediterranean and the Levant (and as far afield as Poland, Hamburg, and even Amsterdam, repudiator of Spinoza) with his claim to be the chosen one who would lead the exiles back to the Holy Land and begin the era of universal peace. His key to revelation was the study of the Kabbalah—more recently revived in fashion by a showbiz woman bizarrely known as Madonna—and his arrival was greeted by hysterical Jewish congregations from his home base in Smyrna to Salonika, Constantinople, and Aleppo. (The rabbis of Jerusalem, having been inconvenienced by premature messianic claims before, were more skeptical.) By the use of Kabbalistic conjury that made his own name the equivalent of "Mosiach" or "Messiah" when unscrambled from a Hebrew anagram, he may have persuaded himself, and certainly persuaded others, that he was the expected one. As one of his disciples phrased it:

> The prophet Nathan prophesied and Sabbatai Sevi preached that whoever did not mend his ways would not behold the comforting of Zion and Jerusalem, and that they would be condemned to shame and to everlasting contempt. And there was a repentance, the like of which has never been seen since the world was created and unto this day.

This was no crude "Millerite" panic. Scholars and learned men debated the question passionately and in writing, and as a consequence we have a very good record of events. All the elements of a true (and a false) prophecy were present. Sabbatai's devotees pointed to his equivalent of John the Baptist, a charismatic rabbi called Nathan of Gaza. Sabbatai's enemies described him as an epileptic and a heretic, and accused him of violating the law. They in turn were stoned by Sabbatai's partisans. Convocations and congregations raged together, and raged against each other. On a voyage to announce himself in Constantinople, Sabbatai's ship was storm-tossed yet he rebuked the waters, and when incarcerated by the Turks his prison was illuminated with holy fires and sweet scents (or not, according to many discrepant accounts). Echoing a very harsh Christian dispute, the supporters of Rabbi Nathan and Sabbatai maintained that without faith, knowledge of the Torah and the performance of good works would be unavailing. Their opponents asserted that the Torah and good works were the main thing. So complete in every respect was the drama that even the stubbornly anti-Sabbatai rabbis in Jerusalem at one point asked to be told if any verifiable miracles or signs had been attached to the claimant who was intoxicating the Jews with joy. Men and women sold all that they had and prepared to follow him to the Promised Land.

The Ottoman imperial authorities had a good deal of experience in dealing with civil unrest among confessional minorities at the time (they were just in the process of wresting Crete from the Venetians) and behaved with much more circumspection than the Romans are supposed to have done. They understood that if Sabbatai was to claim kingdom over all kings, let alone to claim a large tract of their province in Palestine, then he was a secular challenger as well as a religious one. But when he arrived in Constantinople, all they did was lock him up. The ulema, or Muslim religious authority, was likewise sagacious. They counseled against the execution of this turbulent subject, lest his enthused believers "make a new religion."

The script was almost complete when a former disciple of Sabbatai's, one Nehemiah Kohen, came to the grand vizier's headquarters in Edirne and denounced his former master as a practitioner of immorality and heresy. Summoned to the vizier's palace, and allowed to make his way from prison with a procession of hymn-singing supporters, the Messiah was very bluntly asked if he would agree to a trial by ordeal. The archers of the court would use him as a target, and if heaven deflected the arrows he would be adjudged genuine. Should he refuse, he would be impaled. If he wished to decline the choice altogether, he could affirm himself to be a true Muslim and be allowed to live. Sabbatai Zevi did what almost any ordinary mammal would have done, made the standard profession of belief in the one god and his messenger and was awarded a sinecure. He was later deported to an almost *Judenrein* part of the empire, on the Albanian-Montenegrin border, and there expired, supposedly on Yom Kippur 1676, at the precise hour of the evening prayer when Moses is said to have breathed his last. His grave, much sought, has never been conclusively identified.

His distraught followers immediately divided into several factions. There were those who refused to believe in his conversion or apostasy. There were those who argued that he had only become a Muslim in order to be an even greater Messiah. There were those who felt that he had only adopted a disguise. And of course there were those who claimed that he had risen into the heavens. His true disciples eventually adopted the doctrine of "occultation," which, it may not surprise you to learn, involves the belief that the Messiah, invisible to us, has not "died" at all but awaits the moment when humanity will be ready for his magnificent return. ("Occultation" is also the term employed by pious Shia, to describe the present and long-standing condition of the Twelfth Imam or "Mahdi": a child of five who apparently vanished from human view in the year 873.)

So the Sabbatai Sevi religion came to an end, and survives only in the tiny syncretic sect known in Turkey as the Donme, which conceals a Jewish loyalty within an outward Islamic observance. But had its founder been put to death, we should be hearing of it still, and of the elaborate mutual excommunications, stonings, and schisms that its followers would subsequently have engaged in. The nearest approximation in our own day is the Hasidic sect known as Chabad, the Lubavitcher movement once led (and according to some, still led) by Menachem Schneerson. This man's death in Brooklyn in 1994 was confidently expected to produce an age of redemption, which it so far has not. The United States Congress had already established an official "day" in Schneerson's honor in 1983. Just as there are still Jewish sects who maintain that the Nazi "final solution" was a punishment for living in exile from Jerusalem, so there are those who preserve the ghetto policy which maintained a watcher at the gates, whose job it was to alert the others if the Messiah arrived unexpectedly. ("It's steady work," as one of these watchmen is supposed, rather defensively, to have said.) Surveying the not-quite and might-have-been religions, one could experience a slight feeling of pathos, were it not for the constant din of other sermonizers, all of them claiming that it is *their* Messiah, and not anybody else's, who is to be awaited with servility and awe.

Chapter Thirteen

Does Religion Make
People Behave Better?

A little more than a century after Joseph Smith fell victim to the violence and mania that he had helped to unleash, another prophetic voice was raised in the United States. A young black pastor named Dr. Martin Luther King began to preach that his people—the descendants of the very slavery that Joseph Smith and all other Christian churches had so warmly approved—should be free. It is quite impossible even for an atheist like myself to read his sermons or watch recordings of his speeches without profound emotion of the sort that can sometimes bring genuine tears. Dr. King's "Letter from Birmingham Jail," written in response to a group of white Christian clerics who had urged him to show restraint and "patience"—in other words, to know his place—is a model of polemic. Icily polite and generous-minded, it still breathes with an unquenchable conviction that the filthy injustice of racism must be borne no longer.

Taylor Branch's magnificent three-volume biography of Dr. King is successively titled *Parting the Waters*, *Pillar of Fire*, and *At Canaan's Edge*. And the rhetoric with which King addressed his followers was designed to evoke the very story that they all knew best—the one that begins when Moses first tells Pharoah to "Let my people go." In speech after speech he inspired the oppressed, and exhorted and shamed their oppressors. Slowly, the embarrassed religious leadership of the country moved to his side. Rabbi Abraham Heschel asked, "Where in America today do we hear a voice like the voice of the prophets of Israel? Martin Luther King is a sign that God has not forsaken the United States of America."

Most eerie of all, if we follow the Mosaic narrative, was the sermon that King gave on the last night of his life. His work of transforming public opinion and shifting the stubborn Kennedy and Johnson administrations was almost done, and he was in Memphis, Tennessee, to support a long and bitter strike by the city's ground-down garbage collectors, on whose placards appeared the simple words "I Am a Man." In the pulpit at Mason Temple, he reviewed the protracted struggle of the past years and then very suddenly said, "But it doesn't matter with me now." There was silence until he went on. "Because I've been to the mountaintop. And I don't mind. Like anybody I would like to live a long life. Longevity has its place. But I'm not concerned about that now. I just want to do God's will. And he's allowed me to go up the mountain. And I've looked over. And I have *seen* the Promised Land. And I may not get there with you, but I want you to *know, tonight*, that we as a people will get to the Promised Land!" Nobody who was there that night has ever forgotten it, and I daresay the same can be said for anyone who views the film that was so fortunately taken of that transcendent moment. The next best way of experiencing this feeling at second hand is to listen to how Nina Simone sang, that same terrible week, "The King of Love Is Dead." The entire drama has the capacity to unite elements of Moses on Mount Nebo with the agony in the Garden of Gethsemane. The effect is scarcely diminished even when we discover that this was one of his favorite sermons, and one that he had delivered several times before, and into which he could slip as occasion demanded.

But the examples King gave from the books of Moses were,

fortunately for all of us, metaphors and allegories. His most imperative preaching was that of nonviolence. In his version of the story, there are no savage punishments and genocidal bloodlettings. Nor are there cruel commandments about the stoning of children and the burning of witches. His persecuted and despised people were not promised the territory of others, nor were they incited to carry out the pillage and murder of other tribes. In the face of endless provocation and brutality, King beseeched his followers to become what they for a while truly became; the moral tutors of America and of the world beyond its shores. He in effect forgave his murderer in advance: the one detail that would have made his last public words flawless and perfect would have been an actual declaration to that effect. But the difference between him and the "prophets of Israel" could not possibly have been more marked. If the population had been raised from its mother's knee to hear the story of Xenophon's *Anabasis*, and the long wearying dangerous journey of the Greeks to their triumphant view of the sea, that allegory might have done just as well. As it was, though, the "Good Book" was the only point of reference that everybody had in common.

Christian reformism arose originally from the ability of its advocates to contrast the Old Testament with the New. The cobbled-together ancient Jewish books had an ill-tempered and implacable and bloody and provincial god, who was probably more frightening when he was in a good mood (the classic attribute of the dictator). Whereas the cobbled-together books of the last two thousand years contained handholds for the hopeful, and references to meekness, forgiveness, lambs and sheep, and so forth. This distinction is more apparent than real, since it is only in the reported observations of Jesus that we find any mention of hell and eternal punishment. The god of Moses would brusquely call for other tribes, including his favorite one, to suffer massacre and plague and even extirpation, but when the grave closed over his victims he was essentially finished with them unless he remembered to curse their succeeding progeny. Not until the advent of the Prince of Peace do we hear of the ghastly idea of further punishing and torturing the dead. First presaged by the rantings of John the Baptist, the son of god is revealed as one who, if his milder words are not accepted straightaway, will condemn the inattentive to everlasting fire. This has provided texts for clerical sadists ever since, and features very lip-smackingly in the tirades of Islam. At no point did Dr. King—who was once photographed in a bookstore waiting calmly for a physician while the knife of a maniac was sticking straight out of his chest—even hint that those who injured and reviled him were to be threatened with any revenge or punishment, in this world or the next, save the consequences of their own brute selfishness and stupidity. And he even phrased that appeal more courteously than, in my humble opinion, its targets deserved. In no real as opposed to nominal sense, then, was he a Christian.

This does not in the least diminish his standing as a great preacher, any more than does the fact that he was a mammal like the rest of us, and probably plagiarized his doctoral dissertation, and had a notorious fondness for booze and for women a good deal younger than his wife. He spent the remainder of his last evening in orgiastic dissipation, for which I don't blame him. (These things, which of course disturb the faithful, are rather encouraging in that they show that a high moral character is not a precondition for great moral accomplishments.) But if his example is to be deployed, as it often is, to show that religion has an uplifting and liberating effect, then let us examine the wider claim.

Taking the memorable story of black America as our instance, we should find, first, that the enslaved were not captives of some Pharoah but of several Christian states and societies that for many years operated a triangular "trade" between the west coast of Africa, the eastern seaboard of North America, and the capitals of Europe. This huge and terrible industry was blessed by all churches and for a long time aroused absolutely no religious protest. (Its counterpart, the slave trade in the Mediterranean and North Africa, was explicitly endorsed by, and carried out in the name of, Islam.) In the eighteenth century, a few dissenting Mennonites and Quakers in America began to call for abolition, as did some freethinkers like Thomas Paine. Thomas Jefferson, ruminating on the way that slavery corrupted and brutalized the masters as well as exploited and tortured the slaves, wrote, "Indeed, I tremble for my country when I reflect that God is just." This was a statement as incoherent as it is memorable: given the marvel of a god who was also just there would be, in the long term, nothing much to tremble about. At any rate, the Almighty managed to tolerate the situation while several generations were born and died under the lash, and until slavery became less profitable, and even the British Empire began to get rid of it.

This was the spur for the revival of abolitionism. It sometimes took a Christian form, most notably in the case of William Lloyd Garrison, the great orator and founder of the *Liberator*. Mr. Garrison was a splendid man by any standards, but it is probably fortunate that all of his early religious advice was not followed. He based his initial claim on the dangerous verse from Isaiah that calls on the faithful to "come out, and be separated" (this is also the theological basis of Ian Paisley's fundamentalist and bigoted Presbyterianism in Northern Ireland). In Garrison's view, the Union and the United States Constitution were "a covenant with death" and ought both to be destroyed: it was in effect he who called for secession before the Confederates did. (In later life he discovered the work of Thomas Paine and became less of a preacher and a more effective abolitionist, as well as an early supporter of female suffrage.) It was the escaped slave Frederick Douglass, author of the stirring and mordant *Autobiography*, who eschewed apocalyptic language and demanded instead that the United States *live up* to the universalist promises contained in its Declaration and its Constitution. The lionlike John Brown, who also began as a fearsome and pitiless Calvinist, did the same. Later in life, he had Paine's works in his camp and admitted freethinkers to his tiny but epoch-changing army, and even produced and printed a new "Declaration," modeled on that of 1776, on behalf of the enslaved. This was in practice a much more revolutionary as well as a more realistic demand, and prepared the way—as Lincoln admitted—for the Emancipation Proclamation. Douglass was somewhat ambivalent about religion, noting in his *Autiobiography* that the most devout Christians made the most savage slaveholders. The obvious truth of this was underlined when secession really did come and the Confederacy adopted the Latin motto *"Deo Vindice"* or, in effect, "God on Our Side." As Lincoln pointed out in his highly ambivalent second inaugural address, both sides in the quarrel made that claim, at least in their pulpits, just as both were addicted to loud, confident quotations from holy writ.

Lincoln himself was hesitant to claim authority in this manner. In fact, at one point he famously said that such invocations of the divine were wrong, because it was rather a matter of trying to be on god's side. Pressed to issue an immediate Emancipation Proclamation at a gathering of Christians in Chicago, he continued to see both sides of the argument as endorsed by faith, and said that "these are not, however, the days of miracles, and I suppose it will be granted that I am not to expect a direct revelation." This was neatly evasive, yet when he finally did nerve himself to issue the Proclamation he told the remaining waverers that he had promised himself to do so—on condition that god gave victory to the Union forces at Antietam. On that day, the largest ever number of deaths on United States soil was recorded. So it is possible that Lincoln wanted somehow to sanctify and justify that appalling carnage. This would be a noble enough thing, until one reflects that, on the same logic, the same carnage decided the other way would have postponed the freeing of the slaves! As he also said, "The rebel soldiers are praying with a great deal more earnestness, I fear, than our own troops, and expecting God to favor their side; for one of our soldiers, who had been taken prisoner, said that he met with nothing so discouraging as the evident sincerity of those he was among in their prayers." One more bit of battlefield luck for the gray uniforms at Antietam and the president might have become worried that god had deserted the antislavery cause altogether.

We do not know Lincoln's private religious beliefs. He was fond of references to Almighty God, but he never joined any church and his early candidacies were much opposed by clergymen. His friend Herndon knew that he had read Paine and Volney and other freethinkers very closely and formed the opinion that he was privately an outright unbeliever. This seems improbable. However, it would also be inaccurate to say that he was a Christian. Much evidence supports the view that he was a tormented skeptic with a tendency to deism. Whatever may be the case, the very most that can be said for religion in the grave matter of abolition is that after many hundreds of years, and having both imposed and postponed the issue until self-interest had led to a horrifying war, it finally managed to undo some small part of the damage and misery that it had inflicted in the first place.

The same can be said of the King epoch. The southern churches returned to their old ways after Reconstruction, and blessed the new institutions of segregation and discrimination. It was not until after the Second World War and the spread of decolonization and human rights that the cry for emancipation was raised again. In response, it was again very forcefully asserted (on American soil, in the second half of the twentieth century) that the discrepant descendants of Noah were not intended by god to be mixed. This barbaric stupidity had real-world consequences. The late Senator Eugene McCarthy told me that he had once urged Senator Pat Robertson—father of the present television prophet—to support some mild civil rights legislation. "I'd sure like to help the colored," came the response, "but the Bible says I can't." The entire self-definition of "the South" was that it was white, and Christian. This is exactly what gave Dr. King his moral leverage, because he could outpreach the rednecks. But the heavy burden would never have been laid upon him if religiosity had not been so deeply entrenched to begin with. As Taylor Branch shows, many of King's inner circle and entourage were secular Communists and socialists who had been manuring the ground for a civil rights movement for several decades and helping train brave volunteers like Mrs. Rosa Parks for a careful strategy of mass civil disobedience, and these "atheistic" associations were to be used against King all the time, especially from the pulpit. Indeed, one result of his campaign was to generate the "backlash" of white right-wing Christianity which is still such a potent force below the Mason-Dixon line.

When Dr. King's namesake nailed his theses to the door of Wittenberg Cathedral in 1517 and stoutly announced, "Here I stand, I can do no other," he set a standard for intellectual and moral courage. But Martin Luther, who started his religious life being terribly frightened by a near-miss lightning strike, went on to become a bigot and a persecutor in his own right, railing murderously against Jews, screaming about demons, and calling on the German principalities to stamp on the rebellious poor. When Dr. King took a stand on the steps of Mr. Lincoln's memorial and changed history, he too adopted a position that had effectually been forced upon him. But he did so as a profound humanist and nobody could ever use his name to justify oppression or cruelty. He endures for that reason, and his legacy has very little to do with his professed theology. No supernatural force was required to make the case against racism.

Anybody, therefore, who uses the King legacy to justify the role of religion in public life must accept all the corollaries of what they seem to be implying. Even a glance at the whole record will show, first, that person for person, American freethinkers and agnostics and atheists come out the best. The chance that someone's *secular* or freethinking opinion would cause him or her to denounce the whole injustice was extremely high. The chance that someone's religious belief would cause him or her to take a stand against slavery and racism was statistically quite small. But the chance that someone's religious belief would cause him or her to uphold slavery and racism was statistically extremely *high*, and the latter fact helps us to understand why the victory of simple justice took so long to bring about.

As far as I am aware, there is no country in the world today where slavery is still practiced where the justification of it is not derived from the Koran. This returns us to the retort delivered, in the very early days of the Republic, to Thomas Jefferson and John Adams. These two slaveholders had called on the ambassador of Tripoli in London to ask him by what right he and his fellow Barbary potentates presumed to capture and sell American crews and passengers from ships using the Strait of Gibraltar. (It is now estimated that between 1530 and 1780 more than one and a quarter million Europeans were carried off in this way.) As Jefferson reported to Congress:

> The Ambassador answered us that it was founded on the Laws of the Prophet, that it was written in their Koran, that all nations who should not have answered their authority were sinners, that it was their right and duty to make war upon them whenever they could be found and to make slaves of all they could take as prisoners.

Ambassador Abdrahaman went on to mention the requisite price of ransom, the price of protection from kidnapping, and last but not least his own personal commission in these proceedings. (Religion once again betrays its man-made conveniences.) As it happens, he was quite right in what he said about the Koran. The eighth sura, revealed at Medina, deals at some length with the justified spoils of war and dwells continually on the further postmortem "torments of fire" that await those who are defeated by the believers. It was this very sura that was to be used only two centuries later by Saddam Hussein to justify his mass murder and dispossession of the people of Kurdistan.

ANOTHER GRAND HISTORICAL EPISODE—the emancipation of India from colonial rule—is often portrayed as though it involved a connection between religious belief and ethical outcomes. As with the heroic battle of Dr. King, the real story tends to show that something like the opposite is the case.

After the critical weakening of the British Empire by the First World War, and most particularly after the notorious massacre of Indian protestors at the city of Amritsar in April 1919, it became apparent even to the then controllers of the subcontinent that rule from London would come to an end sooner rather than later. It was no longer a matter of "if" but of "when." Had this not been the case, a campaign of peaceful disobedience would have stood no chance. Thus Mohandas K. Gandhi (sometimes known as "the Mahatma" in respect for his standing as a Hindu elder) was in a sense pushing at an open door. There is no dishonor in that, but it is exactly his religious convictions that make his legacy a dubious rather than a saintly one. To state the matter shortly: he wanted India to revert to a village-dominated and primitive "spiritual" society, he made power-sharing with Muslims much harder, and he was quite prepared to make hypocritical use of violence when he thought it might suit him.

The whole question of Indian independence was interleaved with the question of unity: would the former British Raj be reborn as the same country, with the same borders and territorial integrity, and yet still be called India? To this, a certain rugged faction of Muslims answered "no." Under British rule they had enjoyed some protection as a very large minority, not to say a privileged one, and they were not willing to exchange this state of affairs for becoming a large minority in a Hindu-dominated state. Thus the sheer fact that the main force for independence—the Congress Party—was dominated by a conspicuous Hindu made conciliation very difficult. It could be argued, and indeed I would argue, that Muslim intransigence would have played a destructive role in any case. But the task of persuading ordinary Muslims to leave Congress and to join with the partitionist "Muslim League" was made much easier by Gandhi's talk of Hinduism and by the long ostentatious hours he spent in cultish practices and in tending his spinning wheel.

This wheel—which still appears as the symbol on the Indian flag—was the emblem of Gandhi's rejection of modernity. He took to dressing in rags of his own manufacture, and sandals, and to carrying a staff, and expressing hostility to machinery and technology. He rhapsodized about the Indian village, where the millennial rhythms of animals and crops would determine how human life was lived. Millions of people would have mindlessly starved to death if his advice had been followed, and would have continued to worship cows (cleverly denominated by the priests as "sacred" so that the poor ignorant people would not kill and eat their only capital during times of drought and famine). Gandhi deserves credit for his criticism of the inhuman Hindu system of caste, whereby lower orders of humanity were condemned to an ostracism and contempt that was in some ways even more absolute and cruel than slavery. But at just the moment when what India most needed was a modern secular nationalist leader, it got a fakir and guru instead. The crux of this unwelcome realization came in 1941, when the Imperial Japanese Army had conquered Malaya and Burma and was on the frontiers of India itself. Believing (wrongly) that this spelled the end of the Raj, Gandhi chose this moment to boycott the political process and issue his notorious call for the British to "Quit India." He added that they should leave it "To God or to Anarchy," which in the circumstances would have meant much the same thing. Those who naively credit Gandhi with a conscientious or consistent pacifism might wish to ask if this did not amount to letting the Japanese imperialists do his fighting for him.

Among the many bad consequences of the Gandhi/Congress decision to withdraw from negotiations was the opening it gave to Muslim League adherents to "stay on" in the state ministries which they controlled, and thus to enhance their bargaining positions when the moment for independence arrived shortly thereafter. Their insistence that independence take the form of mutilation and amputation, with western Punjab and eastern Bengal hacked away from the national body, became unstoppable. The hideous consequences endure to this day, with further Muslim-on-Muslim bloodbaths in Bangladesh in 1971, the rise of an aggressive Hindu nationalist party, and a confrontation in Kashmir that is still the likeliest provocation for a thermonuclear war.

There was always an alternative, in the form of the secular position taken by Nehru and Rajagopalachari, who would have traded a British promise of immediate postwar independence for a common alliance, on the part of both India and Britain, against fascism. In the event, it was in fact Nehru and not Gandhi who led his country to independence, even at the awful price of partition. For decades, a solid brotherhood between British and Indian secularists and leftists had laid out the case for, and won the argument for, the liberation of India. There was never any need for an obscurantist religious figure to impose his ego on the process and both retard and distort it. The whole case was complete *without that assumption*. One wishes every day that Martin Luther King had lived on and continued to lend his presence and his wisdom to American politics. For "the Mahatma," who was murdered by members of a fanatical Hindu sect for not being devout *enough*, one wishes that he could have lived if only to see what damage he had wrought (and is relieved that he did not live to implement his ludicrous spinning-wheel program).

THE ARGUMENT THAT RELIGIOUS BELIEF improves people, or that it helps to civilize society, is one that people tend to bring up when they have exhausted the rest of their case. Very well, they seem to say, we cease to insist on the Exodus (say), or the Virgin Birth or even the Resurrection, or the "night flight" from Mecca to Jerusalem. But where would people be without faith? Would they not abandon themselves to every kind of license and selfishness? Is it not true, as G. K. Chesterton once famously said, that if people cease to believe in god, they do not believe in nothing but in anything?

The first thing to be said is that virtuous behavior by a believer is no proof at all of—indeed is not even an argument for—the truth of his belief. I might, just for the sake of argument, act more charitably if I believed that Lord Buddha was born from a slit in his mother's side. But would not this make my charitable impulse dependent upon something rather tenuous? By the same token, I do not say that if I catch a Buddhist priest stealing all the offerings left by the simple folk at his temple, Buddhism is thereby discredited. And we forget in any case how contingent all this is. Of the thousands of possible desert religions there were, as with the millions of potential species there were, one branch happened to take root and grow. Passing through its Jewish mutations to its Christian form, it was eventually adopted for political reasons by the Emperor Constantine, and made into an official faith with—eventually—a codified and enforceable form of its many chaotic and contradictory books. As for Islam, it became the ideology of a highly successful conquest that was adopted by successful ruling dynasties, codified and set down in its turn, and promulgated as the law of the land. One or two military victories the other way—as with Lincoln at Antietam—and we in the West would not be the hostages of village disputes that took place in Judaea and Arabia before any serious records were kept. We could have become the votaries of another belief altogether—perhaps a Hindu or an Aztec or a Confucian one—in which case we should still be told that, strictly true or not, it nonetheless helped teach the children the difference between right and wrong. In other words, to believe in a god is in one way to express a *willingness* to believe in anything. Whereas to reject the belief is by no means to profess belief in nothing.

I once watched the late Professor A. J. Ayer, the distinguished author of *Language, Truth and Logic* and a celebrated humanist, debate with a certain Bishop Butler. The chairman was the philosopher Bryan Magee. The exchange proceeded politely enough until the bishop, hearing Ayer assert that he saw no evidence at all for the existence of any god, broke in to say, "Then I cannot see why you do not lead a life of unbridled immorality."

At this point "Freddie," as his friends knew him, abandoned his normal suave urbanity and exclaimed, "I must say that I think that is a perfectly monstrous insinuation." Now, Freddie had certainly broken most commandments respecting the sexual code as adumbrated from Sinai. He was, in a way, justly famous for this. But he was an excellent teacher, a loving parent, and a man who spent much of his spare time pressing for human rights and free speech. To say that his life was an immoral one would be a travesty of the truth.

From the many writers who exemplify the same point in a different way, I shall select Evelyn Waugh, who was of the same faith as Bishop Butler, and who did his best in his fiction to argue for the operations of divine grace. In his novel *Brideshead Revisited* he makes a very acute observation. The two protagonists, Sebastian Flyte and Charles Ryder, the first of whom is heir to an old Catholic nobility, are visited by Father Phipps, who believes that all young men must be passionately interested in cricket. When disabused of this notion, he looks at Charles "with the expression I have seen since in the religious, of innocent wonder that those who expose themselves to the dangers of the world should avail themselves so little of its varied solace."

Thus I rescrutinize Bishop Butler's question. Was he in fact not telling Ayer, in his own naive way, that if freed from the restraints of doctrine *he himself* would choose to lead "a life of unbridled immorality"? One naturally hopes not. But much empirical evidence exists to reinforce the suggestion. When priests go bad, they go very bad indeed, and commit crimes that would make the average sinner pale. One might prefer to attribute this to sexual repression than to the actual doctrines preached, but then one of the actual doctrines preached is sexual repression . . . Thus the connection is unavoidable, and a litany of folkloric jokes have been told by all lay members of the church ever since religion began.

Waugh's own life was far more stained by offenses against chastity and sobriety than was the life of Ayer (only it seemed to bring less happiness to the former than to the latter), and in consequence he was

often asked how he reconciled his private conduct with his public beliefs. His reply has become celebrated: he asked his friends to imagine
how much worse he would be if he were *not* a Catholic. For a believer
in original sin this might have served as a turning of the tables, but
any examination of Waugh's actual life shows that its most wicked
elements arose precisely from his faith. Never mind the sad excesses of
drunkenness and marital infidelity: he once sent a wedding telegram
to a divorced and now remarried friend telling her that her nuptial
night would increase the loneliness of Calvary and add to the spittle
on the face of Christ. He supported fascist movements in Spain and
Croatia, and Mussolini's foul invasion of Abyssinia, because they enjoyed the support of the Vatican, and he wrote in 1944 that only the
Third Reich now stood between Europe and barbarism. These deformities in one of my most beloved authors arose not in spite of his
faith, but because of it. No doubt there were private acts of charity
and contrition, but these could equally well have been performed by a
person of no faith at all. To look no further than the United States, the
great Colonel Robert Ingersoll, who was the nation's leading advocate
of unbelief until his death in 1899, maddened his opponents because
he was a person of immense generosity, a loving and constant husband and father, a gallant officer, and the possessor of what Thomas
Edison with pardonable exaggeration called "all the attributes of a
perfect man."

In my own recent life in Washington, I have been bombarded
with obscene and menacing phone calls from Muslims, promising
to punish my family because I do not support a campaign of lies
and hatred and violence against democratic Denmark. But when
my wife accidentally left a large amount of cash on the backseat of
a taxi, the Sudanese cab driver went to a good deal of trouble and
expense to work out whose property this was, and to drive all the
way to my home to return it untouched. When I made the vulgar
mistake of offering him 10 percent of the money, he made it quietly
but firmly plain that he expected no recompense for performing his

Islamic duty. Which of these two versions of faith is the one to rely upon?

The question is in some ways ultimately undecidable. I would prefer to have Evelyn Waugh's shelf of writing just as it is, and to appreciate that one cannot have the novels without the torments and evils of its author. And if all Muslims conducted themselves like the man who gave up more than a week's salary in order to do the right thing, I could be quite indifferent to the weird exhortations of the Koran. If I search my own life for instances of good or fine behavior I am not overwhelmed by an excess of choice. I did once, shivering with fear, take off my flak jacket in Sarajevo and lend it to an even more frightened woman who I was helping escort to a place of safety (I am not the only one who has been an atheist in a foxhole). I felt at the time that it was the least I could do for her, as well as the most. The people shelling and sniping were Serbian Christians, but then, so was she.

In northern Uganda in late 2005, I sat in a center for the rehabilitation of kidnapped and enslaved children in the land of the Acholi people who live on the northern side of the Nile. The listless, vacant, hardened little boys (and some girls) were all around me. Their stories were distressingly similar. They had been seized, at the age of anything from eight to thirteen, from their schools or homes by a stone-faced militia that was itself originally made up of abducted children. Marched into the bush, they were "initiated" into the force by one (or two) of two methods. They either had to take part in a murder themselves, in order to feel "dirtied up" and implicated, or they had to submit to a prolonged and savage whipping, often of up to three hundred strokes. ("Children who have felt cruelty," said one of the elders of the Acholi people, "know very well how to inflict it.") The misery inflicted by this army of wretches turned zombies was almost beyond computation. It had razed villages, created a vast refugee population, committed hideous crimes such as mutilation and disemboweling, and (in a special touch of evil) had continued to kidnap children so that the Acholi were wary of taking strong countermeasures lest they kill or injure one of their "own."

The name of the militia was the "Lord's Resistance Army" (LRA), and it was led by a man named Joseph Kony, a passionate former altar boy who wanted to subject the area to the rule of the Ten Commandments. He baptized by oil and water, held fierce ceremonies of punishment and purification, and insured his followers against death. His was a fanatical preachment of Christianity. As it happened, the rehabilitation center in which I was sitting was also run by a fundamentalist Christian organization. Having been out into the bush and seen the work of the LRA, I fell to talking with the man who tried to repair the damage. How did he know, I asked him, which of them was the truest believer? Any secular or state-run outfit could be doing what he was doing—fitting prosthetic limbs and providing shelter and "counseling"—but in order to be Joseph Kony one had to have real faith.

To my surprise, he did not dismiss my question. It was true, he said, that Kony's authority arose in part from his background in a priestly Christian family. It was also true that people were apt to believe he could work miracles, by appealing to the spirit world and promising his acolytes that they were death-proof. Even some of those who had run away would still swear that they had seen wonders performed by the man. All that a missionary could do was to try and show people a different face of Christianity.

I was impressed by this man's frankness. There were some other defenses that he might have offered. Joseph Kony is obviously far away from the Christian "mainstream." For one thing, his paymasters and armorers are the cynical Muslims of the Sudanese regime, who use him to make trouble for the government of Uganda, which has in turn supported rebel groups in Sudan. In an apparent reward for this support, Kony at one stage began denouncing the keeping and eating of pigs, which, unless he has become a fundamentalist Jew in his old age, suggests a payoff to his bosses. These Sudanese murderers, in their turn, have for years been conducting a war of extermination not just against the Christians and animists of southern Sudan, but against the non-Arab Muslims of Darfur province. Islam may officially make no distinction between races and nations, but the slaughterers in Darfur are Arab Muslims and their victims are African Muslims. The "Lord's Resistance Army" is nothing but a Christian Khmer Rouge sideshow in this more general horror.

An even more graphic example is afforded by the case of Rwanda, which in 1992 gave the world a new synonym for genocide and sadism. This former Belgian possession is the most Christian country in Africa, boasting the highest percentage of churches per head of population, with 65 percent of Rwandans professing Roman Catholicism and another 15 percent adhering to various Protestant sects. The words "per head" took on a macabre ring in 1992, when at a given signal the racist militias of "Hutu Power," incited by state and church, fell upon their Tutsi neighbors and slaughtered them en masse.

This was no atavistic spasm of bloodletting but a coldly rehearsed African version of the Final Solution, which had been in preparation for some time. The early warning of it came in 1987 when a Catholic visionary with the deceptively folksy name of Little Pebbles began to boast of hearing voices and seeing visions, these deriving from the Virgin Mary. The said voices and visions were distressingly bloody, predicting massacre and apocalypse but also—as if in compensation—the return of Jesus Christ on Easter Sunday, 1992. Apparitions of Mary on a hilltop named Kibeho were investigated by the Catholic Church and announced to be reliable. The wife of the Rwandan president, Agathe Habyarimana, was specially entranced by these visions and maintained a close relationship with the bishop of Kigali, Rwanda's capital city. This man, Monsignor Vincent Nsengiyumva, was also a central-committee member of President Habyarimana's single ruling party, the National Revolutionary Movement for Development, or NRMD. This party, together with other organs of state, was fond of rounding up any women of whom it disapproved as "prostitutes" and of encouraging Catholic activists to trash any stores that sold contraceptives. Over time, the word spread that prophecy would be fulfilled and that the "cockroaches"—the Tutsi minority— would soon get what was coming to them.

When the apocalyptic year of 1994 actually hit, and the premeditated and coordinated massacres began, many frightened Tutsi and dissident Hutu were unwise enough to try and take refuge in churches. This made life considerably easier for the *interahamwe*, or government and military death squads, who knew where to find them and who could rely on priests and nuns to point out the locations. (This is why so many of the mass-grave sites that have been photographed are on consecrated ground, and it is also why several clergymen and nuns are in the dock at the ongoing Rwandan genocide trials.) The notorious Father Wenceslas Munyeshyaka, for example, a leading figure at the Kigali Cathedral of Saint Famille, was smuggled out of the country with the assistance of French priests, but he has since been charged with genocide, with providing lists of civilians to the *interahamwe*, and with the rape of young refugee women. He is by no means the only cleric to have faced similar charges. Lest it be thought that he was merely a "rogue" priest, we have the word of another member of the Rwandan hierarchy, the bishop of Gikongoro, otherwise known as Monsignor Augustin Misago. To quote one careful account of these atrocious events:

> Bishop Misago was often described as a Hutu Power sympathizer; he had been publicly accused of barring Tutsis from places of refuge, criticizing fellow members of the clergy who helped "cockroaches," and asking a Vatican emissary who visited Rwanda in June 1994 to tell the Pope "to find a place for Tutsi priests because the Rwandan people do not want them anymore." What's more, on May 4 of that year, shortly before the last Marian apparition at Kibeho, the bishop appeared there himself with a team of policemen and told a group of ninety Tutsi schoolchildren, who were

being held in preparation for slaughter, not to worry, because the police would protect them. Three days later, the police helped to massacre eighty-two of the children.

Schoolchildren "held in preparation for slaughter" . . . Perhaps you remember the pope's denunciation of this ineffaceable crime, and of the complicity of his church in it? Or perhaps you do not, since no such comment was ever made. Paul Rusesabagina, the hero of *Hotel Rwanda*, remembers Father Wenceslas Munyeshyaka referring even to his own Tutsi mother as a "cockroach." But this did not prevent him, before his arrest in France, from being allowed by the French church to resume his "pastoral duties." As for Bishop Misago, there were those in the postwar Rwandan Ministry of Justice who felt that he should be charged as well. But, as one of the officials of the Ministry phrased it: "The Vatican is too strong, and too unapologetic, for us to go taking on bishops. Haven't you heard of infallibility?"

At a minimum, this makes it impossible to argue that religion causes people to behave in a more kindly or civilized manner. The worse the offender, the more devout he turns out to be. It can be added that some of the most dedicated relief workers are also believers (though as it happens the best ones I have met are secularists who were not trying to proselytize for any faith). But the chance that a person committing the crimes was "faith-based" was almost 100 percent, while the chances that a person of faith was on the side of humanity and decency were about as good as the odds of a coin flip. Extend this back into history, and the odds become more like those of an astrological prediction that just happens to come true. This is because religions could never have got started, let alone thrived, unless for the influence of men as fanatical as Moses or Muhammad or Joseph Kony, while charity and relief work, while they may appeal to tenderhearted believers, are the inheritors of modernism and the Enlightenment. Before that, religion was spread not by example but as an auxiliary to the more old-fashioned methods of holy war and imperialism.

I was a guarded admirer of the late Pope John Paul II, who by any human standards was a brave and serious person capable of displaying both moral and physical courage. He helped the anti-Nazi resistance in his native country as a young man, and in later life did much to assist its emancipation from Soviet rule. His papacy was in some ways shockingly conservative and authoritarian, but showed itself open to science and inquiry (except when the AIDS virus was under discussion) and even in its dogma about abortion made some concessions to a "life ethic" which, for example, began to teach that capital punishment was almost always wrong. On his death, Pope John Paul was praised among other things for the number of apologies he had made. These did not include, as they should have done, an atonement for the million or so put to the sword in Rwanda. However, they did include an apology to the Jews for the centuries of Christian anti-Semitism, an apology to the Muslim world for the Crusades, an apology to Eastern Orthodox Christians for the many persecutions that Rome had inflicted upon them, too, and some general contrition about the Inquisition as well. This seemed to say that the church had mainly been wrong and often criminal in the past, but was now purged of its sin by confession and quite ready to be infallible all over again.

Chapter Fourteen

There Is No "Eastern" Solution

The crisis of organized religion in the West, and the numberless ways in which religious morality has actually managed to fall well *below* the human average, has always led some anxious "seekers" to pursue a softer solution east of Suez. Indeed, I once joined these potential adepts and acolytes, donning orange garb and attending the ashram of a celebrated guru in Poona (or Pune), in the lovely hills above Bombay. I adopted this *sannyas* mode in order to help make a documentary film for the BBC, so you may well question my objectivity if you wish, but the BBC at that time did have a standard of fairness and my mandate was to absorb as much as I could. (One of these days, having in the course of my life been an Anglican, educated at a Methodist school, converted by marriage to Greek Orthodoxy, recognized as an incarnation by the followers of Sai Baba, and remarried by a rabbi, I shall be able to try and update William James's *The Varieties of Religious Experience*.)

The guru in question was named Bhagwan Sri Rajneesh. "Bhagwan" simply means god or godly, and "Sri" means holy. He was a man with huge soulful eyes and a bewitching smile, and a natural if somewhat dirty sense of humor. His sibilant voice, usually deployed through a low-volume microphone at early-morning *dharshan*, possessed a faintly hypnotic quality. This was of some use in alleviating the equally hypnotic platitudinousness of his discourses. Perhaps you have read Anthony Powell's tremendous twelve-volume novel sequence *A Dance to the Music of Time*. In it, a mysterious seer named Dr. Trelawney keeps his group of enlightened followers together in spite of various inevitable difficulties. These initiates can recognize each other not by the individuality of their garb but by an exchange of avowals. On meeting, the first must intone, "The essence of the all is the godhead of the true." The proper response to this is, "The vision of visions heals the blindness of sight." Thus is the spiritual handshake effected. I heard nothing at the Bhagwan's knee (one had to sit cross-legged) that was any more profound than that. There was more emphasis on love, in its eternal sense, than in Dr. Trelawney's circle, and certainly there was more emphasis on sex, in its immediate sense. But on the whole, the instruction was innocuous. Or it would have been, if not for a sign at the entrance to the Bhagwan's preaching-tent. This little sign never failed to irritate me. It read: "Shoes and minds must be left at the gate." There was a pile of shoes and sandals next to it, and in my transcendent condition I could almost picture a heap of abandoned and empty mentalities to round out this literally mindless little motto. I even attempted a brief parody of a Zen koan: "What is the reflection of a mind discarded?"

For the blissed-out visitor or tourist, the ashram presented the outward aspect of a fine spiritual resort, where one could burble about the beyond in an exotic and luxurious setting. But within its holy precincts, as I soon discovered, there was a more sinister principle at work. Many damaged and distraught personalities came to Poona seeking advice and counsel. Several of them were well-off (the clients or pilgrims included a distant member of the British royal family) and were at first urged—as with so many faiths—to part with all their material possessions. Proof of the efficacy of this advice could be seen in the fleet of Rolls-Royce motorcars maintained by the Bhagwan and deemed to be the largest such collection in the world. After this relatively brisk fleecing, initiates were transferred into "group" sessions where the really nasty business began.

Wolfgang Dobrowolny's film *Ashram*, shot in secret by a former devotee and adapted for my documentary, shows the "playful" term *kundalini* in a fresh light. In a representative scene, a young woman is stripped naked and surrounded by men who bark at her, drawing attention to all her physical and psychic shortcomings, until she is abject with tears and apologies. At this point, she is hugged and embraced and comforted, and told that she now has "a family." Sobbing with masochistic relief, she humbly enters the tribe. (It was not absolutely clear what she had to do in order to be given her clothes back, but I did hear some believable and ugly testimony on this point.) In other sessions involving men, things were rough enough for bones to be broken and lives lost: the German princeling of the House of Windsor was never seen again, and his body was briskly cremated without the tedium of an autopsy.

I had been told in respectful and awed tones that "the Bhagwan's body has some allergies," and not long after my sojourn he fled the ashram and then apparently decided that he had no further use for his earthly frame. What happened to the Rolls-Royce collection I never found out, but his acolytes received some kind of message to reconvene in the small town of Antelope, Oregon, in the early months of 1983. And this they did, though now less committed to the pacific and laid-back style. The local inhabitants were disconcerted to find an armed compound being erected in their neighborhood, with unsmiling orange-garbed security forces. An attempt to create "space" for the new ashram was apparently made. In a bizarre episode, food-poisoning matter was found to have been spread over the produce in an Antelope supermarket. Eventually the commune broke up and dispersed amid serial recriminations, and I have occasionally run into empty-eyed refugees from the Bhagwan's long and misleading tuition. (He himself has been reincarnated as "Osho," in whose honor a glossy but stupid magazine was being produced until a few years ago. Possibly a remnant of his following still survives.) I would say that the people of Antelope, Oregon, missed being as famous as Jonestown by a fairly narrow margin.

El sueño de la razón produce monstruos. "The sleep of reason," it has been well said, "brings forth monsters." The immortal Francisco Goya gave us an etching with this title in his series *Los Caprichos*, where a man in defenseless slumber is hag-ridden by bats, owls, and other haunters of the darkness. But an extraordinary number of people appear to believe that the mind, and the reasoning faculty—the only thing that divides us from our animal relatives—is something to be distrusted and even, as far as possible, dulled. The search for nirvana, and the dissolution of the intellect, goes on. And whenever it is tried, it produces a Kool-Aid effect in the real world.

"Make me one with everything." So goes the Buddhist's humble request to the hot-dog vendor. But when the Buddhist hands over a twenty-dollar bill to the vendor, in return for his slathered bun, he waits a long time for his change. Finally asking for it, he is informed that "change comes only from within." All such rhetoric is almost too easy to parody, as is that of missionary Christianity. In the old Anglican cathedral in Calcutta I once paid a visit to the statue of Bishop Reginald Heber, who filled the hymn books of the Church of England with verses like these:

What though the tropic breezes
Blow soft o'er Ceylon's isle
Where every prospect pleases
And only man is vile
What though with loving kindness
The gifts of God are strown
The heathen in his blindness
Bows down to wood and stone.

It is partly in reaction to the condescension of old colonial boobies like this that many westerners have come to revere the apparently more seductive religions of the Orient. Indeed, Sri Lanka (the modern name for the lovely island of Ceylon) is a place of great charm. Its people are remarkable for their kindness and generosity: how dare Bishop Heber have depicted them as vile? However, Sri Lanka is a country now almost utterly ruined and disfigured by violence and repression, and the contending forces are mainly Buddhist and Hindu. The problem begins with the very name of the state: "Lanka" is the old Sinhalese-language name for the island, and the prefix "Sri" simply means "holy," in the Buddhist sense of the word. This postcolonial renaming meant that the Tamils, who are chiefly Hindu, felt excluded at once. (They prefer to call their homeland "Eelam.") It did not take long for this ethnic tribalism, reinforced by religion, to wreck the society.

Though I personally think that the Tamil population had a reasonable grievance against the central government, it is not possible to forgive their guerrilla leadership for pioneering, long before Hezbollah and al-Qaeda, the disgusting tactic of suicide murder. This barbarous technique, which was also used by them to assassinate an elected president of India, does not excuse the Buddhist-led pogroms against Tamils or the murder, by a Buddhist priest, of the first elected president of independent Sri Lanka.

Conceivably, some readers of these pages will be shocked to learn of the existence of Hindu and Buddhist murderers and sadists. Perhaps they dimly imagine that contemplative easterners, devoted to vegetarian diets and meditative routines, are immune to such temptations? It can even be argued that Buddhism is not, in our sense of the word, a "religion" at all. Nonetheless, the perfect one is alleged to have left one of his teeth behind in Sri Lanka, and I once attended a ceremony which involved a rare public showing by priests of this gold-encased object. Bishop Heber did not mention bone in his stupid hymn (though it would have made just as good a rhyme as "stone"), and perhaps this was because Christians have always foregathered to bow down to bones of supposed saints, and to keep them in grisly reliquaries in their churches and cathedrals. However that may be, at the tooth-propitiation I had no feeling at all of peace and inner bliss. To the contrary, I realized that if I was a Tamil I would have a very good chance of being dismembered.

The human species is an animal species without very much variation within it, and it is idle and futile to imagine that a voyage to Tibet, say, will discover an entirely different harmony with nature or eternity. The Dalai Lama, for example, is entirely and easily recognizable to a secularist. In exactly the same way as a medieval princeling, he makes the claim not just that Tibet should be independent of Chinese hegemony—a "perfectly good" demand, if I may render it into everyday English—but that he himself is a hereditary king appointed by heaven itself. How convenient! Dissenting sects within his faith are persecuted; his one-man rule in an Indian enclave is absolute; he makes absurd pronouncements about sex and diet and, when on his trips to Hollywood fund-raisers, anoints major donors like Steven Segal and Richard Gere as holy. (Indeed, even Mr. Gere was moved to whine a bit when Mr. Segal was invested as a *tulku*, or person of high enlightenment. It must be annoying to be outbid at such a spiritual auction.) I will admit that the current "Dalai" or supreme lama is a man of some charm and presence, as I will admit that the present queen of England is a person of more integrity than most of her predecessors, but this does not invalidate the critique of hereditary monarchy, and the first foreign visitors to Tibet were downright appalled at the feudal domination, and hideous punishments, that kept the population in permanent serfdom to a parasitic monastic elite.

How might one easily prove that "Eastern" faith was identical with the unverifiable assumptions of "Western" religion? Here is a decided statement by "Gudo," a very celebrated Japanese Buddhist of the first part of the twentieth century:

As a propagator of Buddhism I teach that "all sentient beings have the Buddha nature" and that "within the Dharma there is equality with neither superior nor inferior." Furthermore, I teach that "all sentient beings are my children." Having taken these golden words as the basis of my faith, I discovered that they are in complete agreement with the principles of socialism. It was thus that I became a believer in socialism.

There you have it again: a baseless assumption that some undefined external "force" has a mind of its own, and the faint but menacing suggestion that anyone who disagrees is in some fashion opposed to the holy or paternal will. I excerpt this passage from Brian Victoria's exemplary book *Zen at War*, which describes the way the majority of Japanese Buddhists decided that Gudo was right in general but wrong in particular. People were indeed to be considered children, as they are by all faiths, but it was actually fascism and not socialism that the Buddha and the dharma required of them.

Mr. Victoria is a Buddhist adept and claims—I leave this to him—to be a priest as well. He certainly takes his faith seriously, and knows a great deal about Japan and the Japanese. His study of the question shows that Japanese Buddhism became a loyal servant—even an advocate—of imperialism and mass murder, and that it did so, not so much because it was Japanese, but because it was Buddhist. In 1938, leading members of the Nichiren sect founded a group devoted to "Imperial-Way Buddhism." It declared as follows:

Imperial-Way Buddhism utilizes the exquisite truth of the Lotus Sutra to reveal the majestic essence of the national polity. Exalting the true spirit of Mahayana Buddhism is a teaching which reverently supports the emperor's work. This is what the great founder of our sect, Saint Nichiren, meant when he referred to the divine unity of Sovereign and Buddha. . . . For this reason the principal image of adoration in Imperial-Way Buddhism is not

Buddha Shakyamuni who appeared in India, but his majesty the emperor, whose lineage extends over ten thousand generations.

Effusions like this are—however wicked they may be—almost beyond criticism. They consist, like most professions of faith, in merely *assuming* what has to be proved. Thus, a bald assertion is then followed with the words "for this reason," as if all the logical work had been done by making the assertion. (All of the statements of the Dalai Lama, who happens not to advocate imperialist slaughter but who did loudly welcome the Indian government's nuclear tests, are also of this non-sequitur type.) Scientists have an expression for hypotheses that are utterly useless even for learning from mistakes. They refer to them as being "not even wrong." Most so-called spiritual discourse is of this type.

You will notice, further, that in the view of this school of Buddhism there are other schools of Buddhism, every bit as "contemplative," that are in error. This is just what an anthropologist of religion would expect to find of something that was, having been manufactured, doomed to be schismatic. But on what basis could a devotee of Buddha Shakyamuni argue that his Japanese co-thinkers were in error themselves? Certainly not by using reasoning or evidence, which are quite alien to those who talk of the "exquisite truth of the Lotus Sutra."

Things went from bad to worse once Japanese generals had mobilized their Zen-obedient zombies into complete obedience. The mainland of China became a killing field, and all the major sects of Japanese Buddhism united to issue the following proclamation:

Revering the imperial policy of preserving the Orient, the subjects of imperial Japan bear the humanitarian destiny of one billion people of color. . . . We believe it is time to effect a major change in the course of human history, which has been centered on Caucasians.

This echoes the line taken by the Shinto—another quasi-religion enjoying state support—that Japanese soldiers really fell for the cause of Asian independence. Every year, there is a famous controversy about whether Japan's civil and spiritual leaders should visit the Yakasuni shrine, which officially ennobles Hirohito's army. Every year, millions of Chinese and Koreans and Burmese protest that Japan was not the enemy of imperialism in the Orient but a newer and more vicious form of it, and that the Yakasuni shrine is a place of horror. How interesting, however, to note that Japanese Buddhists of the time regarded their country's membership of the Nazi/Fascist Axis as a manifestation of liberation theology. Or, as the united Buddhist leadership phrased it at the time:

> In order to establish eternal peace in East Asia, arousing the great benevolence and compassion of Buddhism, we are sometimes accepting and sometimes forceful. We now have no choice but to exercise the benevolent forcefulness of "killing one in order that many may live" (*issatsu tasho*). This is something which Mahayana Buddhism approves of only with the greatest of seriousness.

No "holy war" or "Crusade" advocate could have put it better. The "eternal peace" bit is particularly excellent. By the end of the dreadful conflict that Japan had started, it was Buddhist and Shinto priests who were recruiting and training the suicide bombers, or *Kamikaze* ("Divine Wind"), fanatics, assuring them that the emperor was a "Golden Wheel-Turning Sacred King," one indeed of the four manifestations of the ideal Buddhist monarch and a *Tathagata*, or "fully enlightened being," of the material world. And since "Zen treats life and death indifferently," why not abandon the cares of this world and adopt a policy of prostration at the feet of a homicidal dictator?

This grisly case also helps to undergird my general case for considering "faith" as a threat. It ought to be possible for me to pursue my studies and researches in one house, and for the Buddhist to spin his wheel in another. But contempt for the intellect has a strange way of *not* being passive. One of two things may happen: those who are innocently credulous may become easy prey for those who are less scrupulous and who seek to "lead" and "inspire" them. Or those whose credulity has led their own society into stagnation may seek a solution, not in true self-examination, but in blaming others for their backwardness. Both these things happened in the most consecratedly "spiritual" society of them all.

Although many Buddhists now regret that deplorable attempt to prove their own superiority, no Buddhist since then has been able to demonstrate that Buddhism was wrong in its own terms. A faith that despises the mind and the free individual, that preaches submission and resignation, and that regards life as a poor and transient thing, is ill-equipped for self-criticism. Those who become bored by conventional "Bible" religions, and seek "enlightenment" by way of the dissolution of their own critical faculties into nirvana in any form, had better take a warning. They may think they are leaving the realm of despised materialism, but they are still being asked to put their reason to sleep, and to discard their minds along with their sandals.

Chapter Fifteen

Religion as an Original Sin

There are, indeed, several ways in which religion is not just amoral, but positively immoral. And these faults and crimes are not to be found in the behavior of its adherents (which can sometimes be exemplary) but in its original precepts. These include:

- Presenting a false picture of the world to the innocent and the credulous
- The doctrine of blood sacrifice
- The doctrine of atonement
- The doctrine of eternal reward and/or punishment
- The imposition of impossible tasks and rules

The first point has already been covered. All the creation myths of all peoples have long been known to be false, and have fairly recently been replaced by infinitely superior and more magnificent explanations. To its list of apologies, religion should simply add an apology for foisting man-made parchments and folk myths upon the unsuspecting, and for taking so long to concede that this had been done. One senses a reluctance to make this admission, since it might tend to explode the whole religious worldview, but the longer it is delayed the more heinous the denial will become.

BLOOD SACRIFICE

Before monotheism arose, the altars of primitive society reeked of blood, much of it human and some of it infant. The thirst for this, at least in animal form, is still with us. Pious Jews are at this moment trying to breed the spotlessly pure "red heifer" mentioned in the book of Numbers, chapter 19, which if slaughtered again according to the exact and meticulous ritual will bring about the return of animal sacrifices in the Third Temple, and hasten the end of time and the coming of the Messiah. This may appear merely absurd, but a team of like-minded Christian maniac farmers are attempting as I write to help their co-fundamentalists by employing special breeding techniques (borrowed or stolen from modern science) to produce a perfect "Red Angus" beast in Nebraska. Meanwhile in Israel, the Jewish biblical fanatics are also trying to raise a human child, in a pure "bubble" free from contamination, who will at the attainment of the right age be privileged to cut that heifer's throat. Ideally, this should be done on the Temple Mount, awkwardly the site of the Muslim holy places but nonetheless the very spot where Abraham is alleged to have drawn the knife over the live body of his own child. Other sacramental guttings and throat-cuttings, particularly of lambs, occur every year in the Christian and Muslim world, either to celebrate Easter or the feast of Eid.

The latter, which honors Abraham's willingness to make a human sacrifice of his son, is common to all three monotheisms, and descends from their primitive ancestors. There is no softening the plain meaning of this frightful story. The prelude involves a series of vilenesses and delusions, from the seduction of Lot by both his daughters to the marriage of Abraham to his stepsister, the birth of Isaac to Sarah when Abraham was a hundred years old, and many other credible and incredible rustic crimes and misdemeanors. Perhaps afflicted by a poor conscience, but at any rate believing himself commanded by god, Abraham agreed to murder his son. He prepared the kindling, laid the tied-up boy upon it (thus showing that he knew the procedure), and took up the knife in order to kill the child like an animal. At the last available moment his hand was stayed, not by god as it happens, but by an angel, and he was praised from the clouds for showing his sturdy willingness to murder an innocent in expiation of his own crimes. As a reward for his fealty, he was promised a long and large posterity.

Not long after this (though the Genesis narrative is not very well illustrated in point of time) his wife Sarah expired at the age of one hundred and twenty-seven, and her dutiful husband found her a place of burial in a cave in the town of Hebron. Having outlived her by attaining the fine old age of one hundred and seventy-five, and having fathered six more children meanwhile, Abraham was eventually buried in the same cave. To this day, religious people kill each other and kill each other's children for the right to exclusive property in this unidentifiable and unlocatable hole in a hill.

There was a terrible massacre of Jewish residents of Hebron during the Arab revolt of 1929, when sixty-seven Jews were slaughtered. Many of these were Lubavitchers, who regard all non-Jews as racially inferior and who had moved to Hebron because they believed the Genesis myth, but this does not excuse the pogrom. Remaining outside the border of Israel until 1967, the town was captured that year with much fanfare by Israeli forces and became part of the occupied West Bank. Jewish settlers began to "return," under the leadership of a particularly violent and obnoxious rabbi named Moshe Levinger, and to build an armed settlement named Kiryat Arba above the town, as well as some smaller settlements within it. The Muslims among the mainly Arab inhabitants continued to claim that the praiseworthy Abraham indeed had been willing to murder his son, but only for *their* religion and not for the Jews. This is what "submission" means. When

I visited the place I found that the supposed "Cave of the Patriarchs," or "Cave of Machpela," had separate entrances and separate places of worship for the two warring claimants to the right to celebrate this atrocity in their own names.

A short while before I arrived, another atrocity had occurred. An Israeli zealot named Dr. Baruch Goldstein had come to the cave and, unslinging the automatic weapon that he was allowed to carry, discharged it into the Muslim congregation. He killed twenty-seven worshippers and injured countless others before being overwhelmed and beaten to death. It turned out that many people already knew that Dr. Goldstein was dangerous. While serving as a physician in the Israeli army he had announced that he would not treat non-Jewish patients, such as Israeli Arabs, especially on the Sabbath. As it happens, he was obeying rabbinic law in declining to do this, as many Israeli religious courts have confirmed, so an easy way to spot an inhumane killer was to notice that he was guided by a sincere and literal observance of the divine instruction. Shrines in his name have been set up by the more doggedly observant Jews ever since, and of those rabbis who condemned his action, not all did so in unequivocal terms. The curse of Abraham continues to poison Hebron, but the religious warrant for blood sacrifice poisons our entire civilization.

Atonement

Previous sacrifices of humans, such as the Aztec and other ceremonies from which we recoil, were common in the ancient world and took the form of propitiatory murder. An offering of a virgin or an infant or a prisoner was assumed to appease the gods: once again, not a very good advertisement for the moral properties of religion. "Martyrdom," or a deliberate sacrifice of oneself, can be viewed in a slightly different light, though when practiced by the Hindus in the form of suttee, or the strongly suggested "suicide" of widows, it was put down by the British in India for imperial as much as for Christian reasons. Those "martyrs" who wish to kill others as well as themselves, in an act of religious exaltation, are viewed more differently still: Islam is ostensibly opposed to suicide per se but cannot seem to decide whether to condemn or recommend the act of such a bold *shahid*.

However, the idea of a *vicarious* atonement, of the sort that so much troubled even C. S. Lewis, is a further refinement of the ancient superstition. Once again we have a father demonstrating love by subjecting a son to death by torture, but this time the father is not trying to impress god. He *is* god, and he is trying to impress humans. Ask yourself the question: how moral is the following? I am told of a human sacrifice that took place two thousand years ago, without my wishing it and in circumstances so ghastly that, had I been present and in possession of any influence, I would have been duty-bound to try and stop it. In consequence of this murder, my own manifold sins are forgiven me, and I may hope to enjoy everlasting life.

Let us just for now overlook all the contradictions between the tellers of the original story and assume that it is basically true. What are the further implications? They are not as reassuring as they look at first sight. For a start, and in order to gain the benefit of this wondrous offer, I have to accept that I am *responsible* for the flogging and mocking and crucifixion, in which I had no say and no part, and agree that every time I decline this responsibility, or that I sin in word or deed, I am intensifying the agony of it. Furthermore, I am required to believe that the agony was *necessary* in order to compensate for an earlier crime in which I also had no part, the sin of Adam. It is useless to object that Adam seems to have been created with insatiable discontent and curiosity and then forbidden to slake it: all this was settled long before even Jesus himself was born. Thus my own guilt in the matter is deemed "original" and inescapable. However, I am still granted free will with which to reject the offer of vicarious redemption. Should I exercise this choice, however, I face an eternity of torture much more awful than anything endured at Calvary, or anything threatened to those who first heard the Ten Commandments.

The tale is made no easier to follow by the necessary realization that Jesus both *wished* and *needed* to die and came to Jerusalem at Passover in order to do so, and that all who took part in his murder were unknowingly doing god's will, and fulfilling ancient prophecies. (Absent the gnostic version, this makes it hopelessly odd that Judas, who allegedly performed the strangely redundant act of identifying a very well-known preacher to those who had been hunting for him, should suffer such opprobrium. Without him, there could have been no "Good Friday," as the Christians naively call it even when they are not in a vengeful mood.)

There is a charge (found in only one of the four Gospels) that the Jews who condemned Jesus asked for his blood to be "on their heads" for future generations. This is not a problem that concerns only the Jews, or those Catholics who are worried by the history of Christian anti-Semitism. Suppose that the Jewish Sanhedrin *had* in fact made such a call, as Maimonides thought they had, and should have. How could that call possibly be binding upon successor generations? Remember that the Vatican did not assert that it was *some Jews* who had killed Christ. It asserted that it was *the Jews* who had ordered his death, and that the Jewish people as a whole were the bearers of a collective responsibility. It seems bizarre that the church could not bring itself to drop the charge of generalized Jewish "deicide" until very recently. But the key to its reluctance is easy to find. If you once admit that the descendants of Jews are not implicated, it becomes very hard to argue that anyone else not there present was implicated, either. One rent in the fabric, as usual, threatens to tear the whole thing apart (or to make it into something simply man-made and woven, like the discredited Shroud of Turin). The collectivization of guilt, in short, is immoral in itself, as religion has been occasionally compelled to admit.

ETERNAL PUNISHMENT AND IMPOSSIBLE TASKS

The Gospel story of the Garden of Gethsemane used to absorb me very much as a child, because its "break" in the action and its human whimper made me wonder if some of the fantastic scenario might after all be true. Jesus asks, in effect, "Do I *have* to go through with this?" It is an impressive and unforgettable question, and I long ago decided that I would cheerfully wager my own soul on the belief that the only right answer to it is "no." We cannot, like fear-ridden peasants of antiquity, hope to load all our crimes onto a goat and then drive the hapless animal into the desert. Our everyday idiom is quite sound in regarding "scapegoating" with contempt. And religion is scapegoating writ large. I can pay your debt, my love, if you have been imprudent, and if I were a hero like Sidney Carton in *A Tale of Two Cities* I could even serve your term in prison or take your place on the scaffold. Greater love hath no man. But I cannot absolve you of your responsibilities. It would be immoral of me to offer, and immoral of you to accept. And if the same offer is made from another time and another world, through the mediation of middlemen and accompanied by inducements, it loses all its grandeur and becomes debased into wish-thinking or, worse, a combination of blackmailing with bribery.

The ultimate degeneration of all this into a mere bargain was made unpleasantly obvious by Blaise Pascal, whose theology is not far short of sordid. His celebrated "wager" puts it in hucksterish form: what have you got to lose? If you believe in god and there is a god, you win. If you believe in him and you are wrong—so what? I once wrote a response to this cunning piece of bet-covering, which took two forms. The first was a version of Bertrand Russell's hypothetical reply to the hypothetical question: what will you say if you die and are confronted with your Maker? His response? "I should say, Oh God, you did not give us enough evidence." My own reply: Imponderable Sir, I presume from some if not all of your many reputations that you might prefer honest and convinced unbelief to the hypocritical and self-interested affectation of faith or the smoking tributes of bloody altars. But I would not count on it.

Pascal reminds me of the hypocrites and frauds who abound in Talmudic Jewish rationalization. Don't do any work on the Sabbath yourself, but pay someone else to do it. You obeyed the letter of the law: who's counting? The Dalai Lama tells us that you can visit a prostitute as long as someone else pays her. Shia Muslims offer "temporary marriage," selling men the permission to take a wife for an hour or two with the usual vows and then divorce her when they are done. Half of the splendid buildings in Rome would never have been raised if the sale of indulgences had not been so profitable: St. Peter's itself was financed by a special one-time offer of that kind. The newest pope, the former Joseph Ratzinger, recently attracted Catholic youths to a festival by offering a certain "remission of sin" to those who attended.

This pathetic moral spectacle would not be necessary if the original rules were ones that it would be possible to obey. But to the totalitarian edicts that begin with revelation from absolute authority, and that are enforced by fear, and based on a sin that had been committed long ago, are added regulations that are often immoral and impossible at the same time. The essential principle of totalitarianism is to make laws that are *impossible to obey.* The resulting tyranny is even more impressive if it can be enforced by a privileged caste or party which is highly zealous in the detection of error. Most of humanity, throughout its history, has dwelt under a form of this stupefying dictatorship, and a large portion of it still does. Allow me to give a few examples of the rules that must, yet cannot, be followed.

The commandment at Sinai which forbade people even to *think* about coveting goods is the first clue. It is echoed in the New Testament by the injunction which says that a man who looks upon a woman in the wrong way has actually committed adultery already. And it is almost equaled by the current Muslim and former Christian prohibition against lending out money at interest. All of these, in their different fashion, attempt to place impossible restraints on human initiative. They can only be met in one of two ways. The first is by a continual scourging and mortification of the flesh, accompanied by incessant wrestling with "impure" thoughts which become actual as soon as they are named, or even imagined. From this come hysterical confessions of guilt, false promises of improvement, and loud, violent denunciations of other backsliders and sinners: a spiritual police state. The second solution is organized hypocrisy, where forbidden foods are rebaptized as something else, or where a donation to the religious authorities will purchase some wiggle-room, or where ostentatious orthodoxy will buy some time, or where money can be paid into one account and then paid back—with perhaps a slight percentage added in a non-usurious manner—into another. This we might term the spiritual banana republic. Many theocracies, from medieval Rome to modern Wahhabi Saudi Arabia, have managed to be spiritual police states *and* spiritual banana republics at the same time.

This objection applies even to some of the noblest and some of the basest rules. The order to "love thy neighbor" is mild and yet stern: a reminder of one's duty to others. The order to "love thy neighbor *as thyself*" is too extreme and too strenuous to be obeyed, as is the hard-to-interpret instruction to love others "as I have loved you." Humans are not so constituted as to care for others as much as themselves: the thing simply cannot be done (as any intelligent "creator" would well understand from studying his own design). Urging humans to be superhumans, on pain of death and torture, is the urging of terrible self-abasement at their repeated and inevitable failure to keep the rules. What a grin, meanwhile, on the face of those who accept the cash donations that are made in lieu! The so-called Golden Rule, sometimes needlessly identified with a folktale about the Babylonian Rabbi Hillel, simply enjoins us to treat others as one would wish to be treated by them. This sober and rational precept, which one can teach to any child with its innate sense of fairness (and which predates all Jesus's "beatitudes" and parables), is well within the compass of any atheist and does not require masochism and hysteria, or sadism and hysteria, when it is breached. It is gradually learned, as part of the painfully slow evolution of the species, and once grasped is never forgotten. Ordinary conscience will do, without any heavenly wrath behind it.

As to the basest rules, one need only consult the argument from design once more. People wish to enrich and better themselves, and though they may well lend or even give money to a friend or relative in need and ask for nothing but its eventual return or its grateful acknowledgment, they will not advance money to perfect strangers without expecting interest. By a nice chance, cupidity and avarice are the spur to economic development. No student of the subject from David Ricardo to Karl Marx to Adam Smith has been unaware of this fact. It is "not from the benevolence" of the baker, observed Smith in his shrewd Scots manner, that we expect our daily bread, but from his self-interest in baking and selling it. In any case, one may choose to be altruistic, whatever that may mean, but by definition one may not be *compelled* into altruism. Perhaps we would be better mammals if we were not "made" this way, but surely nothing could be sillier than having a "maker" who then forbade the very same instinct he instilled.

"Free will," reply the casuists. You do not have to obey the laws against murder or theft either. Well, one may be genetically programmed for a certain amount of aggression and hatred and greed, and yet also evolved enough to beware of following every prompting. If we gave in to our every base instinct every time, civilization would have been impossible and there would be no writing in which to continue this argument. However, there can be no question that a human being, whether standing up or lying down, finds his or her hand resting just next to the genitalia. Useful no doubt in warding off primeval aggressors once our ancestors decided to take the risk of going erect and exposing the viscera, this is both a privilege and a provocation denied to most quadrupeds (some of whom can compensate by getting their mouths to the same point that we can reach with our fingers and palms). Now: who devised the rule that this easy apposition between the manual and the genital be forbidden, even as a thought? To put it more plainly, who ordered that you *must* touch (for other reasons having nothing to do with sex or reproduction) but that you also *must not*? There does not even seem to be any true scriptural authority here, yet almost all religions have made the prohibition a near-absolute one.

One could write an entire book that was devoted only to the grotesque history of religion and sex, and to holy dread of the procreative act and its associated impulses and necessities, from the emission of semen to the effusion of menstrual blood. But a convenient way of condensing the whole fascinating story may be to ask one single provocative question.

Chapter Sixteen

Is Religion Child Abuse?

"Tell me straight out, I call on you—answer me: imagine that you
yourself are building the edifice of human destiny with the object
of making people happy in the finale, of giving them peace and rest
at last, but for that you must inevitably and unavoidably torture just
one tiny creature, that same child who was beating her chest with her
little fist, and raise your edifice on the foundation of her unrequited
tears—would you agree to be the architect on such conditions? Tell
me the truth."

—Ivan to Alyosha in *The Brothers Karamazov*

W hen we consider whether religion has "done more harm
than good"—not that this would say anything *at all* about
its truth or authenticity—we are faced with an imponderably large
question. How can we ever know how many children had their psychological and physical lives irreparably maimed by the compulsory
inculcation of faith? This is almost as hard to determine as the number of spiritual and religious dreams and visions that came "true,"
which in order to possess even a minimal claim to value would have
to be measured against all the unrecorded and unremembered ones
that did not. But we can be sure that religion has always hoped to
practice upon the unformed and undefended minds of the young, and
has gone to great lengths to make sure of this privilege by making alliances with secular powers in the material world.

One of the great instances of moral terrorism in our literature is the sermon preached by Father Arnall in James Joyce's *Portrait of the Artist as a Young Man*. This disgusting old priest is readying Stephen Dedalus and his other young "charges" for a retreat in honor of Saint Francis Xavier (the man who brought the Inquisition to Asia and whose bones are still revered by those who choose to revere bones). He decides to impress them with a long and gloating account of eternal punishment, of the sort which the church used to mandate when it still had the confidence to do so. It is impossible to quote the entire rant, but two particularly vivid elements—concerning the nature of torture and the nature of time—are of interest. It is easy to see that the priest's words are designed *precisely* to frighten children. In the first place, the images are themselves childlike. In the torture section, the very devil himself makes a mountain shrivel like wax. Every frightening malady is summoned, and the childlike worry that this pain might go on forever is deftly played upon. When it comes to the picture of a unit of time, we see a child on the beach playing with grains of sand, and then the infantile magnification of units ("Daddy, what if there were a million million million squillion kittens: would they fill up the whole *world?*"), and then, adding further multiplicities, the evocation of nature's leaves, and the easily conjured fur and feathers and scales of the family pet. For centuries, grown men have been paid to frighten children in this way (and to torture and beat and violate them as well, as they also did in Joyce's memory and the memory of countless others).

The other man-made stupidities and cruelties of the religious are easy to detect as well. The idea of torture is as old as the nastiness of mankind, which is the only species with the imagination to guess what it might feel like when imposed upon another. We cannot blame religion for this impulse, but we can condemn it for institutionalizing and refining the practice. The museums of medieval Europe, from Holland to Tuscany, are crammed with instruments and devices upon which holy men labored devoutly, in order to see how long they could keep someone alive while being roasted. It is not needful to go into further details, but there were also religious books of instruction in this art, and guides for the detection of heresy by pain. Those who were not lucky enough to be allowed to take part in the auto-da-fé (or "act of faith," as a torture session was known) were permitted free rein to fantasize as many lurid nightmares as they could, and to inflict them verbally in order to keep the ignorant in a state of permanent fear. In an era where there was little enough by way of public entertainment, a good public burning or disembowelment or breaking on the wheel was often as much recreation as the saintly dared to allow. Nothing proves the man-made character of religion as obviously as the sick mind that designed hell, unless it is the sorely limited mind that has failed to describe heaven—except as a place of either worldly comfort, eternal tedium, or (as Tertullian thought) continual relish in the torture of others.

Pre-Christian hells were highly unpleasant too, and called upon the same sadistic ingenuity for their invention. However, some of the early ones we know of—most notably the Hindu—were limited in time. A sinner, for example, might be sentenced to a given number of years in hell, where every day counted as 6,400 human years. If he slew a priest, the sentence thus adjusted would be 149,504,000,000 years. At this point, he was allowed nirvana, which seems to mean annihilation. It was left to Christians to find a hell from which there was no possible appeal. (And the idea is easily plagiarized: I once heard Louis Farrakhan, leader of the heretical black-only "Nation of Islam," as he drew a hideous roar from a mob in Madison Square Garden. Hurling spittle at the Jews, he yelled, "And don't you forget—when it's God who puts you in the ovens, it's FOREVER!")

The obsession with children, and with rigid control over their upbringing, has been part of every system of absolute authority. It may have been a Jesuit who was first actually quoted as saying, "Give me the child until he is ten, and I will give you the man," but the idea is very much older than the school of Ignatius Loyola. Indoctrination of the young often has the reverse effect, as we also know from the fate of many secular ideologies, but it seems that the religious will run this risk in order to imprint the average boy or girl with enough propaganda. What else can they hope to do? If religious instruction were not allowed until the child had attained the age of reason, we would be living in a quite different world. Faithful parents are divided over this, since they naturally hope to share the wonders and delights of Christmas and other fiestas with their offspring (and can also make good use of god, as well as of lesser figures like Santa Claus, to help tame the unruly) but mark what happens if the child should stray to another faith, let alone another cult, even in early adolescence. The parents will tend to proclaim that this is taking advantage of the innocent. All monotheisms have, or used to have, a very strong prohibition against apostasy for just this reason. In her *Memories of a Catholic Girlhood*, Mary McCarthy remembers her shock at learning from a Jesuit preacher that her Protestant grandfather—her guardian and friend—was doomed to eternal punishment because he had been baptized in the wrong way. A precociously intelligent child, she would not let the matter drop until she had made the Mother Superior consult some higher authorities and discover a loophole in the writings of Bishop Athanasius, who held that heretics were only damned if they rejected the true church with full awareness of what they were doing. Her grandfather, then, might be sufficiently unaware of the true church to evade hell. But what an agony to which to subject an eleven-year-old girl! And only think of the number of less curious children who simply accepted this evil teaching without questioning it. Those who lie to the young in this way are wicked in the extreme.

Two instances—one of immoral teaching and the other of immoral practice—may be adduced. The immoral teaching concerns abortion. As a materialist, I think it has been demonstrated that an embryo is a separate body and entity, and not merely (as some really did used to argue) a growth on or in the female body. There used to be feminists who would say that it was more like an appendix or even—this was seriously maintained—a tumor. That nonsense seems to have stopped. Of the considerations that have stopped it, one is the fascinating and moving view provided by the sonogram, and another is the survival of "premature" babies of featherlike weight, who have achieved "viability" outside the womb. This is yet another way in which science can make common cause with humanism. Just as no human being of average moral capacity could be indifferent to the sight of a woman being kicked in the stomach, so nobody could fail to be far more outraged if the woman in question were pregnant. Embryology confirms morality. The words "unborn child," even when used in a politicized manner, describe a material reality.

However, this only opens the argument rather than closes it. There may be many circumstances in which it is not desirable to carry a fetus to full term. Either nature or god appears to appreciate this, since a very large number of pregnancies are "aborted," so to speak, because of malformations, and are politely known as "miscarriages." Sad though this is, it is probably less miserable an outcome than the vast number of deformed or idiot children who would otherwise have been born, or stillborn, or whose brief lives would have been a torment to themselves and others. As with evolution in general, therefore, in utero we see a microcosm of nature and evolution itself. In the first place we begin as tiny forms that are amphibian, before gradually developing lungs and brains (and growing and shedding that now useless coat of fur) and then struggling out and breathing fresh air after a somewhat difficult transition. Likewise, the system is fairly pitiless in eliminating those who never had a very good chance of surviving in the first place: our ancestors on the savannah were not going to survive in their turn if they had a clutch of sickly and lolling infants to protect against predators. Here the analogy of evolution might not be to Adam Smith's "invisible hand" (a term that I have always distrusted) so much as to Joseph Schumpeter's model of "creative destruction," whereby we accustom ourselves to a certain amount of natural failure, taking into account the pitilessness of nature and extending back to the remote prototypes of our species.

Thus, not all conceptions are, or ever were, going to lead to births. And ever since the mere struggle for existence began to abate, it has been an ambition of the human intelligence to gain control over the rate of reproduction. Families who are at the mercy of mere nature, with its inevitable demand for profusion, will be tied to a cycle that is not much better than animal. The best way of achieving a measure of control is by prophylaxis, which has been restlessly sought since records were kept and which has in our own time become relatively foolproof and painless. The second-best fallback solution, which may sometimes be desirable for other reasons, is termination of pregnancy: an expedient which is regretted by many even when it has been undertaken in dire need. All thinking people recognize a painful conflict of rights and interests in this question, and strive to achieve a balance. The only proposition that is completely useless, either morally or practically, is the wild statement that sperms and eggs are all potential lives which must not be prevented from fusing and that, when united however briefly, have souls and must be protected by law. On this basis, an intrauterine device that prevents the attachment of the egg to the wall of the uterus is a murder weapon, and an ectopic pregnancy (the disastrous accident that causes the egg to begin growing inside the Fallopian tube) is a human life instead of an already doomed egg that is also an urgent threat to the life of the mother.

Every single step toward the clarification of this argument has been opposed root and branch by the clergy. The attempt even to educate people in the possibility of "family planning" was anathematized from the first, and its early advocates and teachers were arrested (like John Stuart Mill) or put in jail or thrown out of their jobs. Only a few years ago, Mother Teresa denounced contraception as the moral equivalent of abortion, which "logically" meant (since she regarded abortion as murder) that a sheath or a pill was a murder weapon also. She was a little more fanatical even than her church, but here again we can see that the strenuous and dogmatic is the moral enemy of the good. It demands that we believe the impossible, and practice the unfeasible. The whole case for extending protection to the unborn, and to expressing a bias in favor of life, has been wrecked by those who use unborn children, as well as born ones, as mere manipulable objects of their doctrine.

As to immoral practice, it is hard to imagine anything more grotesque than the mutilation of infant genitalia. Nor is it easy to imagine anything more incompatible with the argument from design. We must assume that a designer god would pay especial attention to the reproductive organs of his creatures, which are so essential for the continuation of the species. But religious ritual since the dawn of time has insisted on snatching children from the cradle and taking sharp stones or knives to their pudenda. In some animist and Muslim societies, it is the female babies who suffer the worst, with the excision of the labia and the clitoris. This practice is sometimes postponed to adolescence and, as earlier described, accompanied by infibulation, or the sewing up of the vagina with only a small aperture for the passage of blood and urine. The aim is clear—to kill or dull the girl's sexual instinct and destroy the temptation to experiment with any man save the one to whom she will be given (and who will have the privilege of rending those threads on the dreaded nuptial night). Meanwhile, she will be taught that her monthly visitation of blood is a curse (all religions have expressed a horror of it, and many still prohibit menstruating women from attending service) and that she is an unclean vessel.

In other cultures, notably the "Judeo-Christian," it is the sexual mutilation of small boys that is insisted upon. (For some reason, little girls can be Jewish without genital alteration: it is useless to look for consistency in the covenants that people believe they have made with god.) Here, the original motives appear to be twofold. The shedding of blood—which is insisted upon at circumcision ceremonies—is most probably a symbolic survival from the animal and human sacrifices which were such a feature of the gore-soaked landscape of the Old

Testament. By adhering to the practice, parents could offer to sacrifice a part of the child as a stand-in for the whole. Objections to interference with something that god must have designed with care—the human penis—were overcome by the invented dogma that Adam was born circumcised and in the image of god. Indeed, it is argued by some rabbis that Moses, too, was born circumcised, though this claim may result from the fact that his own circumcision is nowhere mentioned in the Pentateuch.

The second purpose—very unambivalently stated by Maimonides—was the same as for girls: the destruction as far as possible of the pleasurable side of sexual intercourse. Here is what the sage tells us in his *Guide to the Perplexed*:

> With regard to circumcision, one of the reasons for it is, in my opinion, the wish to bring about a decrease in sexual intercourse and a weakening of the organ in question, so that this activity be diminished and the organ be in as quiet a state as possible. It has been thought that circumcision perfects what is defective congenitally. . . . How can natural things be defective so that they need to be perfected from outside, all the more because *we know how useful the foreskin is for that member*? In fact this commandment has not been prescribed with a view to perfecting what is defective congenitally, but to perfecting what is defective morally. The bodily pain caused to that member is the real purpose of circumcision. . . . The fact that circumcision weakens the faculty of sexual excitement and sometimes perhaps diminishes the pleasure is indubitable. For if at birth this member has been made to bleed and has had its covering taken away from it, it must indubitably be weakened.

Maimonides did not seem particularly impressed by the promise (made to Abraham in Genesis 17) that circumcision would lead to his having a vast progeny at the age of ninety-nine. Abraham's decision to circumcise his slaves as well as his male household was a side issue or perhaps an effect of enthusiasm, since these non-Jews were not part of the covenant. But he did circumcise his son Ishmael, who was then thirteen. (Ishmael only had to part with his foreskin: his younger brother Isaac—oddly described as Abraham's "only" son in Genesis 22—was circumcised when he was eight days old but later offered as a sacrifice in his whole person.)

Maimonides also argued that circumcision would be a means of reinforcing ethnic solidarity, and he laid particular stress on the need to perform the operation on babies rather than on those who had reached the age of reason:

> The first [argument] is that if the child were let alone until he grew up, he would sometimes not perform it. The second is that a child does not suffer as much pain as a grown-up man because his membrane is still soft and his imagination weak; for a grown-up man would regard the thing, which he would imagine before it occurred, as terrible and hard. The third is that the parents of a child that is just born take lightly matters concerning it, for up to that time the imaginative form that compels the parents to love it is not yet consolidated. . . . Consequently if it were left uncircumcised for two or three years, this would necessitate the abandonment of circumcision because of the father's love and affection for it. At the time of its birth, on the other hand, this imaginative form is very weak, especially as far as concerns the father upon whom this commandment is imposed.

In ordinary words, Maimonides is perfectly aware that, if not supposedly mandated by god, this hideous procedure would, even in the most devout parent—he stipulates only a father—create a natural revulsion in favor of the child. But he represses this insight in favor of "divine" law.

In more recent times, some pseudosecular arguments have been adduced for male circumcision. It has been argued that the process is more hygienic for the male and thus more healthy for females in helping them avoid, for example, cervical cancer. Medicine has exploded these claims, or else revealed them as problems which can just as easily be solved by a "loosening" of the foreskin. Full excision, originally ordered by god as the blood price for the promised future massacre of the Canaanites, is now exposed for what it is—a mutilation of a powerless infant with the aim of ruining its future sex life. The connection between religious barbarism and sexual repression could not be plainer than when it is "marked in the flesh." Who can count the number of lives that have been made miserable in this way, especially since Christian doctors began to adopt ancient Jewish folklore in their hospitals? And who can bear to read the medical textbooks and histories which calmly record the number of boy babies who died from infection after their eighth day, or who suffered gross and unbearable dysfunction and disfigurement? The record of syphilitic and other infection, from rotting rabbinical teeth or other rabbinical indiscretions, or of clumsy slitting of the urethra and sometimes a vein, is simply dreadful. And it is permitted in New York in 2006! If religion and its arrogance were not involved, no healthy society would permit this primitive amputation, or allow any surgery to be practiced on the genitalia without the full and informed consent of the person concerned.

Religion is also to be blamed for the hideous consequences of the masturbation taboo (which also furnished yet another excuse for circumcision among the Victorians). For decades, millions of young men and boys were terrified in adolescence by supposedly "medical" advice that warned them of blindness, nervous collapse, and descent into insanity if they resorted to self-gratification. Stern lectures from clergymen, replete with nonsense about semen as an irreplaceable and finite energy source, dominated the upbringing of generations. Robert Baden-Powell composed an entire obsessive treatise on the subject, which he used to reinforce the muscular Christianity of his Boy Scout movement. To this day, the madness persists on Islamic Web sites purporting to offer counsel to the young. Indeed, it seems that the mullahs have been poring over the same discredited texts, by Samuel Tissot and others, which used to be wielded by their Christian predecessors to such dire effect. The identical weird and dirty-minded misinformation is on offer, especially from Abd al-Aziz bin Baz, the late grand mufti of Saudi Arabia, whose warnings against onanism are repeated on many Muslim sites. The habit will disrupt the digestive system, he warns, damage the eyesight, inflame the testicles, erode the spinal cord ("the place from which sperm originates"!), and lead to tremors and shakes. Nor are the "cerebral glands" unaffected, with concomitant decline in IQ and eventual insanity. Last of all, and still tormenting millions of healthy youngsters with guilt and worry, the mufti tells them that their semen will grow thin and insipid and prevent them from becoming fathers later on. The Inter-Islam and Islamic Voice sites recycle this tripe, as if there were not already enough repression and ignorance among young males in the Muslim world, who are often kept apart from all female company, taught in effect to despise their mothers and sisters, and subjected to stultifying rote recitation of the Koran. Having met some of the products of this "education" system, in Afghanistan and elsewhere, I can only reiterate that their problem is not so much that they desire virgins as that they *are* virgins: their emotional and psychic growth irremediably stunted in the name of god, and the safety of many others menaced as a consequence of this alienation and deformation.

Sexual innocence, which can be charming in the young if it is not needlessly protracted, is positively corrosive and repulsive in the mature adult. Again, how shall we reckon the harm done by dirty old men and hysterical spinsters, appointed as clerical guardians to supervise the innocent in orphanages and schools? The Roman Catholic Church in particular is having to answer this question in the most painful of ways, by calculating the monetary value of child abuse in terms of compensation. Billions of dollars have already been awarded, but there is no price to be put on the generations of boys and girls who were introduced to sex in the most alarming and disgusting ways by those whom they and their parents trusted. "Child abuse" is really a silly and pathetic euphemism for what has been going on: we are talking about the systematic rape and torture of children, positively aided and abetted by a hierarchy which knowingly moved the grossest offenders to parishes where they would be safer. Given what has come to light in modern cities in recent times, one can only shudder to think what was happening in the centuries where the church was above all criticism. But what did people expect would happen when the vulnerable were controlled by those who, misfits and inverts themselves, were required to affirm hypocritical celibacy? And who were taught to state grimly, as an article of belief, that children were "imps of" or "limbs of" Satan? Sometimes the resulting frustration expressed itself in horrible excesses of corporal punishment, which is bad enough in itself. But when the artificial inhibitions really collapse, as we have seen them do, they result in behavior which no average masturbating, fornicating sinner could even begin to contemplate without horror. This is not the result of a few delinquents among the shepherds, but an outcome of an ideology which sought to establish clerical control by means of control of the sexual instinct and even of the sexual organs. It belongs, like the rest of religion, to the fearful childhood of our species. Alyosha's answer to Ivan's question about the sacred torture of a child was to say ("softly")—"No, I do not agree." Our reply, to the repellent original offer of the defenseless boy Isaac on the pyre, right up to the current abuses and repressions, must be the same, only not delivered so softly.

Chapter Seventeen

An Objection Anticipated: The Last-Ditch "Case" Against Secularism

I f I cannot definitively prove that the usefulness of religion is in the past, and that its foundational books are transparent fables, and that it is a man-made imposition, and that it has been an enemy of science and inquiry, and that it has subsisted largely on lies and fears, and been the accomplice of ignorance and guilt as well as of slavery, genocide, racism, and tyranny, I can most certainly claim that religion is now fully aware of these criticisms. It is also fully aware of the ever-mounting evidence, concerning the origins of the cosmos and the origin of species, which consign it to marginality if not to irrelevance. I have tried to deal with most faith-based objections as they occur in the unfolding argument, but there is one remaining argument that one may not avoid.

When the worst has been said about the Inquisition and the witch trials and the Crusades and the Islamic imperial conquests and the horrors of the Old Testament, is it not true that secular and atheist regimes have committed crimes and massacres that are, in the scale of things, at least as bad if not worse? And does not the corollary hold, that men freed from religious awe will act in the most unbridled and abandoned manner? Dostoyevsky in his *Brothers Karamazov* was extremely critical of religion (and lived under a despotism that was sanctified by the church) and he also represented his character Smerdyakov as a vain and credulous and stupid figure, but Smerdyakov's maxim, that "if there is no God there is no morality," understandably resonates with those who look back on the Russian Revolution through the prism of the twentieth century.

One could go further and say that secular totalitarianism has actually provided us with the *summa* of human evil. The examples most in common use—those of the Hitler and Stalin regimes—show us with terrible clarity what can happen when men usurp the role of gods. When I consult with my secular and atheist friends, I find that this has become the most common and frequent objection that they encounter from religious audiences. The point deserves a detailed reply.

To begin with a slightly inexpensive observation, it is interesting to find that people of faith now seek defensively to say that they are no worse than fascists or Nazis or Stalinists. One might hope that religion had retained more sense of its dignity than that. I would not say that the ranks of secularism and atheism are exactly crammed with Communists or fascists, but it can be granted for the sake of argument that, just as secularists and atheists have withstood clerical and theocratic tyrannies, so religious believers have resisted pagan and materialistic ones. But this would only be to split the difference.

The word "totalitarian" was probably first used by the dissident Marxist Victor Serge, who had become appalled by the harvest of Stalinism in the Soviet Union. It was popularized by the secular Jewish intellectual Hannah Arendt, who had fled the hell of the Third Reich and who wrote *The Origins of Totalitarianism*. It is a useful term, because it separates "ordinary" forms of despotism—those which merely exact obedience from their subjects—from the absolutist systems which demand that citizens become wholly subjects and surrender their private lives and personalities entirely to the state, or to the supreme leader.

If we accept that latter definition, then the first point to be made is likewise an easy one. For most of human history, the idea of the total or absolute state was intimately bound up with religion. A baron or king might compel you to pay taxes or serve in his army, and he would usually arrange to have priests on hand to remind you that this was your duty, but the truly frightening despotisms were those which also wanted the contents of your heart and your head. Whether we examine the oriental monarchies of China or India or Persia, or the empires of the Aztec or the Incas, or the medieval courts of Spain and Russia and France, it is almost unvaryingly that we find that these dictators were also gods, or the heads of churches. More than mere obedience was owed them: any criticism of them was profane by definition, and millions of people lived and died in pure fear of a ruler who could select you for a sacrifice, or condemn you to eternal punishment, on a whim. The slightest infringement—of a holy day, or a holy object, or an ordinance about sex or food or caste—could bring calamity. The totalitarian principle, which is often represented as "systematic," is also closely bound up with caprice. The rules might change or be extended at any moment, and the rulers had the advantage of knowing that their subjects could never be sure if they were obeying the latest law or not. We now value the few exceptions from antiquity—such as Periclean Athens with all its deformities—precisely because there were a few moments when humanity did not live in permanent terror of a Pharoah or Nebuchadnezzar or Darius whose least word was holy law.

This was even true when the divine right of despots began to give way to versions of modernity. The idea of a utopian state on earth, perhaps modeled on some heavenly ideal, is very hard to efface and has led people to commit terrible crimes in the name of the ideal. One of the very first attempts to create such an ideal Edenic society, patterned on the scheme of human equality, was the totalitarian socialist state estab-

lished by the Jesuit missionaries in Paraguay. It managed to combine
the maximum of egalitarianism with the maximum of unfreedom, and
could only be kept going by the maximum of fear. This ought to have
been a warning to those who sought to perfect the human species. Yet
the object of perfecting the species—which is the very root and source
of the totalitarian impulse—is in essence a religious one.

George Orwell, the ascetic unbeliever whose novels gave us an ineradicable picture of what life in a totalitarian state might truly feel
like, was in no doubt about this. "From the totalitarian point of view,"
he wrote in "The Prevention of Literature" in 1946, "history is something to be created rather than learned. *A totalitarian state is in effect
a theocracy*, and its ruling caste, in order to keep its position, has to be
thought of as infallible." (You will notice that he wrote this in a year
when, having fought for more than a decade against fascism, he was
turning his guns even more on the sympathizers of Communism.)

In order to be a part of the totalitarian mind-set, it is not necessary
to wear a uniform or carry a club or a whip. It is only necessary to *wish*
for your own subjection, and to delight in the subjection of others.
What is a totalitarian system if not one where the abject glorification
of the perfect leader is matched by the surrender of all privacy and
individuality, especially in matters sexual, and in denunciation and
punishment—"for their own good"—of those who transgress? The
sexual element is probably decisive, in that the dullest mind can grasp
what Nathaniel Hawthorne captured in *The Scarlet Letter*: the deep
connection between repression and perversion.

In the early history of mankind, the totalitarian principle was
the regnant one. The state religion supplied a complete and "total"
answer to all questions, from one's position in the social hierarchy to
the rules governing diet and sex. Slave or not, the human was property, and the clerisy was the reinforcement of absolutism. Orwell's
most imaginative projection of the totalitarian idea—the offense
of "thoughtcrime"—was a commonplace. An impure thought, let
alone a heretical one, could lead to your being flayed alive. To be

accused of demonic possession or contact with the Evil One was to be convicted of it. Orwell's first realization of the hellishness of this came to him early in life, when he was enclosed in a hermetic school run by Christian sadists in which it was not possible to know when you had broken the rules. Whatever you did, and however many precautions you took, the sins of which you were unaware could always be made to find you out.

It was possible to leave that awful school (traumatized for life, as millions of children have been) but it is not possible, in the religious totalitarian vision, to escape this world of original sin and guilt and pain. An infinity of punishment awaits you even after you die. According to the really extreme religious totalitarians, such as John Calvin, who borrowed his awful doctrine from Augustine, an infinity of punishment can be awaiting you even before you are born. Long ago it was written which souls would be chosen or "elected" when the time came to divide the sheep from the goats. No appeal against this primordial sentence is possible, and no good works or professions of faith can save one who has not been fortunate enough to be picked. Calvin's Geneva was a prototypical totalitarian state, and Calvin himself a sadist and torturer and killer, who burned Servetus (one of the great thinkers and questioners of the day) while the man was still alive. The lesser wretchedness induced in Calvin's followers, compelled to waste their lives worrying if they had been "elected" or not, is well caught in George Eliot's *Adam Bede*, and in an old English plebeian satire against the other sects, from Jehovah's Witnesses to Plymouth Brethren, who dare to claim that they are of the elect, and that they alone know the exact number of those who will be plucked from the burning:

> *We are the pure and chosen few, and all the rest are damned.*
> *There's room enough in hell for you—we don't want heaven crammed.*

I had an innocuous but weak-spirited uncle whose life was ruined and made miserable in just this way. Calvin may seem like a far-off figure to us, but those who used to grab and use power in his name are still among us and go by the softer names of Presbyterians and Baptists. The urge to ban and censor books, silence dissenters, condemn outsiders, invade the private sphere, and invoke an exclusive salvation is the very essence of the totalitarian. The fatalism of Islam, which believes that all is arranged by Allah in advance, has some points of resemblance in its utter denial of human autonomy and liberty, as well as in its arrogant and insufferable belief that its faith already contains everything that anyone might ever need to know.

Thus, when the great antitotalitarian anthology of the twentieth century came to be published in 1950, its two editors realized that it could only have one possible name. They called it *The God That Failed.* I slightly knew and sometimes worked for one of these two men—the British socialist Richard Crossman. As he wrote in his introduction to the book:

> For the intellectual, material comforts are relatively unimportant; what he cares about most is spiritual freedom. The strength of the Catholic Church has always been that it demands the sacrifice of that freedom uncompromisingly, and condemns spiritual pride as a deadly sin. The Communist novice, subjecting his soul to the canon law of the Kremlin, felt something of the release which Catholicism also brings to the intellectual, wearied and worried by the privilege of freedom.

The only book that had warned of all this in advance, a full thirty years earlier, was a small but brilliant volume published in 1919 and entitled *The Practice and Theory of Bolshevism.* Long before Arthur Koestler and Richard Crossman had begun to survey the wreckage in retrospect, the whole disaster was being predicted in terms that still command admiration for their prescience. The mordant analyst of the new religion was Bertrand Russell, whose atheism made him more far-seeing than many naive "Christian socialists" who claimed to detect in Russia the beginnings of a new paradise on earth. He was also more far-seeing than the Anglican Christian establishment in his native England, whose newspaper of record the London *Times* took the view that the Russian Revolution could be explained by *The Protocols of the Learned Elders of Zion*. This revolting fabrication by Russian Orthodox secret policemen was republished by Eyre and Spottiswoode, the official printers to the Church of England.

GIVEN ITS OWN RECORD of succumbing to, and of promulgating, dictatorship on earth and absolute control in the life to come, how did religion confront the "secular" totalitarians of our time? One should first consider, in order, fascism, Nazism, and Stalinism.

Fascism—the precursor and model of National Socialism—was a movement that believed in an organic and corporate society, presided over by a leader or guide. (The "fasces"—symbol of the "lictors" or enforcers of ancient Rome—were a bundle of rods, tied around an axe, that stood for unity and authority.) Arising out of the misery and humiliation of the First World War, fascist movements were in favor of the defense of traditional values against Bolshevism, and upheld nationalism and piety. It is probably not a coincidence that they arose first and most excitedly in Catholic countries, and it is certainly not a coincidence that the Catholic Church was generally sympathetic to fascism as an idea. Not only did the church regard Communism as a lethal foe, but it also saw its old Jewish enemy in the most senior ranks of Lenin's party. Benito Mussolini had barely seized power in Italy before the Vatican made an official treaty with him, known as the Lateran Pact of 1929. Under the terms of this deal, Catholicism became the only recognized religion in Italy, with monopoly powers over matters such as birth, marriage, death, and education, and in return urged its followers to vote for Mussolini's party. Pope Pius XI described Il Duce ("the leader") as "a man sent by providence." Elections were not to be a feature of Italian life for very long, but the church nonetheless brought about the dissolution of lay Catholic centrist parties and helped sponsor a pseudoparty called "Catholic Action" which was emulated in several countries. Across southern Europe, the church was a reliable ally in the instatement of fascist regimes in Spain, Portugal, and Croatia. General Franco in Spain was allowed to call his invasion of the country, and his destruction of its elected republic, by the honorific title *La Crujada*, or "the crusade." The Vatican either supported or refused to criticize Mussolini's operatic attempt to re-create a pastiche of the Roman Empire by his invasions of Libya, Abyssinia (today's Ethiopia), and Albania: these territories being populated either by non-Christians or by the wrong kind of Eastern Christian. Mussolini even gave, as one of his justifications for the use of poison gas and other gruesome measures in Abyssinia, the persistence of its inhabitants in the heresy of Monophysitism: an incorrect dogma of the Incarnation that had been condemned by Pope Leo and the Council of Chalcedon in 451.

In central and eastern Europe the picture was hardly better. The extreme right-wing military coup in Hungary, led by Admiral Horthy, was warmly endorsed by the church, as were similar fascistic movements in Slovakia and Austria. (The Nazi puppet regime in Slovakia was actually led by a man in holy orders named Father Tiso.) The cardinal of Austria proclaimed his enthusiasm at Hitler's takeover of his country at the time of the Anschluss.

In France, the extreme right adopted the slogan of *"Meilleur Hitler Que Blum"*—in other words, better to have a German racist dictator than an elected French socialist Jew. Catholic fascist organizations such as Charles Maurras's Action Française and the Croix de Feu campaigned violently against French democracy and made no bones about their grievance, which was the way in which France had been going downhill since the acquittal of the Jewish captain Alfred Dreyfus in 1899. When the German conquest of France arrived, these forces eagerly collaborated in the rounding up and murder of French Jews, as well as in the deportation to forced labor of a huge number of other Frenchmen. The Vichy regime conceded to clericalism by wiping the slogan of 1789—*"Liberte, Egalite, Fraternite"*—off the national currency and replacing it with the Christian ideal motto of *"Famille, Travail, Patrie."* Even in a country like England, where fascist sympathies were far less prevalent, they still managed to get an audience in respectable circles by the agency of Catholic intellectuals such as T. S. Eliot and Evelyn Waugh.

In neighboring Ireland, the Blue Shirt movement of General O'Duffy (which sent volunteers to fight for Franco in Spain) was little more than a dependency of the Catholic Church. As late as April 1945, on the news of the death of Hitler, President Eamon de Valera put on his top hat, called for the state coach, and went to the German embassy in Dublin to offer his official condolences. Attitudes like this meant that several Catholic-dominated states, from Ireland to Spain to Portugal, were ineligible to join the United Nations when it was first founded. The church has made efforts to apologize for all this, but its complicity with fascism is an ineffaceable mark on its history, and was not a short-term or a hasty commitment so much as a working alliance which did not break down until *after* the fascist period had itself passed into history.

The case of the church's surrender to German National Socialism is considerably more complicated but not very much more elevating. Despite sharing two important principles with Hitler's movement— those of anti-Semitism and anti-Communism—the Vatican could see that Nazism represented a challenge to itself as well. In the first place, it was a quasi-pagan phenomenon which in the long run sought to replace Christianity with pseudo-Nordic blood rites and sinister race myths, based upon the fantasy of Aryan superiority. In the second place, it advocated an exterminationist attitude to the unwell, the unfit, and the insane, and began quite early on to apply this policy not to Jews but to Germans. To the credit of the church, it must be said that its German pulpits denounced this hideous eugenic culling from a very early date.

But if ethical principle had been the guide, the Vatican would not have had to spend the next fifty years vainly trying to account for, or apologize for, its contemptible passivity and inaction. "Passivity" and "inaction," in fact, may be the wrong choice of words here. To decide to do nothing is itself a policy and a decision, and it is unfortunately easy to record and explain the church's alignment in terms of a realpolitik that sought, not the defeat of Nazism, but an accommodation with it.

The very *first* diplomatic accord undertaken by Hitler's government was consummated on July 8, 1933, a few months after the seizure of power, and took the form of a treaty with the Vatican. In return for unchallenged control of the education of Catholic children in Germany, the dropping of Nazi propaganda against the abuses inflicted in Catholic schools and orphanages, and the concession of other privileges to the church, the Holy See instructed the Catholic Center Party to disband, and brusquely ordered Catholics to abstain from any political activity on any subject that the regime chose to define as off-limits. At the first meeting of his cabinet after this capitulation was signed, Hitler announced that these new circumstances would be "especially significant in the struggle against international Jewry." He was not wrong about this. In fact, he could have been excused for disbelieving his own luck. The twenty-three million Catholics living in the Third Reich, many of whom had shown great individual courage in resisting the rise of Nazism, had been gutted and gelded as a political force. Their own Holy Father had in effect told them to render everything unto the worst Caesar in human history. From then on, parish records were made available to the Nazi state in order to establish who was and who was not "racially pure" enough to survive endless persecution under the Nuremberg laws.

Not the least appalling consequence of this moral surrender was the parallel moral collapse of the German Protestants, who sought to preempt a special status for Catholics by publishing their own accommodation with the führer. None of the Protestant churches,

however, went as far as the Catholic hierarchy in ordering an annual celebration for Hitler's birthday on April 20. On this auspicious
date, on papal instructions, the cardinal of Berlin regularly transmitted "warmest congratulations to the führer in the name of the
bishops and dioceses in Germany," these plaudits to be accompanied
by "the fervent prayers which the Catholics of Germany are sending to heaven on their altars." The order was obeyed, and faithfully
carried out.

To be fair, this disgraceful tradition was not inaugurated until 1939,
in which year there was a change of papacy. And to be fair again, Pope
Pius XI had always harbored the most profound misgivings about the
Hitler system and its evident capacity for radical evil. (During Hitler's
first visit to Rome, for example, the Holy Father rather ostentatiously
took himself out of town to the papal retreat at Castelgandolfo.) However, this ailing and weak pope was continually outpointed, throughout
the 1930s, by his secretary of state, Eugenio Pacelli. We have good reason to think that at least one papal encyclical, expressing at least a modi-
cum of concern about the maltreatment of Europe's Jews, was readied
by His Holiness but suppressed by Pacelli, who had another strategy in
mind. We now know Pacelli as Pope Pius XII, who succeeded to the office after the death of his former superior in February 1939. Four days
after his election by the College of Cardinals, His Holiness composed
the following letter to Berlin:

> To the Illustrious Herr Adolf Hitler, Fuhrer and Chancellor of
> the German Reich! Here at the beginning of Our Pontificate
> We wish to assure you that We remain devoted to the spiritual
> welfare of the German people entrusted to your leadership. . . .
> During the many years We spent in Germany, We did all in Our
> power to establish harmonious relations between Church and
> State. Now that the responsibilities of Our pastoral function have
> increased Our opportunities, how much more ardently do We
> pray to reach that goal. May the prosperity of the German people

and their progress in every domain come, with God's help, to fruition!

Within six years of this evil and fatuous message, the once prosperous and civilized people of Germany could gaze around themselves and see hardly one brick piled upon another, as the godless Red Army swept toward Berlin. But I mention this conjuncture for another reason. Believers are supposed to hold that the pope is the vicar of Christ on earth, and the keeper of the keys of Saint Peter. They are of course free to believe this, and to believe that god decides when to end the tenure of one pope or (more important) to inaugurate the tenure of another. This would involve believing in the death of an anti-Nazi pope, and the accession of a pro-Nazi one, as a matter of divine will, a few months before Hitler's invasion of Poland and the opening of the Second World War. Studying that war, one can perhaps accept that 25 percent of the SS were practicing Catholics and that no Catholic was ever even threatened with excommunication for participating in war crimes. (Joseph Goebbels *was* excommunicated, but that was earlier on, and he had after all brought it on himself for the offense of marrying a Protestant.) Human beings and institutions are imperfect, to be sure. But there could be no clearer or more vivid proof that holy institutions are man-made.

The collusion continued even after the war, as wanted Nazi criminals were spirited to South America by the infamous "rat line." It was the Vatican itself, with its ability to provide passports, documents, money, and contacts, which organized the escape network and also the necessary shelter and succor at the other end. Bad as this was in itself, it also involved another collaboration with extreme-right dictatorships in the Southern Hemisphere, many of them organized on the fascist model. Fugitive torturers and murderers like Klaus Barbie often found themselves second careers as servants of these regimes, which until they began to collapse in the last decades of the twentieth century had also enjoyed a steady relationship of support from the local Catholic clergy. The connection of the church to fascism and Nazism actually outlasted the Third Reich itself.

Many Christians gave their lives to protect their fellow creatures in this midnight of the century, but the chance that they did so on orders from any priesthood is statistically almost negligible. This is why we revere the memory of the very few believers, like Dietrich Bonhoeffer and Martin Niemoller, who acted in accordance only with the dictates of conscience. The papacy took until the 1980s to find a candidate for sainthood in the context of the "final solution," and even then could only identify a rather ambivalent priest who—after a long record of political anti-Semitism in Poland—had apparently behaved nobly in Auschwitz. An earlier nominee—a simple Austrian named Franz Jagerstatter—was unfortunately unqualified. He had indeed refused to join Hitler's army on the grounds that he was under higher orders to love his neighbor, but while in prison facing execution had been visited by his confessors who told him that he ought to be obeying the law. The secular left in Europe comes far better out of the anti-Nazi struggle than that, even if many of its adherents believed that there was a worker's paradise beyond the Ural Mountains.

It is often forgotten that the Axis triad included another member— the Empire of Japan—which had not only a religious person as its head of state, but an actual deity. If the appalling heresy of believing that Emperor Hirohito was god was ever denounced from any German or Italian pulpit or by any prelate, I have been unable to discover the fact. In the sacred name of this ridiculously overrated mammal, huge areas of China and Indochina and the Pacific were plundered and enslaved. In his name, too, millions of indoctrinated Japanese were martyred and sacrificed. So imposing and hysterical was the cult of this god-king that it was believed that the whole Japanese people might resort to suicide if his person was threatened at the end of the war. It was accordingly decided that he could "stay on," but that he would henceforward have to claim to be an emperor only, and perhaps somewhat divine, but not strictly speaking a god. This deference to the strength of religious opinion must involve the admission that faith and worship can make people behave very badly indeed.

THUS, THOSE WHO INVOKE "SECULAR" TYRANNY in contrast to religion are hoping that we will forget two things: the connection between the Christian churches and fascism, and the capitulation of the churches to National Socialism. This is not just my assertion: it has been admitted by the religious authorities themselves. Their poor conscience on the point is illustrated by a piece of bad faith that one still has to combat. On religious Web sites and in religious propaganda, you may come across a statement purportedly made by Albert Einstein in 1940:

> Being a lover of freedom, when the revolution came to Germany, I looked to the universities to defend it, knowing that they had always boasted of their devotion to the cause of truth; but, no, the universities immediately were silenced. Then I looked to the great editors of the newspapers whose flaming editorials in days gone by had proclaimed their love of freedom; but they, like the universities were silenced in a few short weeks. . . . Only the Church stood squarely across the path of Hitler's campaign for suppressing truth. I never had any special interest in the Church before, but now I feel a great affection and admiration because the Church alone has had the courage and persistence to stand for intellectual truth and moral freedom. I am forced thus to confess that what I once despised I now praise unreservedly.

Originally printed in *Time* magazine (without any verifiable attribution), this supposed statement was once cited in a national broadcast by the famous American Catholic spokesman and cleric Fulton Sheen, and remains in circulation. As the analyst William Waterhouse has pointed out, it does not sound like Einstein at all. Its rhetoric is too florid, for one thing. It makes no mention of the persecution of the Jews. And it makes the cool and careful Einstein look silly, in that he claims to have once "despised" something in which he also "never had any special interest." There is another difficulty, in that the statement never appears in any anthology of Einstein's written or spoken remarks. Eventually, Waterhouse was able to find an unpublished letter in the Einstein Archives in Jerusalem, in which the old man in 1947 complained of having once made a remark praising some German "churchmen" (*not* "churches") which had since been exaggerated beyond all recognition.

Anyone wanting to know what Einstein *did* say in the early days of Hitler's barbarism can easily look him up. For example:

> I hope that healthy conditions will soon supervene in Germany and that in future her great men like Kant and Goethe will not merely be commemorated from time to time but that the principles which they taught will also prevail in public life and in the general consciousness.

It is quite clear from this that he put his "faith," as always, in the Enlightenment tradition. Those who seek to misrepresent the man who gave us an alternative theory of the cosmos (as well as those who remained silent or worse while his fellow Jews were being deported and destroyed) betray the prickings of their bad consciences.

Turning to Soviet and Chinese Stalinism, with its exorbitant cult of personality and depraved indifference to human life and human rights, one cannot expect to find too much overlap with preexisting religions. For one thing, the Russian Orthodox Church had been the main prop of the czarist autocracy, while the czar himself was regarded as the formal head of the faith and something a little more than merely human. In China, the Christian churches were overwhelm-ingly identified with the foreign "concessions" extracted by imperial powers, which were among the principal causes of the revolution in the first place. This is not to explain or excuse the killing of priests and nuns and the desecration of churches—any more than one should excuse the burning of churches and the murder of clergy in Spain during the struggle of the Spanish republic against Catholic fascism—but the long association of religion with corrupt secular power has meant that most nations have to go through at least one anticlerical phase, from Cromwell through Henry VIII to the French Revolution to the Risorgimento, and in the conditions of warfare and collapse that obtained in Russia and China these interludes were exceptionally brutal ones. (I might add, though, that no serious Christian ought to hope for the restoration of religion *as it was* in either country: the church in Russia was the protector of serfdom and the author of anti-Jewish pogroms, and in China the missionary and the tight-fisted trader and concessionaire were partners in crime.)

Lenin and Trotsky were certainly convinced atheists who believed that illusions in religion could be destroyed by acts of policy and that in the meantime the obscenely rich holdings of the church could be seized and nationalized. In the Bolshevik ranks, as among the Jacobins of 1789, there were also those who saw the revolution as a sort of alternative religion, with connections to myths of redemption and messianism. For Joseph Stalin, who had trained to be a priest in a seminary in Georgia, the whole thing was ultimately a question of power. "How many divisions," he famously and stupidly inquired, "has the pope?" (The true answer to his boorish sarcasm was, "More than you think.") Stalin then pedantically repeated the papal routine of making science conform to dogma, by insisting that the shaman and charlatan Trofim Lysenko had disclosed the key to genetics and promised extra harvests of specially inspired vegetables. (Millions of innocents died of gnawing internal pain as a consequence of this "revelation.") This Caesar unto whom all things were dutifully rendered took care, as his regime became a more nationalist and statist one, to maintain at least a puppet church that could attach its traditional appeal to his. This was especially true during the Second World War, when the "Internationale" was dropped as the Russian anthem and replaced by the sort of hymnal propaganda that had defeated Bonaparte in 1812 (this at a time when "volunteers" from several European fascist states were invading Russian territory under the holy banner of a crusade against "godless" Communism). In a much-neglected passage of *Animal Farm*, Orwell allowed Moses the raven, long the croaking advocate of a heaven beyond the skies, to return to the farm and preach to the more credulous creatures after Napoleon had vanquished Snowball. His analogy to Stalin's manipulation of the Russian Orthodox Church was, as ever, quite exact. (The postwar Polish Stalinists had recourse to much the same tactic, legalizing a Catholic front organization called Pax Christi and giving it seats in the Warsaw parliament, much to the delight of fellow-traveling Catholic Communists such as Graham Greene.) Antireligious propaganda in the Soviet Union was of the most banal materialist sort: a shrine to Lenin often had stained glass while in the official museum of atheism there was testimony offered by a Russian astronaut, who had seen no god in outer space. This idiocy expressed at least as much contempt for the gullible yokels as any wonder-working icon. As the great laureate of Poland, Czeslaw Milosz, phrased it in his antitotalitarian classic *The Captive Mind*, first published in 1953:

> I have known many Christians—Poles, Frenchmen, Spaniards—
> who were strict Stalinists in the field of politics but who retained
> certain inner reservations, believing God would make corrections
> once the bloody sentences of the all-mighties of History were car-
> ried out. They pushed their reasoning rather far. They argue that
> history develops according to immutable laws that exist by the
> will of God; one of these laws is the class struggle; the twentieth
> century marks the victory of the proletariat, which is led in its
> struggle by the Communist Party; Stalin, the leader of the Com-

munist Party, fulfils the law of history, or in other words acts by the will of God, therefore one must obey him. Mankind can be renewed only on the Russian pattern; that is why no Christian can oppose the one—cruel, it is true—idea which will create a new kind of man over the entire planet. Such reasoning is often used by clerics who are Party tools. "Christ is a new man. The new man is the Soviet man. Therefore Christ is a Soviet man!" said Justinian Marina, the Rumanian patriarch.

Men like Marina were hateful and pathetic no doubt, and hateful and pathetic simultaneously, but this is no worse in principle than the numberless pacts made between church and empire, church and monarchy, church and fascism, and church and state, all of them justified by the need of the faithful to make temporal alliances for the sake of "higher" goals, while rendering unto Caesar (the word from which "czar" is derived) even if he is "godless."

A political scientist or anthropologist would have little difficulty in recognizing what the editors and contributors of *The God That Failed* put into such immortal secular prose: Communist absolutists did not so much negate religion, in societies that they well understood were saturated with faith and superstition, as seek to *replace* it. The solemn elevation of infallible leaders who were a source of endless bounty and blessing; the permanent search for heretics and schismatics; the mummification of dead leaders as icons and relics; the lurid show trials that elicited incredible confessions by means of torture . . . none of this was very difficult to interpret in traditional terms. Nor was the hysteria during times of plague and famine, when the authorities unleashed a mad search for any culprit but the real one. (The great Doris Lessing once told me that she left the Communist Party when she discovered that Stalin's inquisitors had plundered the museums of Russian Orthodoxy and czarism and reemployed the old instruments of torture.) Nor was the ceaseless invocation of a "Radiant Future," the arrival of which would one day justify all crimes and dissolve all petty doubts.

"Extra ecclesiam, nulla salus," as the older faith used to say. "Within the revolution anything," as Fidel Castro was fond of remarking. "Outside the revolution—nothing." Indeed, within Castro's periphery there evolved a bizarre mutation known oxymoronically as "liberation theology," where priests and even some bishops adopted "alternative" liturgies enshrining the ludicrous notion that Jesus of Nazareth was really a dues-paying socialist. For a combination of good and bad reasons (Archbishop Romero of El Salvador was a man of courage and principle, in the way that some Nicaraguan "base community" clerics were not), the papacy put this down as a heresy. Would that it could have condemned fascism and Nazism in the same unhesitating and unambiguous tones.

In a very few cases, such as Albania, Communism tried to extirpate religion completely and to proclaim an entirely atheist state. This only led to even more extreme cults of mediocre human beings, such as the dictator Enver Hoxha, and to secret baptisms and ceremonies that proved the utter alienation of the common people from the regime. There is nothing in modern secular argument that even hints at any ban on religious observance. Sigmund Freud was quite correct to describe the religious impulse, in *The Future of an Illusion*, as essentially ineradicable until or unless the human species can conquer its fear of death and its tendency to wish-thinking. Neither contingency seems very probable. All that the totalitarians have demonstrated is that the religious impulse—the need to worship—can take even more monstrous forms if it is repressed. This might not necessarily be a compliment to our worshipping tendency.

In the early months of this century, I made a visit to North Korea. Here, contained within a hermetic quadrilateral of territory enclosed either by sea or by near-impenetrable frontiers, is a land entirely given over to adulation. Every waking moment of the citizen—the subject—is consecrated to praise of the Supreme Being and his Father. Every schoolroom resounds with it, every film and opera and play is devoted to it, every radio and television transmission is given up to it.

So are all books and magazines and newspaper articles, all sporting events and all workplaces. I used to wonder what it would be like to have to sing everlasting praises, and now I know. Nor is the devil forgotten: the unsleeping evil of outsiders and unbelievers is warded off with a perpetual vigilance, which includes daily moments of ritual in the workplace in which hatred of the "other" is inculcated. The North Korean state was born at about the same time that *Nineteen Eighty-Four* was published, and one could almost believe that the holy father of the state, Kim Il Sung, was given a copy of the novel and asked if he could make it work in practice. Yet even Orwell did not dare to have it said that "Big Brother's" birth was attended by miraculous signs and portents—such as birds hailing the glorious event by singing in human words. Nor did the Inner Party of Airstrip One/Oceania spend billions of scarce dollars, at a time of horrific famine, to prove that the ludicrous mammal Kim Il Sung and his pathetic mammal son, Kim Jong Il, were two incarnations of the same person. (In this version of the Arian heresy so much condemned by Athanasius, North Korea is unique in having a dead man as head of state: Kim Jong Il is the head of the party and the army but the presidency is held in perpetuity by his deceased father, which makes the country a necrocracy or mausolocracy as well as a regime that is only one figure short of a Trinity.) The afterlife is not mentioned in North Korea, because the idea of a defection in any direction is very strongly discouraged, but as against that it is not claimed that the two Kims will continue to dominate you after you are dead. Students of the subject can easily see that what we have in North Korea is not so much an extreme form of Communism—the term is hardly mentioned amid the storms of ecstatic dedication—as a debased yet refined form of Confucianism and ancestor worship.

When I left North Korea, which I did with a sense of mingled relief, outrage, and pity so strong that I can still summon it, I was leaving a totalitarian state and also a religious one. I have since talked with many of the brave people who are trying to undermine this atrocious system from within and without. Let me admit at once that some of the bravest of these resisters are fundamentalist Christian anti-Communists. One of these courageous men gave an interview not long ago in which he was honest enough to say that he had a difficult time preaching the idea of a savior to the half-starved and terrified few who had managed to escape their prison-state. The whole idea of an infallible and all-powerful redeemer, they said, struck them as a bit too familiar. A bowl of rice and some exposure to some wider culture, and a little relief from the hideous din of compulsory enthusiasm, would be the most they could ask for, for now. Those who are fortunate enough to get as far as South Korea, or the United States, may find themselves confronted with yet another Messiah. The jailbird and tax evader Sun Myung Moon, undisputed head of the "Unification Church" and major contributor to the extreme right in the United States, is one of the patrons of the "intelligent design" racket. A leading figure of this so-called movement, and a man who never fails to award his god-man guru his proper name of "Father," is Jonathan Wells, the author of a laughable antievolutionist diatribe entitled *The Icons of Evolution.* As Wells himself touchingly put it, "Father's words, my studies, and my prayers convinced me that I should devote my life to destroying Darwinism, just as many of my fellow Unificationists had already devoted their lives to destroying Marxism. When Father chose me (along with about a dozen other seminary graduates) to enter a Ph.D. program in 1978, I welcomed the opportunity to do battle." Mr. Wells's book is unlikely even to rate a footnote in the history of piffle, but having seen "fatherhood" at work in both of the two Koreas, I have an idea of what the "Burned-Over District" of upstate New York must have looked and felt like when the believers had everything their own way.

Religion even at its meekest has to admit that what it is proposing is a "total" solution, in which faith must be to some extent blind, and in which all aspects of the private and public life must be submitted to a permanent higher supervision. This constant surveillance and con-

tinual subjection, usually reinforced by fear in the shape of infinite
vengeance, does not invariably bring out the best mammalian characteristics. It is certainly true that emancipation from religion does not
always produce the best mammal either. To take two salient examples: one of the greatest and most enlightening scientists of the twentieth century, J. D. Bernal, was an abject votary of Stalin and wasted
much of his life defending the crimes of his leader. H. L. Mencken,
one of the best satirists of religion, was too keen on Nietzsche and
advocated a form of "social Darwinism" which included eugenics and
a contempt for the weak and sick. He also had a soft spot for Adolf
Hitler and wrote an unpardonably indulgent review of *Mein Kampf*.
Humanism has many crimes for which to apologize. But it can apologize for them, and also correct them, in its own terms and without
having to shake or challenge the basis of any unalterable system of
belief. Totalitarian systems, whatever outward form they may take,
are fundamentalist and, as we would now say, "faith-based."

In her magisterial examination of the totalitarian phenomenon,
Hannah Arendt was not merely being a tribalist when she gave a special place to anti-Semitism. The idea that a group of people—whether
defined as a nation or as a religion—could be condemned for all time
and without the possibility of an appeal was (and is) essentially a totalitarian one. It is horribly fascinating that Hitler began by being a
propagator of this deranged prejudice, and that Stalin ended by being
both a victim and an advocate of it. But the virus was kept alive for
centuries by religion. Saint Augustine positively relished the myth of
the Wandering Jew, and the exile of the Jews in general, as a proof of
divine justice. The Orthodox Jews are not blameless here. By claiming to be "chosen" in a special exclusive covenant with the Almighty,
they invited hatred and suspicion and evinced their own form of racism. However, it was the secular Jews above all who were and are
hated by the totalitarians, so no question of "blaming the victim" need
arise. The Jesuit order, right up until the twentieth century, refused
by statute to admit a man unless he could prove that he had no "Jew-

ish blood" for several generations. The Vatican preached that all Jews inherited the responsibility for deicide. The French church aroused the mob against Dreyfus and "the intellectuals." Islam has never forgiven "the Jews" for encountering Muhammad and deciding that he was not the authentic messenger. For emphasizing tribe and dynasty and racial provenance in its holy books, religion must accept the responsibility for transmitting one of mankind's most primitive illusions down through the generations.

The connection between religion, racism, and totalitarianism is also to be found in the other most hateful dictatorship of the twentieth century: the vile system of apartheid in South Africa. This was not just the ideology of a Dutch-speaking tribe bent on extorting forced labor from peoples of a different shade of pigmentation, it was also a form of Calvinism in practice. The Dutch Reformed Church preached as a dogma that black and white were biblically forbidden to mix, let alone to coexist in terms of equality. Racism is totalitarian by definition: it marks the victim in perpetuity and denies him, or her, the right to even a rag of dignity or privacy, even the elemental right to make love or marry or produce children with a loved one of the "wrong" tribe, without having love nullified by law . . . And this was the life of millions living in the "Christian West" in our own time. The ruling National Party, which was also heavily infected with anti-Semitism and had taken the Nazi side in the Second World War, relied on the ravings of the pulpit to justify its own blood myth of a Boer "Exodus" that awarded it exclusive rights in a "promised land." As a result, an Afrikaner permutation of Zionism created a backward and despotic state, in which the rights of all other peoples were abolished and in which eventually the survival of Afrikaners themselves was threatened by corruption, chaos, and brutality. At that point the bovine elders of the church had a revelation which allowed the gradual abandonment of apartheid. But this can never permit forgiveness for the evil that religion did while it felt strong enough to do so. It is to the credit of many secular Christians and Jews, and many atheist and agnostic militants of the African National Congress, that South African society was saved from complete barbarism and implosion.

The last century saw many other improvisations on the old idea of a dictatorship that could take care of more than merely secular or everyday problems. These ranged from the mildly offensive and insulting—the Greek Orthodox Church baptized the usurping military junta of 1967, with its eyeshades and steel helmets, as "a Greece for Christian Greeks"—to the all-enslaving "Angka" of the Khmer Rouge in Cambodia, which sought its authority in prehistoric temples and legends. (Their sometime friend and sometime rival, the aforementioned King Sihanouk, who took a playboy's refuge under the protection of the Chinese Stalinists, was also adept at being a god-king when it suited him.) In between lies the shah of Iran, who claimed to be "the shadow of god" as well as "the light of the Aryans," and who repressed the secular opposition and took extreme care to be represented as the guardian of the Shiite shrines. His megalomania was succeeded by one of its close cousins, the Khomeinist heresy of the *velayet-i-faqui*, or total societal control by mullahs (who also display their deceased leader as their founder, and assert that his holy words can never be rescinded). At the very extreme edge can be found the primeval puritanism of the Taliban, which devoted itself to discovering new things to forbid (everything from music to recycled paper, which might contain a tiny fleck of pulp from a discarded Koran) and new methods of punishment (the burial alive of homosexuals). The alternative to these grotesque phenomena is not the chimera of secular dictatorship, but the defense of secular pluralism and of the right *not* to believe or be compelled to believe. This defense has now become an urgent and inescapable responsibility: a matter of survival.

Chapter Eighteen

A Finer Tradition: The Resistance of the Rational

I am thus one of the very few examples, in this country, of one who has, not thrown off religious belief, but never had it. . . . This point in my early education had however incidentally one bad consequence deserving notice. In giving me an opinion contrary to that of the world, my father thought it necessary to give it as one which could not prudently be avowed to the world. This lesson of keeping my thoughts to myself, at that early age, was attended with some moral disadvantages."

—JOHN STUART MILL, *AUTOBIOGRAPHY*

Le silence éternel de ces espaces infinis m'effraie.
(The eternal silence of these infinite spaces makes me afraid.)

—BLAISE PASCAL, *PENSÉES*

The book of Psalms can be deceiving. The celebrated opening of psalm 121, for example—"I shall lift up mine eyes unto the hills, from whence cometh my help"—is rendered in English as a statement but in the original takes the form of a question: where is the help coming from? (Never fear: the glib answer is that the believers will be immune from all danger and suffering.) Whoever the psalmist turns out to have been, he was obviously pleased enough with the polish and address of psalm 14 to repeat it virtually word for word as

253

psalm 53. Both versions begin with the identical statement that "The fool has said in his heart, there is no God." For some reason, this null remark is considered significant enough to be recycled throughout all religious apologetics. All that we can tell for sure from the otherwise meaningless assertion is that unbelief—not just heresy and backsliding but unbelief—must have been known to exist even in that remote epoch. Given the then absolute rule of unchallenged and brutally punitive faith, it would perhaps have been a fool who did *not* keep this conclusion buried deep inside himself, in which case it would be interesting to know how the psalmist knew it was there. (Dissidents used to be locked up in Soviet lunatic asylums for "reformist delusions," it being quite naturally and reasonably assumed that anybody mad enough to propose reforms had lost all sense of self-preservation.)

Our species will never run out of fools but I dare say that there have been at least as many credulous idiots who professed faith in god as there have been dolts and simpletons who concluded otherwise. It might be immodest to suggest that the odds rather favor the intelligence and curiosity of the atheists, but it is the case that some humans have always noticed the improbability of god, the evil done in his name, the likelihood that he is man-made, and the availability of less harmful alternative beliefs and explanations. We cannot know the names of all these men and women, because they have in all times and all places been subject to ruthless suppression. For the identical reason, nor can we know how many ostensibly devout people were secretly unbelievers. As late as the eighteenth and nineteenth centuries, in relatively free societies such as Britain and the United States, unbelievers as secure and prosperous as James Mill and Benjamin Franklin felt it advisable to keep their opinions private. Thus, when we read of the glories of "Christian" devotional painting and architecture, or "Islamic" astronomy and medicine, we are talking about advances of civilization and culture—some of them anticipated by Aztecs and Chinese—that have as much to do with "faith" as their predecessors had to do with human sacrifice and imperialism. And we have no means of knowing, except in a very few special cases, how many of these architects and painters and scientists were preserving their innermost thoughts from the scrutiny of the godly. Galileo might have been unmolested in his telescopic work if he had not been so unwise as to admit that it had cosmological implications.

Doubt, skepticism, and outright unbelief have always taken the same essential form as they do today. There were always observations on the natural order which took notice of the absence or needlessness of a prime mover. There were always shrewd comments on the way in which religion reflected human wishes or human designs. It was never that difficult to see that religion was a cause of hatred and conflict, and that its maintenance depended upon ignorance and superstition. Satirists and poets, as well as philosophers and men of science, were capable of pointing out that if triangles had gods their gods would have three sides, just as Thracian gods had blond hair and blue eyes.

The original collision between our reasoning faculties and any form of organized faith, though it must have occurred before in the minds of many, is probably exemplified in the trial of Socrates in 399 BC. It does not matter at all to me that we have no absolute certainty that Socrates even existed. The records of his life and his words are secondhand, almost but not quite as much as are the books of the Jewish and Christian Bible and the hadiths of Islam. Philosophy, however, has no need of such demonstrations, because it does not deal in "revealed" wisdom. As it happens, we have some plausible accounts of the life in question (a stoic soldier somewhat resembling Schweik in appearance; a shrewish wife; a tendency to attacks of catalepsy), and these will do. On the word of Plato, who was perhaps an eyewitness, we may accept that during a time of paranoia and tyranny in Athens, Socrates was indicted for godlessness and knew his life to be forfeit. The noble words of the *Apology* also make it plain that he did not care to save himself by affirming, like a later man faced with an inquisition, anything that he did not believe. Even though he was not in fact an atheist, he was quite correctly considered unsound for his advocacy of free thought and unrestricted inquiry, and his refusal to give assent to any dogma. All he really "knew," he said, was the extent of his own ignorance. (This to me is still the definition of an educated person.) According to Plato, this great Athenian was quite content to observe the customary rites of the city, testified that the Delphic oracle had instructed him to become a philosopher, and on his deathbed, condemned to swallow the hemlock, spoke of a possible afterlife in which those who had thrown off the world by mental exercise might yet continue to lead an existence of pure mind. But even then, he remembered as always to qualify himself by adding that this might well not be the case. The question, as always, was worth pursuing. Philosophy begins where religion ends, just as by analogy chemistry begins where alchemy runs out, and astonomy takes the place of astrology.

From Socrates, also, we can learn how to argue two things that are of the highest importance. The first is that conscience is innate. The second is that the dogmatic faithful can easily be outpointed and satirized by one who pretends to take their preachings at face value.

Socrates believed that he had a daimon, or oracle, or internal guide, whose good opinion was worth having. Everybody but the psychopath has this feeling to a greater or lesser extent. Adam Smith described a permanent partner in an inaudible conversation, who acted as a check and scrutineer. Sigmund Freud wrote that the voice of reason was small, but very persistent. C. S. Lewis tried to prove too much by opining that the presence of a conscience indicated the divine spark. Modern vernacular describes conscience—not too badly—as whatever it is that makes us behave well when nobody is looking. At any event, Socrates absolutely refused to say anything of which he was not morally sure. He would sometimes, if he suspected himself of casuistry or crowd-pleasing, break off in the very middle of a speech. He told his judges that at no point in his closing plea had his "oracle" hinted at him to stop. Those who believe that the existence of conscience is a proof of a godly design are advancing an argument that simply cannot be disproved because there is no evidence for or against it. The case of Socrates, however, demonstrates that men and women of real conscience will often have to assert it against faith.

He was facing death but had the option, even if convicted, of a lesser sentence if he chose to plead for it. In almost insulting tones, he offered to pay a negligible fine instead. Having thus given his angry judges no alternative but the supreme penalty, he proceeded to explain why murder at their hands was meaningless to him. Death had no terror: it was either perpetual rest or the chance of immortality—and even of communion with great Greeks like Orpheus and Homer who had predeceased him. In such a happy case, he observed drily, one might even wish to die and die again. It need not matter to us that the Delphic oracle is no more, and that Orpheus and Homer are mythical. The point is that Socrates was mocking his accusers in their own terms, saying in effect: I do not know for certain about death and the gods—but I am as certain as I can be that *you* do not know, either.

Some of the antireligious effect of Socrates and his gentle but relentless questioning can be gauged from a play that was written and performed in his own lifetime. *The Clouds*, composed by Aristophanes, features a philosopher named Socrates who keeps up a school of skepticism. A nearby farmer manages to come up with all the usual dull questions asked by the faithful. For one thing, if there is no Zeus, who brings the rain to water the crops? Inviting the man to use his head for a second, Socrates points out that if Zeus could make it rain, there would or could be rain from cloudless skies. Since this does not happen, it might be wiser to conclude that the clouds are the cause of the rainfall. All right then, says the farmer, who moves the clouds into position? That must surely be Zeus. Not so, says Socrates, who explains about winds and heat. Well in that case, replies the old rustic, where does the lightning come from, to punish liars and other wrongdoers? The lightning, it is gently pointed out to him, does not seem to discriminate between the just and the unjust. Indeed, it has often been noticed to strike the temples of Olympian Zeus himself. This is enough to win the farmer over, though he later recants his impiety and burns down the school with Socrates inside it. Many are the free-thinkers who have gone the same way, or escaped very narrowly. All major confrontations over the right to free thought, free speech, and free inquiry have taken the same form—of a religious attempt to assert the literal and limited mind over the ironic and inquiring one.

In essence, the argument with faith begins and ends with Socrates, and you may if you wish take the view that the city prosecutors did right in protecting Athenian youth from his troublesome speculations. However, it cannot be argued that he brought much science to bear against superstition. One of his prosecutors alleged that he had called the sun a piece of stone and the moon a piece of earth (the latter of which would have been true), but Socrates turned aside the charge, saying that it was a problem for Anaxagoras. This Ionian philosopher had in fact been prosecuted earlier for saying that the sun was a red-hot piece of rock and the moon a piece of earth, but he was not as insightful as Leucippus and Democritus, who proposed that everything was made of atoms in perpetual motion. (Incidentally, it is also quite possible that Leucippus never existed, and nothing important depends on whether or not he actually did.) The important thing about the brilliant "atomist" school is that it regarded the question of first cause or origin as essentially irrelevant. At the time, this was as far as any mind could reasonably go.

This left the problem of the "gods" unresolved. Epicurus, who took up the theory of Democritus concerning atoms, could not quite disbelieve in "their" existence, but he did find it impossible to convince himself that the gods played any role in human affairs. For one thing, why would "they" bother with the tedium of human existence, let alone the tedium of human government? They avoid unnecessary pain, and humans are wise to do likewise. Thus there is nothing to be feared in death, and in the meantime all attempts to read the gods' intentions, such as studying the entrails of animals, are an absurd waste of time.

In some ways, the most attractive and the most charming of the founders of antireligion is the poet Lucretius, who lived in the first century before Christ and admired the work of Epicurus beyond measure. Reacting to a revival of ancient worship by the Emperor Augustus, he composed a witty and brilliant poem entitled *De Rerum Natura*, or "On the Nature of Things." This work was nearly destroyed by Christian fanatics in the Middle Ages, and only one printed manuscript survived, so we are fortunate even to know that a person writing in the time of Cicero (who first published the poem) and Julius Caesar had managed to keep alive the atomic theory. Lucretius anticipated David Hume in saying that the prospect of future annihilation was no worse than the contemplation of the nothingness from which one came, and also anticipated Freud in ridiculing the idea of prearranged burial rites and memorials, all of them expressing the vain and useless wish to be present in some way at one's own funeral. Following Aristophanes, he thought that the weather was its own explanation and that nature, "rid of all gods," did the work that foolish and self-centered people imagined to be divinely inspired, or directed at their puny selves:

> *Who can wheel all the starry spheres, and blow*
> *Over all land the fruitful warmth from above*
> *Be ready in all places and all times,*
> *Gather black clouds and shake the quiet sky*
> *With terrible thunder, to hurl down bolts which often*
> *Rattle his own shrines, to rage in the desert, retreating*
> *For target drill, so that his shafts can pass*
> *The guilty by, and slay the innocent?*

Atomism was viciously persecuted throughout Christian Europe for many centuries, on the not unreasonable ground that it offered a far better explanation of the natural world than did religion. But, like a tenuous thread of thought, the work of Lucretius managed to persist in a few learned minds. Sir Isaac Newton may have been a believer—in all sorts of pseudoscience as well as in Christianity—but when he came to set out his *Principia* he included ninety lines of *De Rerum Natura* in the early drafts. Galileo's 1623 volume *Saggiatore*, while it does not acknowledge Epicurus, was so dependent on his atomic theories that both its friends and its critics referred to it as an Epicurean book.

In view of the terror imposed by religion on science and scholarship throughout the early Christian centuries (Augustine maintained that the pagan gods did exist, but only as devils, and that the earth was less than six thousand years old) and the fact that most intelligent people found it prudent to make an outward show of conformity, one need not be surprised that the revival of philosophy was often originally expressed in quasi-devout terms. Those who followed the various schools of philosophy that were permitted in Andalusia during its brief flowering—a synthesis between Aristotelianism, Judaism, Christianity, and Islam—were permitted to speculate about duality in truth, and a possible balance between reason and revelation. This concept of "double truth" was advanced by supporters of Averroes but strongly opposed by the church for obvious reasons. Francis Bacon, writing during the reign of Queen Elizabeth, liked to say— perhaps following Tertullian's assertion that the greater the absurdity the stronger his belief in it—that faith is at its greatest when its teachings are least amenable to reason. Pierre Bayle, writing a few decades later, was fond of stating all the claims of reason against a given belief, only to add "so much the greater is the triumph of faith in nevertheless believing." We can be fairly sure that he did not do this merely in order to escape punishment. The time when irony would punish and confuse the literal and the fanatical was about to dawn.

But this was not to happen without many revenges and rearguard actions from the literal and the fanatical. For a brief but splendid time in the seventeenth century, the staunch little nation of Holland was the tolerant host of many freethinkers such as Bayle (who moved there to be safe) and René Descartes (who moved there for the same reason). It was also the birthplace, one year before the arraignment of Galileo by the Inquisition, of the great Baruch Spinoza, a son of the Spanish and Portuguese Jewry who had themselves originally emigrated to Holland to be free of persecution. On July 27, 1656, the elders of the Amsterdam synagogue made the following *cherem*, or damnation, or fatwa, concerning his work:

> With the judgment of the angels and of the saints we excommunicate, cut off, curse, and anathematize Baruch de Espinoza, with the consent of the elders and of all this holy congregation, in the presence of the holy books: by the 613 precepts which are written therein, with the anathema wherewith Joshua cursed Jericho, with the curse which Elisha laid upon the children, and with all the curses which are written in the law. Cursed be he by day and cursed be he by night. Cursed be he in sleeping and cursed be he in waking, cursed in going out and cursed in coming in. The Lord shall not pardon him, the wrath and fury of the Lord shall henceforth be kindled against this man, and shall lay upon him all the curses which are written in the book of the law. The Lord shall destroy his name under the sun, and cut him off for his undoing from all the tribes of Israel, with all the curses of the firmament which are written in the book of the law.

The multiple malediction concluded with an order requiring all Jews to avoid any contact with Spinoza, and to refrain on pain of punishment from reading "any paper composed or written by him." (Incidentally, "the curse which Elisha laid upon the children" refers to the highly elevating biblical story in which Elisha, annoyed by children who teased him for his baldness, called upon god to send some she-bears to rend the children limb from limb. Which, so says the story, the bears dutifully did. Perhaps Thomas Paine was not wrong in saying that he could not believe in any religion that shocked the mind of a child.)

The Vatican, and the Calvinist authorities in Holland, heartily approved of this hysterical Jewish condemnation and joined in the Europe-wide suppression of all Spinoza's work. Had the man not questioned the immortality of the soul, and called for the separation of church and state? Away with him! This derided heretic is now credited with the most original philosophical work ever done on the mind/body distinction, and his meditations on the human condition have provided more real consolation to thoughtful people than has any religion. Argument continues about whether Spinoza was an atheist: it now seems odd that we should have to argue as to whether pantheism is atheism or not. In its own expressed terms it is actually theistic, but Spinoza's definition of a god made manifest throughout the natural world comes very close to defining a *religious* god out of existence. And if there is a pervasive, preexisting cosmic deity, who is part of what he creates, then there is no space left for a god who intervenes in human affairs, let alone for a god who takes sides in vicious hamlet-wars between different tribes of Jews and Arabs. No text can have been written or inspired by him, for one thing, or can be the special property of one sect or tribe. (One recalls the question that was asked by the Chinese when the first Christian missionaries made their appearance. If god has revealed himself, how is it that he has allowed so many centuries to elapse before informing the Chinese? "Seek knowledge even if it is in China," said the Prophet Muhammad, unconsciously revealing that the greatest civilization in the world at that time was on the very outer rim of his awareness.) As with Newton and Galileo building on Democritus and Epicurus, we find Spinoza projected forward into the mind of Einstein, who answered a question from a rabbi by stating firmly that he believed only in "Spinoza's god," and not at all in a god "who concerns himself with the fates and actions of human beings."

Spinoza de-Judaized his name by changing it to Benedict, outlasted the Amsterdam anathema by twenty years, and died with extreme stoicism, always persisting in calm and rational conversation, as a consequence of the powdered glass that entered his lungs. His was a career devoted to the grinding and polishing of lenses for telescopes and medicine: an appropriate scientific activity for one who taught humans to see with greater acuity. "All our modern philosophers," wrote Heinrich Heine, "though often perhaps unconsciously, see through the glasses which Baruch Spinoza ground." Heine's poems were later to be thrown on a pyre by gibbering Nazi bully-boys who did not believe that even an assimilated Jew could have been a true German. The frightened, backward Jews who ostracized Spinoza had thrown away a pearl richer than all their tribe: the body of their bravest son was stolen after his death and no doubt subjected to other rituals of desecration.

Spinoza had seen some of this coming. In his correspondence he would write the word *Caute!* (Latin for "take care") and place a little rose underneath. This was not the only aspect of his work that was sub rosa: he gave a false name for the printer of his celebrated *Tractatus* and left the author's page blank. His prohibited work (much of which might not have survived his death if not for the bravery and initiative of a friend) continued to have a subterranean existence in the writing of others. In Pierre Bayle's 1697 critical *Dictionnaire* he earned the longest entry. Montesquieu's 1748 *Spirit of the Laws* was considered so dependent on Spinoza's writing that its author was compelled by the church authorities in France to repudiate this Jewish monster and to make a public statement announcing his belief in a (Christian) creator. The great French *Encyclopédie* that came to define the Enlightenment, edited by Denis Diderot and d'Alembert, contains an immense entry on Spinoza.

I do not wish to repeat the gross mistake that Christian apologists have made. They expended huge and needless effort to show that wise men who wrote before Christ were in effect prophets and prefigurations of his coming. (As late as the nineteenth century, William Ewart Gladstone covered reams of wasted paper trying to prove this about the ancient Greeks.) I have no right to claim past philosophers as putative ancestors of atheism. I do, however, have the right to point out that because of religious intolerance we cannot know what they really thought privately, and were very nearly prevented from learning what they wrote publicly. Even the relatively conformist Descartes, who found it advisable to live in the freer atmosphere of the Netherlands, proposed a few lapidary words for his own headstone: "He who hid well, lived well."

In the cases of Pierre Bayle and Voltaire, for example, it is not easy to determine whether they were seriously irreligious or not. Their method certainly tended to be irreverent and satirical, and no reader clinging to uncritical faith could come away from their works without having that faith severely shaken. These same works were the best-sellers of their time, and made it impossible for the newly literate classes to go on believing in things like the literal truth of the biblical stories. Bayle in particular caused a huge but wholesome uproar when he examined the deeds of David the supposed "psalmist" and showed them to be the career of an unscrupulous bandit. He also pointed out that it was absurd to believe that religious faith caused people to conduct themselves better, or that unbelief made them behave worse. A vast accumulation of observable experience testified to this common sense, and Bayle's delineation of it is the reason why he has been praised or blamed for oblique, surreptitious atheism. Yet he accompanied or bodyguarded this with many more orthodox affirmations, which probably allowed his successful work to enjoy a second edition. Voltaire balanced his own savage ridicule of religion with some devotional gestures, and smilingly proposed that his own tomb (how these men did rattle on about the view of their own funerals) be built so as to be half inside and half outside the church. But in one of his most celebrated defenses of civil liberty and the rights of conscience, Voltaire had also seen his client Jean Calas broken on the wheel with hammers, and then hanged, for the "offense" of trying to convert someone in his household to Protestantism. Not even an aristocrat like himself could be counted safe, as he knew from seeing the inside of the Bastille. Let us at least not fail to keep this in mind.

Immanuel Kant believed for a time that all the planets were populated and that these populations improved in character the farther
away they were. But even while beginning from this rather charm-
ingly limited cosmic base, he was able to make convincing arguments
against any theistic presentation that depended upon reason. He
showed that the old argument from design, then as now a perennial
favorite, might possibly be stretched to imply an architect but not a creator. He overthrew the cosmological proof of god—which suggested
that one's own existence must posit another necessary existence—by
saying that it only restated the ontological argument. And he undid
the ontological argument by challenging the simpleminded notion
that if god can be conceived as an idea, or stated as a predicate, he
must therefore possess the quality of existence. This traditional tripe
is accidentally overthrown by Penelope Lively in her much-garlanded
novel *Moon Tiger*. Describing her daughter Lisa as a "dull child," she
nonetheless delights in the infant's dim but imaginative questions:

> "Are there dragons?" she asked. I said that there were not. "Have
> there ever been?" I said all the evidence was to the contrary. "But
> if there is a word dragon," she said, "then once there must have
> been dragons."

Who has not protected an innocent from the disproof of such
ontology? But for the sake of pith, and since we do not have all our
lives to waste simply in growing up, I quote Bertrand Russell here:
"Kant objects that existence is *not* a predicate. A hundred thalers that
I merely imagine, he says, have all the same predicates as a hundred
real thalers." I have stated Kant's disproofs in reverse order so as to
notice the case, recorded by the Inquisition in Venice in 1573, of a man
named Matteo de Vincenti, who opined on the doctrine of the "real
presence" of Christ in the Mass that: "It's nonsense, having to believe
these things—they're stories. I would rather believe I had money in
my pocket." Kant did not know of this predecessor of his among the

common people, and when he switched to the more rewarding topic of ethics he may not have known that his "categorical imperative" had an echo of Rabbi Hillel's "Golden Rule." Kant's principle enjoins us to "act as if the maxim of your action were to become through your will a general natural law." In this summary of mutual interest and solidarity, there is no requirement for any enforcing or supernatural authority. And why should there be? Human decency is not derived from religion. It precedes it.

It is of great interest to see, in the period of the eighteenth-century Enlightenment, how many great minds thought alike, and intersected with each other, and also took great care to keep their opinions cautiously expressed, or confined as far as possible to a circle of educated sympathizers. One of my choice instances would be that of Benjamin Franklin, who, if he did not exactly discover electricity, was certainly one of those who helped uncover its principles and practical applications. Among the latter were the lightning rod, which was to decide forever the question of whether god intervened to punish us in sudden random flashes. There is no steeple or minaret now standing that does not boast one. Announcing his invention to the public, Franklin wrote:

> It has pleased God in his Goodness to Mankind, at length to discover to them the Means of Securing their Habitations and other Buildings from Mischief by Thunder and Lightning. The Method is this. . . .

He then goes on to elaborate the common household equipment—brass wire, a knitting needle, "a few small staples"—that is required to accomplish the miracle.

This shows perfect outward conformity with received opinion, but is embellished with a small yet obvious dig in the words "at length." You may choose to believe, of course, that Franklin sincerely meant every word of it, and desired people to believe that he credited the

Almighty with relenting after all these years and finally handing over the secret. But the echo of Prometheus, stealing the fire from the gods, is too plain to miss. And Private Prometheans in those days still had to be watchful. Joseph Priestley, the virtual discoverer of oxygen, had his Birmingham laboratory smashed by a Tory-inspired mob yelling "for Church and King," and had to take his Unitarian convictions across the Atlantic in order to begin work again. (Nothing is perfect in these accounts: Franklin took as strong an interest in Freemasonry as Newton had in alchemy, and even Priestley was a devotee of the phlogiston theory. Remember that we are examining the childhood of our species.)

Edward Gibbon, who was revolted by what he discovered about Christianity during the labor of his massive *Decline and Fall of the Roman Empire*, dispatched an early copy to David Hume, who warned him that there would be trouble, which there was. Hume received Benjamin Franklin as a guest in Edinburgh, and traveled to Paris to meet with the editors of the *Encyclopédie*. These sometimes flamboyantly irreligious men were at first disappointed when their careful Scottish guest remarked on the absence of atheists and therefore on the possible absence of such a thing as atheism. They might have liked him better if they had read his *Dialogue Concerning Natural Religion* a decade or so later.

Based on a Ciceronian dialogue, with Hume himself apparently (but cautiously) taking the part of Philo, the traditional arguments about the existence of god are qualified a little by the availability of more modern evidence and reasoning. Borrowing perhaps from Spinoza—much of whose own work was still only available at second hand—Hume suggested that the profession of belief in a perfectly simple and omnipresent supreme being was in fact a covert profession of atheism, because such a being could possess nothing that we could reasonably call a mind, or a will. Moreover, if "he" did chance to possess such attributes, then the ancient inquiry of Epicurus would still stand:

Is he willing to prevent evil but not able? Then is he impotent.
Is he able but not willing? Then is he malevolent. Is he both able
and willing? Whence then is evil?

Atheism cuts through this non-quandary like the razor of Ockham.
It is absurd, even for a believer, to imagine that god should owe him
an explanation. But a believer nonetheless takes on the impossible task
of interpreting the will of a person unknown, and thus brings these
essentially absurd questions upon himself. Let the assumption lapse,
though, and we shall see where we are and be able to apply our intelligence, which is all that we have. (To the inescapable question—where
do all the creatures come from?—Hume's answer anticipates Darwin
by saying that in effect they evolve: the efficient ones survive and the
inefficient ones die out.) At the close, he chose, as had Cicero, to split
the difference between the deist Cleanthes and the skeptic Philo. This
could have been playing it safe, as Hume tended to do, or it could have
represented the apparent appeal of deism in the age before Darwin.

Even the great Thomas Paine, a friend to Franklin and Jefferson, repudiated the charge of atheism that he was not afraid to invite. Indeed, he set out to expose the crimes and horrors of the Old
Testament, as well as the foolish myths of the New, as part of a vindication of god. No grand and noble deity, he asserted, should have
such atrocities and stupidities laid to his charge. Paine's *Age of Reason*
marks almost the first time that frank contempt for organized religion was openly expressed. It had a tremendous worldwide effect.
His American friends and contemporaries, partly inspired by him to
declare independence from the Hanoverian usurpers and their private
Anglican Church, meanwhile achieved an extraordinary and unprec-
edented thing: the writing of a democratic and republican constitution that made no mention of god and that mentioned religion only
when guaranteeing that it would always be separated from the state.
Almost all of the American founders died without any priest by their
bedside, as also did Paine, who was much pestered in his last hours by

religious hooligans who demanded that he accept Christ as his savior. Like David Hume, he declined all such consolation and his memory has outlasted the calumnious rumor that he begged to be reconciled with the church at the end. (The mere fact that such deathbed "repentances" were sought by the godly, let alone subsequently fabricated, speaks volumes about the bad faith of the faith-based.)

Charles Darwin was born within the lifetime of Paine and Jefferson and his work was eventually able to transcend the limitations of ignorance, concerning the origins of plants and animals and other phenomena, under which they had had to labor. But even Darwin, when he began his quest as a botanist and natural historian, was quite sure that he was acting in a way that was consistent with god's design. He had wanted to be a clergyman. And the more discoveries he made, the more he tried to "square" them with faith in a higher intelligence. Like Edward Gibbon, he anticipated a controversy upon publication, and (a bit less like Gibbon) he made some protective and defensive notes. In fact, he at first argued with himself very much as some of today's "intelligent design" boobies are wont to do. Faced with the unarguable facts of evolution, why not claim that those prove how much greater is god than we even thought he was? The discovery of natural laws "should exalt our notion of the power of the omniscient Creator." Not quite convinced by this in his own mind, Darwin feared that his first writings on natural selection would be the end of his reputation, equivalent to "confessing a murder." He also appreciated that, if he ever found adaptation conforming to environment, he would have to confess to something even more alarming: the absence of a first cause or grand design.

The symptoms of old-style between-the-lines encoded concealment are to be found throughout the first edition of *The Origin of Species*. The term "evolution" never appears, while the word "creation" is employed frequently. (Fascinatingly, his first 1837 notebooks were given the provisional title *The Transmutation of Species*, almost as if Darwin were employing the archaic language of alchemy.) The title page of the eventual *Origin* bore a comment, significantly drawn from the apparently respectable Francis Bacon, about the need to study not just the word of god but also his "work." In *The Descent of Man* Darwin felt able to push matters a little further, but still submitted to some editorial revisions by his devout and beloved wife Emma. Only in his autobiography, which was not intended for publication, and in some letters to friends, did he admit that he had no remaining belief. His "agnostic" conclusion was determined as much by his life as by his work: he had suffered many bereavements and could not reconcile these with any loving creator let alone with the Christian teaching concerning eternal punishment. Like so many people however brilliant, he was prone to that solipsism that either makes or breaks faith, and which imagines that the universe is preoccupied with one's own fate. This, however, makes his scientific rigor the more praiseworthy, and fit to be ranked with Galileo, since it did not arise from any intention but that of finding out the truth. It makes no difference that this intention included the false and disappointed expectation that that same truth would finally resound *ad majorem dei gloriam*.

After his death, Darwin too was posthumously insulted by fabrications from a hysterical Christian, who claimed that the great and honest and tormented investigator had been squinting at the Bible at the last. It took a little while to expose the pathetic fraud who had felt that this would be a noble thing to do.

WHEN ACCUSED OF SCIENTIFIC PLAGIARISM, of which he was quite probably guilty, Sir Isaac Newton made the guarded admission—which was itself plagiarized—that he had in his work had the advantage of "standing on the shoulders of giants." It would seem only minimally gracious, in the first decade of the twenty-first century, to concede the same. As and when I wish, I can use a simple laptop to acquaint myself with the life and work of Anaxagoras and Erasmus, Epicurus and Wittgenstein. Not for me the poring in the library by candlelight, the shortage of texts, or the difficulties of contact with like-minded persons in other ages or societies. And not for me (except when the telephone sometimes rings and I hear hoarse voices condemning me to death, or hell, or both) the persistent fear that something I write will lead to the extinction of my work, the exile or worse of my family, the eternal blackening of my name by religious frauds and liars, and the painful choice between recantation or death by torture. I enjoy a freedom and an access to knowledge that would have been unimaginable to the pioneers. Looking back down the perspective of time, I therefore cannot help but notice that the giants upon whom I depend, and upon whose massive shoulders I perch, were all of them forced to be a little weak in the crucial and highly (and poorly) evolved joints of their knees. Only one member of the giant and genius category ever truly spoke his mind without any apparent fear or excess of caution. I therefore cite Albert Einstein, so much misrepresented, once again. He is addressing a correspondent who is troubled by yet another of those many misrepresentations:

> It was, of course, a lie what you read about my religious convictions, a lie which is being systematically repeated. I do not believe in a personal God and I have never denied this but expressed it clearly. If something is in me which can be called religious then it is the unbounded admiration for the structure of the world so far as our science can reveal it.

Years later he answered another query by stating:

> I do not believe in the immortality of the individual, and I consider ethics to be an exclusively human concern with no superhuman authority behind it.

These words stem from a mind, or a man, who was rightly famed for his care and measure and scruple, and whose sheer genius had laid bare a theory that might, in the wrong hands, have obliterated not only this world but also its whole past and the very possibility of its future. He devoted the greater part of his life to a grand refusal of the role of a punitive prophet, preferring to spread the message of enlightenment and humanism. Decidedly Jewish, and exiled and defamed and persecuted as a consequence, he preserved what he could of ethical Judaism and rejected the barbaric mythology of the Pentateuch. We have more reason to be grateful to him than to all the rabbis who have ever wailed, or who ever will. (Offered the first presidency of the state of Israel, Einstein declined because of his many qualms about the way Zionism was tending. This was much to the relief of David Ben-Gurion, who had nervously asked his cabinet, "What are we going to do if he says 'yes'?")

Wreathed in the widow's weeds of grief, the greatest Victorian of all is said to have appealed to her favorite prime minister to ask if he could produce one unanswerable argument for the existence of god. Benjamin Disraeli hesitated briefly before his queen—the woman whom he had made "Empress of India"—and replied, "The Jews, Ma'am." It seemed to this worldly but superstitious political genius that the survival of the Jewish people, and their admirably stubborn adherence to their ancient rituals and narratives, showed the invisible hand at work. In fact, he was changing ships on a falling tide. Even as he spoke, the Jewish people were emerging from two different kinds of oppression. The first and most obvious was the ghettoization that had been imposed on them by ignorant and bigoted Christian authorities. This has been too well documented to need any elaboration from me. But the second oppression was self-imposed. Napoleon Bonaparte, for example, had with some reservations removed the discriminatory laws against Jews. (He may well have hoped for their financial support, but no matter.) Yet when his armies invaded Russia, the rabbis urged their flock to rally to the side of the very czar who had been defaming and flogging and fleecing and murdering them. Better this Jew-baiting despotism, they said, than even a whiff of the unholy French Enlightenment. This is why the silly, ponderous melodrama in that Amsterdam synagogue was and remains so important. Even in a country as broad-minded as Holland, the elders had preferred to make common cause with Christian anti-Semites and other obscurantists, rather than permit the finest of their number to use his own free intelligence.

When the walls of the ghettos fell, therefore, the collapse liberated the inhabitants from the rabbis as well as "the gentiles." There ensued a flowering of talent such as has seldom been seen in any epoch. A formerly stultified population proceeded to make immense contributions to medicine, science, law, politics, and the arts. The reverberations are still being felt: one need only instance Marx, Freud, Kafka, and Einstein, though Isaac Babel, Arthur Koestler, Billy Wilder, Lenny Bruce, Saul Bellow, Philip Roth, Joseph Heller, and countless others are also the product of this dual emancipation.

If one could nominate an absolutely tragic day in human history, it would be the occasion that is now commemorated by the vapid and annoying holiday known as "Hannukah." For once, instead of Christianity plagiarizing from Judaism, the Jews borrow shamelessly from Christians in the pathetic hope of a celebration that coincides with "Christmas," which is itself a quasi-Christian annexation, complete with burning logs and holly and mistletoe, of a pagan Northland solstice originally illuminated by the Aurora Borealis. Here is the terminus to which banal "multiculturalism" has brought us. But it was nothing remotely multicultural that induced Judah Maccabeus to reconsecrate the Temple in Jerusalem in 165 BC, and to establish the date which the soft celebrants of Hannukah now so emptily commemorate. The Maccabees, who founded the Hasmonean dynasty, were forcibly restoring Mosaic fundamentalism against the many Jews of Palestine and elsewhere who had become attracted by Hellenism. These true early multiculturalists had become bored by "the law," offended by circumcision, interested by Greek literature, drawn by the physical and intellectual exercises of the gymnasium, and rather adept at philosophy. They could feel the pull exerted by Athens, even if only by way of Rome and by the memory of Alexander's time, and were impatient with the stark fear and superstition mandated by the Pentateuch. They obviously seemed too cosmopolitan to the votaries of the old Temple—and it must have been easy to accuse them of "dual loyalty" when they agreed to have a temple of Zeus on the site where smoky and bloody altars used to propitiate the unsmiling deity of yore. At any rate, when the father of Judah Maccabeus saw a Jew about to make a Hellenic offering on the old altar, he lost no time in murdering him. Over the next few years of the Maccabean "revolt," many more assimilated Jews were slain, or forcibly circumcised, or both, and the women who had flirted with the new Hellenic dispensation suffered even worse. Since the Romans eventually preferred the violent and dogmatic Maccabees to the less militarized and fanatical Jews who had shone in their togas in the Mediterranean light, the scene was set for the uneasy collusion between the old-garb ultra-Orthodox Sanhedrin and the imperial governorate. This lugubrious relationship was eventually to lead to Christianity (yet another Jewish heresy) and thus ineluctably to the birth of Islam. We could have been spared the whole thing.

No doubt there would still have been much foolishness and solipsism. But the connection between Athens and history and humanity would not have been so sundered, and the Jewish people might have been the carriers of philosophy instead of arid monotheism, and the ancient schools and their wisdom would not have become prehistoric to us. I once sat in the Knesset office of the late Rabbi Meir Kahane, a vicious racist and demagogue among whose supporters the mad Dr. Baruch Goldstein and other violent Israeli settlers were to be found. Kahane's campaign against mixed marriages, and for the expulsion of all non-Jews from Palestine, had earned him the contempt of many Israelis and diaspora Jews, who compared his program to that of the Nuremberg laws in Germany. Kahane raved for a bit in response to this, saying that any Arab could remain if he converted to Judaism by a strictly *halacha* test (not a concession, admittedly, that Hitler would have permitted), but then became bored and dismissed his Jewish opponents as mere "Hellenized" riffraff. [To this day, the Orthodox Jewish curse word for a heretic or apostate is *apikoros*, meaning "follower of Epicurus."] And he was correct in a formal sense: his bigotry had little to do with "race" and everything to do with "faith." Sniffing this insanitary barbarian, I had a real pang about the world of light and color that we had lost so long ago, in the black-and-white nightmares of his dreary and righteous ancestors. The stench of Calvin and Torquemada and bin Laden came from the dank, hunched figure whose Kach Party goons patrolled the streets looking for Sabbath violations and unauthorized sexual contacts. Again to take the metaphor of the Burgess shale, here was a poisonous branch that should have been snapped off long ago, or allowed to die out, before it could infect any healthy growth with its junk DNA. But yet we still dwell in its unwholesome, life-killing shadow. And little Jewish children celebrate Hannukah, so as not to feel left out of the tawdry myths of Bethlehem, which are now being so harshly contested by the more raucous propaganda of Mecca and Medina.

Chapter Nineteen

In Conclusion:
The Need for a
New Enlightenment

The true value of a man is not determined by his possession, supposed or real, of Truth, but rather by his sincere exertion to get to the Truth. It is not possession of the Truth, but rather the pursuit of Truth by which he extends his powers and in which his ever-growing perfectibility is to be found. Possession makes one passive, indolent, and proud. If God were to hold all Truth concealed in his right hand, and in his left only the steady and diligent drive for Truth, albeit with the proviso that I would always and forever err in the process, and to offer me the choice, I would with all humility take the left hand.
—GOTTHOLD LESSING, *ANTI-GOEZE* (1778)

"The Messiah Is Not Coming—and He's Not Even Going to Call!"
—ISRAELI HIT TUNE IN 2001

T
he great Lessing put it very mildly in the course of his exchange of polemics with the fundamentalist preacher Goeze. And his becoming modesty made it seem as if he had, or could have, a choice in the matter. In point of fact, we do not have the option of "choosing" absolute truth, or faith. We only have the right to say,

of those who *do* claim to know the truth of revelation, that they are deceiving themselves and attempting to deceive—or to intimidate—others. Of course, it is better and healthier for the mind to "choose" the path of skepticism and inquiry in any case, because only by continual exercise of these faculties can we hope to achieve anything. Whereas religions, wittily defined by Simon Blackburn in his study of Plato's *Republic*, are merely "fossilized philosophies," or philosophy with the questions left out. To "choose" dogma and faith over doubt and experiment is to throw out the ripening vintage and to reach greedily for the Kool-Aid.

Thomas Aquinas once wrote a document on the Trinity and, modestly regarding it as one of his more finely polished efforts, laid it on the altar at Notre Dame so that god himself could scrutinize the work and perhaps favor "the Angelic doctor" with an opinion. (Aquinas here committed the same mistake as those who made nuns in convents cover their baths with canvas during ablutions: it was felt that god's gaze would be deflected from the undraped female forms by such a modest device, but forgotten that he could supposedly "see" anything, anywhere, at any time by virtue of his omniscience and omnipresence, and further forgotten that he could undoubtedly "see" through the walls and ceilings of the nunnery before being baffled by the canvas shield. One supposes that the nuns were actually being prevented from peering at their own bodies, or rather at one another's.)

However that may be, Aquinas later found that god indeed had given his treatise a good review—he being the only author ever to have claimed this distinction—and was discovered by awed monks and novices to be blissfully levitating around the interior of the cathedral. Rest assured that we have eyewitnesses for this event.

On a certain day in the spring of 2006, President Ahmadinejad of Iran, accompanied by his cabinet, made a procession to the site of a well between the capital city of Tehran and the holy city of Qum. This is said to be the cistern where the Twelfth or "occulted" or "hidden" Imam took refuge in the year 873, at the age of five, never to be seen again until his long-awaited and beseeched reappearance will astonish and redeem the world. On arrival, Ahmadinejad took a scroll of paper and thrust it down the aperture, so as to update the occulted one on Iran's progress in thermonuclear fission and the enrichment of uranium. One might have thought that the imam could keep abreast of these developments wherever he was, but it had in some way to be the well that acted as his dead-letter box. One might add that President Ahmadinejad had recently returned from the United Nations, where he had given a speech that was much covered on both radio and television as well as viewed by a large "live" audience. On his return to Iran, however, he told his supporters that he had been suffused with a clear green light—green being the preferred color of Islam—all throughout his remarks, and that the emanations of this divine light had kept everybody in the General Assembly quite silent and still. Private to him as this phenomenon was—it appears to have been felt by him alone—he took it as a further sign of the imminent return of the Twelfth Imam, not so say a further endorsement of his ambition to see the Islamic Republic of Iran, sunk as it was in beggary and repression and stagnation and corruption, as nonetheless a nuclear power. But like Aquinas, he did not trust the Twelfth or "hidden" Imam to be able to scan a document unless it was put, as it were, right in front of him.

Having often watched Shia ceremonies and processions, I was not surprised to learn that they are partly borrowed, in their form and liturgy, from Catholicism. Twelve imams, one of them now "in occultation" and awaiting reappearance or reawakening. A frenzied cult of martyrdom, especially over the agonizing death of Hussein, who was forsaken and betrayed on the arid and bitter plains of Karbala. Processions of flagellants and self-mortifiers, awash in grief and guilt at the way in which their sacrificed leader had been abandoned. The masochistic Shia holiday of Ashura bears the strongest resemblances to the sort of *Semana Santa*, or "Holy Week," in which the cowls and crosses and hoods and torches are borne through the streets of Spain.

Yet again it is demonstrated that monotheistic religion is a plagiarism of a plagiarism of a hearsay of a hearsay, of an illusion of an illusion, extending all the way back to a fabrication of a few nonevents.

Another way of putting this is to say that, as I write, a version of the Inquisition is about to lay hands on a nuclear weapon. Under the stultified rule of religion, the great and inventive and sophisticated civilization of Persia has been steadily losing its pulse. Its writers and artists and intellectuals are mainly in exile or stifled by censorship; its women are chattel and sexual prey; its young people are mostly half-educated and without employment. After a quarter century of theocracy, Iran still exports the very things it exported when the theocrats took over—pistachio nuts and rugs. Modernity and technology have passed it by, save for the one achievement of nuclearization.

This puts the confrontation between faith and civilization on a whole new footing. Until relatively recently, those who adopted the clerical path had to pay a heavy price for it. Their societies would decay, their economies would contract, their best minds would go to waste or take themselves elsewhere, and they would consistently be outdone by societies that had learned to tame and sequester the religious impulse. A country like Afghanistan would simply rot. Bad enough as this was, it became worse on September 11, 2001, when from Afghanistan the holy order was given to annex two famous achievements of modernism—the high-rise building and the jet aircraft—and use them for immolation and human sacrifice. The succeeding stage, very plainly announced in hysterical sermons, was to be the moment when apocalyptic nihilists coincided with Armageddon weaponry. Faith-based fanatics could not design anything as useful or beautiful as a skyscraper or a passenger aircraft. But, continuing their long history of plagiarism, they could borrow and steal these things and use them as a negation.

This book has been about the oldest argument in human history, but almost every week that I was engaged in writing it, I was forced to break off and take part in the argument as it was actually continuing.

These arguments tended to take ugly forms: I was not so often leaving my desk to go and debate with some skillful old Jesuit at Georgetown, but rather hurrying out to show solidarity at the embassy of Denmark, a small democratic country in northern Europe whose other embassies were going up in smoke because of the appearance of a few caricatures in a newspaper in Copenhagen. This last confrontation was an especially depressing one. Islamic mobs were violating diplomatic immunity and issuing death threats against civilians, yet the response from His Holiness the Pope and the archbishop of Canterbury was to condemn—the cartoons! In my own profession, there was a rush to see who could capitulate the fastest, by reporting on the disputed images without actually showing them. And this at a time when the mass media has become almost exclusively picture-driven. Euphemistic noises were made about the need to show "respect," but I know quite a number of the editors concerned and can say for a certainty that the chief motive for "restraint" was simple fear. In other words, a handful of religious bullies and bigmouths could, so to speak, outvote the tradition of free expression in its Western heartland. And in the year 2006, at that! To the ignoble motive of fear one must add the morally lazy practice of relativism: no group of nonreligious people threatening and practicing violence would have been granted such an easy victory, or had their excuses—not that they offered any of their own—made for them.

Then again, on another day, one might open the newspaper to read that the largest study of prayer ever undertaken had discovered yet again that there was no correlation of any kind between "intercessory" prayer and the recovery of patients. (Well, perhaps *some* correlation: patients who knew that prayers were being said for them had more postoperative complications than those who did not, though I would not argue that this proved anything.) Elsewhere, a group of dedicated and patient scientists had located, in a remote part of the Canadian Arctic, several skeletons of a large fish that, 375 million years ago, exhibited the precursor features of digits, proto-wrists, elbows, and shoulders. The

Tiktaalik, named at the suggestion of the local Nunavut people, joins the Archaeopteryx, a transitional form between dinosaurs and birds, as one of the long-sought so-called missing links that are helping us to enlighten ourselves about our true nature. Meanwhile, the hoarse proponents of "intelligent design" would be laying siege to yet another school board, demanding that tripe be taught to children. In my mind, these contrasting events began to take on the characteristics of a race: a tiny step forward by scholarship and reason; a huge menacing lurch forward by the forces of barbarism—the people who *know* they are right and who wish to instate, as Robert Lowell once phrased it in another context, "a reign of piety and iron."

Religion even boasts a special branch of itself, devoted to the study of the end. It calls itself "eschatology," and broods incessantly on the passing away of all earthly things. This death cult refuses to abate, even though we have every reason to think that "earthly things" are all that we have, or are ever going to have. Yet in our hands and within our view is a whole universe of discovery and clarification, which is a pleasure to study in itself, gives the average person access to insights that not even Darwin or Einstein possessed, and offers the promise of near-miraculous advances in healing, in energy, and in peaceful exchange between different cultures. Yet millions of people in all societies still prefer the myths of the cave and the tribe and the blood sacrifice. The late Stephen Jay Gould generously wrote that science and religion belong to "non-overlapping *magisteria*." They most certainly do not overlap, but this does not mean that they are not antagonistic.

Religion has run out of justifications. Thanks to the telescope and the microscope, it no longer offers an explanation of anything important. Where once it used to be able, by its total command of a worldview, to *prevent* the emergence of rivals, it can now only impede and retard—or try to turn back—the measurable advances that we have made. Sometimes, true, it will artfully concede them. But this is to offer itself the choice between irrelevance and obstruction, impotence or outright reaction, and, given this choice, it is programmed to select the worse of the two. Meanwhile, confronted with undreamed-of vistas inside our own evolving cortex, in the farthest reaches of the known universe, and in the proteins and acids which constitute our nature, religion offers either annihilation in the name of god, or else the false promise that if we take a knife to our foreskins, or pray in the right direction, or ingest pieces of wafer, we shall be "saved." It is as if someone, offered a delicious and fragrant out-of-season fruit, matured in a painstakingly and lovingly designed hothouse, should throw away the flesh and the pulp and gnaw moodily on the pit.

Above all, we are in need of a renewed Enlightenment, which will base itself on the proposition that the proper study of mankind is man, and woman. This Enlightenment will not need to depend, like its predecessors, on the heroic breakthroughs of a few gifted and exceptionally courageous people. It is within the compass of the average person. The study of literature and poetry, both for its own sake and for the eternal ethical questions with which it deals, can now easily depose the scrutiny of sacred texts that have been found to be corrupt and confected. The pursuit of unfettered scientific inquiry, and the availability of new findings to masses of people by easy electronic means, will revolutionize our concepts of research and development. Very importantly, the divorce between the sexual life and fear, and the sexual life and disease, and the sexual life and tyranny, can now at last be attempted, on the sole condition that we banish all religions from the discourse. And all this and more is, for the first time in our history, within the reach if not the grasp of everyone.

However, only the most naive utopian can believe that this new humane civilization will develop, like some dream of "progress," in a straight line. We have first to transcend our prehistory, and escape the gnarled hands which reach out to drag us back to the catacombs and the reeking altars and the guilty pleasures of subjection and abjection. "Know yourself," said the Greeks, gently suggesting the consolations of philosophy. To clear the mind for this project, it has become necessary to know the enemy, and to prepare to fight it.

Acknowledgments

I have been writing this book all my life and intend to keep on writing it, but it would have been impossible to produce this version without the extraordinary collaboration between agent and publisher—I mean to say Steve Wasserman and Jonathan Karp—that enabled me. All authors ought to have such careful and literate friends and allies. All authors ought also to have book-finders as astute and determined as Windsor Mann.

My old schoolfriend Michael Prest was the first person to make it plain to me that while the authorities could compel us to attend prayers, they could not force us to pray. I shall always remember his upright posture while others hypocritically knelt or inclined themselves, and also the day that I decided to join him. All postures of submission and surrender should be part of our prehistory.

I have been fortunate in having many moral tutors, formal and informal, many of whom had to undergo considerable intellectual trial, and evince notable courage, in order to break with the faith of their tribes. Some of these would still be in some danger if I were to name them, but I must admit my debt to the late Dr. Israel Shahak, who introduced me to Spinoza; to Salman Rushdie, who bravely witnessed for reason and humor and language in a very dark time; to Ibn Warraq and Irfan Khawaja, who also know something about the price of the ticket; and to Dr. Michael Shermer, the very model of the reformed and recovered Christian fundamentalist. Among the many others who have shown that life and wit and inquiry begin just at the point where faith ends, I ought to salute Penn and Teller, that other amazing myth- and fraud-buster James Randi (Houdini of our time), and Tom Flynn, Andrea Szalanski and all the other staffers at *Free Inquiry* magazine. Jennifer Michael Hecht put me immensely in her debt when she sent me a copy of her extraordinary *Doubt: A History.*

To all those who I do not know, and who live in the worlds where superstition and barbarism are still dominant, and into whose hands I hope this little book may fall, I offer the modest encouragement of an older wisdom. It is in fact this, and not any arrogant preaching, that comes to us out of the whirlwind: *Die Stimme der Vernunft ist leise.* Yes, "The voice of Reason is soft." *But it is very persistent.* In this, and in the lives and minds of combatants known and unknown, we repose our chief hope.

Over many years I have pursued these questions with Ian McEwan, whose body of fiction shows an extraordinary ability to elu- cidate the numinous without conceding anything to the supernatural. He has subtly demonstrated that the natural is wondrous enough for anyone. It was in some discussions with Ian, first on that remote Uru- guayan coast where Darwin so boldly put ashore and took samples, and later in Manhattan, that I felt this essay beginning to germinate. I am very proud to have sought and received his permission to dedicate the ensuing pages to him.

REFERENCES

CHAPTER TWO
RELIGION KILLS

[p. 17–18] Mother Teresa was interviewed by Daphne Barak, and her comments on Princess Diana can be found in *Ladies' Home Journal*, April 1996.

[p. 24] The details of the murder of Yusra al-Azami in Bethlehem can be found in "Gaza Taliban?," editorial, *New Humanist* 121:1 (January 2006), http://www.newhumanist.org.uk/volume121issue1_comments.php?id=1860 _0 _ 40 _ 0 _C. See also Isabel Kershner, "The Sheikh's Revenge," *Jerusalem Report*, March 20, 2006.

[p. 27] For Abu Musab al-Zarqawi's letter to Osama bin Laden, see http://www.state.gov/p/nea/rls/31694.htm.

[p. 33] For the story of the born-again Air Force Academy cadets and MeLinda Morton, see Faye Fiore and Mark Mazzetti, "School's Religious Intolerance Misguided, Pentagon Reports," *Los Angeles Times*, June 23, 2005, p. 10; Laurie Goodstein, "Air Force Academy Staff Found Promoting Religion," *New York Times*, June 23, 2005, p. A12; David Van Biema, "Whose God Is Their Co-Pilot?," *Time*, June 27, 2005, p. 61; and United States Air Force, *The Report of the Headquarters Review Group Concerning the Religious Climate at the U.S. Air Force Academy*, June 22, 2005, http://www.afmil/shared/media/document/AFD-051014-008.pdf

[p. 33] For James Madison on the constitutionality of religious establishment in government or public service, see Brooke Allen, *Moral Minority: Our Skeptical Founding Fathers* (Chicago: Ivan R. Dee, 2006), pp. 116–117.

[p. 35] For Charles Stanley and Tim LaHaye, see Charles Marsh, "Wayward Christian Soldiers," *New York Times*, January 20, 2006.

CHAPTER FOUR
A NOTE ON HEALTH, TO WHICH
RELIGION CAN BE HAZARDOUS

[p. 45] For the Bishop Cifuentes sermon, see the BBC-TV production *Panorama*, aired June 27, 2004.

[p. 46] The *Foreign Policy* quotation comes from Laura M. Kelley and Nicholas Eberstadt, "The Muslim Face of AIDS," *Foreign Policy*, July/August 2005, http://www.foreignpolicy.com/story/cms.php?story_id=3081.

[p. 47] For Daniel Dennett's criticisms of religion, see his *Breaking the Spell: Religion as a Natural Phenomenon* (New York: Viking Adult, 2006).

[p. 57] For the Tim LaHaye and Jerry B. Jenkins quote, see their *Glorious Appearing: The End of Days* (Wheaton, IL: Tyndale House, 2004), pp. 250, 260.

[p. 59] Pervez Hoodbhoy's comments on the Pakistani nuclear tests can be found in *Free Inquiry*, spring 2002.

CHAPTER FIVE
THE METAPHYSICAL CLAIMS OF
RELIGION ARE FALSE

[p. 68] E. P. Thompson, *The Making of the English Working Class* (New York: Vintage, 1966), p. 12.

[p. 69] Father Coplestone's commentary is from his *History of Philosophy*, vol. iii (Kent, England: Search Press, 1953).

CHAPTER SIX
ARGUMENTS FROM DESIGN

[pp. 81–83] On the evolution of the eye and why it argues against intelligent design, see Michael Shermer, *Why Darwin Matters: The Case Against Intelligent Design* (New York: Times Books, 2006), p. 17. The emphasis is in the original. See also *Climbing Mount Improbable*, by Richard Dawkins (New York: W. W. Norton, 1996), pp. 138–197.

[p. 87] For the University of Oregon "irreducible complexity" study, see Jamie T. Bridgham, Sean M. Carroll, and Joseph W. Thornton, "Evolution of Hormone-Receptor Complexity by Molecular Exploitation," *Science* 312:5770 (April 7, 2006): pp. 97–101.

[p. 93] For Stephen Jay Gould's quotation on the Burgess shale, see his *Wonderful Life: The Burgess Shale and the Nature of History* (New York: W. W. Norton, 1989), p. 323.

[p. 95] For the University of Chicago human genome study, see Nicholas Wade, "Still Evolving, Human Genes Tell New Story," *New York Times*, March 7, 2006.

[p. 96] Voltaire's statement—*Si Dieu n'existait pas, il faudrait l'inventer*—is taken from his "À l'auteur du livre des trois imposteurs," *Epîtres*, no. 96 (1770).

[p. 96] Sam Harris's observation on Jesus being born of a virgin can be found in his *The End of Faith: Religion, Terror, and the Future of Reason* (New York: W. W. Norton, 2005).

CHAPTER SEVEN
REVELATION: THE NIGHTMARE OF THE
"OLD" TESTAMENT

[p. 102] For Finkelstein and Silberman's work, see Israel Finkelstein and Neil Asher Silberman, *The Bible Unearthed: Archaeology's*

New Vision of Ancient Israel and the Origin of Its Sacred Texts (New York: Touchstone, 2002).

[p. 103] For Sigmund Freud on religion's incurable deficiency, see *The Future of an Illusion*, translated by W. D. Robson-Scott, revised and newly edited by James Strachey (New York: Anchor, 1964).

[p. 104] The Thomas Paine quotation is from *The Age of Reason* in Eric Foner, ed., *Collected Writings* (Library of America, 1995).

Chapter Eight
The "New" Testament Exceeds the Evil of the "Old" One

[p. 110] For H. L. Mencken's assessment of the New Testament, see his *Treatise on the Gods* (Baltimore: Johns Hopkins University Press, 1997), p. 176.

[p. 118] For C. S. Lewis's quotation beginning "Now, unless the speaker is God," see his *Mere Christianity* (New York: Harper-Collins, 2001), pp. 51–52.

[p. 119] For C. S. Lewis's quotation beginning "That is the one thing we must not say," see *Mere Christianity*, p. 52. For his quotation beginning "Now it seems to me obvious," see p. 53.

[p. 122] For Bart Ehrman, see his *Misquoting Jesus: The Story Behind Who Changed the Bible and Why* (New York: HarperCollins, 2005).

Chapter Nine
The Koran Is Borrowed from Both Jewish and Christian Myths

[p. 124] For why Muslims must recite the Koran in its original Arabic, see Ziauddin Sardar and Zafar Abbas Malik, *Introducing Mohammed* (Totem Books, 1994), p. 47.

[p. 136]   The Karen Armstrong quotation comes from her *Islam: A Short History* (New York: Modem Library, 2000), p. 10.

CHAPTER TEN
THE TAWDRINESS OF THE MIRACULOUS AND THE DECLINE OF HELL

[pp. 145–146]   The Malcolm Muggeridge and Ken Macmillan anecdotes regarding Mother Teresa are included in my *Missionary Position: Mother Teresa in Theory and Practice* (Verso, 1995), pp. 25–26.

[p. 147]   The information on Monica Besra's tumor and recovery comes from Aroup Chatterjee, *Mother Teresa: The Final Verdict* (Calcutta: Meteor Books, 2003), pp. 403–406.

CHAPTER ELEVEN
"THE LOWLY STAMP OF THEIR ORIGIN": RELIGION'S CORRUPT BEGINNINGS

[p. 164]   Mark Twain's "chloroform in print" comes from his *Roughing It* (New York: Signet Classics, 1994), p. 102.

[p. 165]   On the possible utility of religion in curing disease, see Daniel Dennett, *Breaking the Spell: Religion as a Natural Phenomenon* (New York: Viking Adult, 2006).

[p. 165]   For Sir James George Frazer's *The Golden Bough* (1922), see http://www.bartleby.com/196/.

CHAPTER TWELVE
A CODA: HOW RELIGIONS END

[p. 170]   For the story of Sabbatai Sevi, see John Freely, *The Last Messiah* (New York: Viking Penguin, 2001).

CHAPTER THIRTEEN
DOES RELIGION MAKE PEOPLE BEHAVE BETTER?

[p. 177] The information on William Lloyd Garrison can be found in his letter to Rev. Samuel J. May, July 17, 1845, in Walter M. Merrill, ed., *The Letters of William Lloyd Garrison* (1973) 3:303, and in *The Liberator*, May 6, 1842.

[p. 178] The information on Lincoln comes from Susan Jacoby, *Freethinkers: A History of American Secularism* (New York: Metropolitan Books, 2004), p. 118.

[p. 181] Barbary ambassador Abdrahaman's justification for slavery is included in my *Thomas Jefferson: Author of America* (New York: HarperCollins, 2003), p. 128.

[p. 191] The material on Rwandan genocide is derived primarily from Philip Gourevitch, *We Wish to Inform You That Tomorrow We Will Be Killed with Our Families: Stories from Rwanda* (New York: Farrar, Straus and Giroux, 1998) pp. 69–141.

[pp. 201–202] The philosophy of "Gudo" and the Nichiren declaration are excerpted from Brian Victoria's *Zen at War* (Weatherhill, 1997), pp. 41 and 84, respectively; the Japanese Buddhist wartime proclamations are from pp. 86–87.

CHAPTER SIXTEEN
IS RELIGION CHILD ABUSE?

[p. 220] Mary McCarthy, *Memories of a Catholic Girlhood* (New York: Harcourt, 1946).

[p. 221] Joseph Schumpeter's model of "creative destruction" can be found in his *Capitalism, Socialism, and Democracy* (London: George Allen & Unwin, 1976), pp. 81–86.

[p. 224] For Maimonides on circumcision, see Leonard B. Glick, *Marked in Your Flesh: Circumcision from Ancient Judea to Modern America* (New York: Oxford University Press, 2005), pp. 64–66 [emphasis added].

Chapter Seventeen
An Objection Anticipated: The Last-Ditch "Case" Against Secularism

[p. 239–240] On the Vatican's endorsement of Nazi Germany, see John Cornwell, *Hitler's Pope: The Secret History of Pius XII* (New York: Viking Adult, 1999).

[p. 242] On the misrepresentation of Einstein, see William Waterhouse, "Misquoting Einstein," in *Skeptic* vol. 12, no. 3, pp. 60–61.

[p. 250] For H. L. Mencken's social Darwinism, see his *Treatise on the Gods* (Baltimore: Johns Hopkins University Press, 1997), p. 176.

[p. 250] Hannah Arendt, *The Origins of Totalitarianism* (New York: Harcourt, 1994).

Chapter Eighteen
A Finer Tradition: The Resistance of the Rational

[p. 262] Einstein's statement on "Spinoza's god" can be found in Jennifer Michael Hecht's *Doubt: A History* (New York: HarperCollins, 2003), p. 447. See also Ronald W. Clark, *Einstein: The Life and Times* (New York: Avon, 1984), p. 502.

[p. 263] The Heinrich Heine quotation can be found in Jennifer Michael Hecht, *Doubt: A History*, p. 376. See also Heine as cited in Joseph Ratner's introduction to *The Philosophy of Spinoza: Selections from His Works* (New York: Modern Library, 1927).

[p. 264] The information about Pierre Bayle can be found in Ruth Whelan, "Bayle, Pierre," in Tom Flynn, ed., *The New Encyclopedia of Unbelief* (Amherst, NY: Prometheus Books, 2006).

[p. 265]   The Matteo de Vincenti quotation can be found in Jennifer Michael Hecht, *Doubt: A History*, p. 287. See also Nicholas Davidson, "Unbelief and Atheism in Italy, 1500-1700," in Michael Hunter and David Wootton, ed., *Atheism from the Reformation to the Enlightenment* (Oxford, UK: Clarendon, 1992), p. 63.

[p. 266]   Benjamin Franklin's quotation on the lightning rod can be found in *The Autobiography and Other Writings* (New York: Penguin, 1986), p. 213.

[p. 268]   Hume's quotation can be found in Jennifer Michael Hecht, *Doubt: A History*, p. 351.

[p. 268]   The information on Paine and his religious views comes from Jennifer Michael Hecht, *Doubt: A History*, pp. 356–57.

[p. 271]   The Albert Einstein quotation beginning "It was, of course, a lie" can be found in Jennifer Michael Hecht, *Doubt: A History*, p. 447. See also Helen Dukas and Banesh Hoffinan, eds., *Albert Einstein, the Human Side: New Glimpses from His Archives*, (Princeton, NJ: Princeton University Press, 1979), p. 43. The quotation beginning "I do not believe in the immortality of the individual" can be found in Hecht, *Doubt: A History*, p. 447. See also Dukas and Hoffman, *Albert Einstein, the Human Side*, p. 39.

CHAPTER NINETEEN
IN CONCLUSION: THE NEED FOR
A NEW ENLIGHTENMENT

[p. 282]   For the Robert Lowell quotation, see Walter Kirn, "The Passion of Robert Lowell," *New York Times*, June 26, 2005, http://www.nytimes.com/2005/06/26/books/review/26KIR-NL.html.

INDEX